School Finance and Teacher Quality:

Exploring the Connections

2003 Yearbook of the American Education Finance Association

Margaret L. Plecki and David H. Monk
Editors

EYE ON EDUCATION
6 DEPOT WAY WEST, SUITE 106
LARCHMONT, NY 10538
(914) 833–0551
(914) 833–0761 fax
www.eyeoneducation.com

Library of Congress Cataloging-in-Publication Data

ISSN pending

10 9 8 7 6 5 4 3 2 1

#52825239

Editorial and production services provided by
Richard H. Adin Freelance Editorial Services
52 Oakwood Blvd., Poughkeepsie, NY 12603-4112
(914-471-3566)

Also Available from Eye On Education

Cost-Effectiveness and Educational Policy
2002 Yearbook of the American Education Finance Association
Edited by Henry M. Levin and Patrick J. McEwan

Education Finance in the New Millennium
2001 Yearbook of the American Education Finance Association
Edited by Stephen Chaikind and William J. Fowler, Jr.

Balancing Local Control and State Responsibility for K-12 Education
2000 Yearbook of the American Education Finance Association
Edited by Neil D. Theobald and Betty Malen

Money and Schools, Second Edition
David C. Thompson and R. Craig Wood

Instructional Supervision
Applying Tools and Concepts
Sally J. Zepeda

Introduction of Educational Leadership and Organizational Behavior
Theory into Practice
Patti L. Chance And Edward W. Chance

The Emerging Principalship
Linda Skrla, David Erlandson, Eileen Reed and Alfred Wilson

The School Portfolio Toolkit
A Planning, Implementation and Evaluation Guide
for Continuous School Improvement
Victoria L. Bernhardt

Data Analysis for Comprehensive Schoolwide Improvement
Victoria L. Bernhardt

Human Resources Administration: A School-Based Perspective, 2/e
Richard E. Smith

School Community Relations
Douglas J. Fiore

Research on Educational Innovations, Third Edition
Arthur K. Ellis and Jeffery T. Fouts

Resource Allocation: Managing Money and People
M. Scott Norton and Larry K. Kelly

Working in a Legal and Regulatory Environment:
A Handbook for School Leaders
David J. Sperry

Editors and Contributors

Editors

Margaret L. Plecki is Associate Professor in the Area of Educational Leadership and Policy Studies at the University of Washington, Seattle. Her teaching and research activities focus on school finance, the economics of education, and education policy evaluation. Her experience in education includes 15 years of service as a special education teacher, a staff development specialist, and a public school administrator. She has also worked in the private sector as a management consultant. She earned her Ph.D. from the University of California, Berkeley. Currently, she is working on studies of the relationships between resource allocation practices, teaching quality, and student achievement. She is Deputy Director of the Center for the Study of Teaching and Policy, and is Principal Investigator for a study of the conditions of teaching in Washington State. Marge has been an active member of AEFA since 1989 and served on the AEFA Board of Directors from 1999–2002.

David H. Monk is professor of educational administration and dean of the College of Education at The Pennsylvania State University. He earned his Ph.D. in 1979 at the University of Chicago and was a member of the Cornell University faculty for 20 years. He has also taught in a visiting capacity at the University of Rochester and the University of Burgundy in Dijon, France. Monk is the author of *Educational Finance: An Economic Approach* (1990); *Raising Money for Education: A Guide to the Property Tax* (1997) (with Brian O. Brent); and *Cost Adjustments in Education* (2001) (with William J. Fowler, Jr.) in addition to numerous articles in scholarly journals. He is a co-editor for *Leadership and Policy in Schools* and serves on the editorial boards of *The Economics of Education Review, The Journal of Education Finance, Educational Policy,* and the *Journal of Research in Rural Education.* He consults widely on matters related to educational productivity and the organizational structuring of schools and school districts and is a Past President of the American Education Finance Association.

Contributors

Donald Boyd is the deputy director of the Center for Policy Research at the State University of New York at Albany, focusing on education research. Current education research at the Center includes analysis of teacher labor markets, teacher mobility, and the geographic distribution of teacher qualifications. Boyd holds a Ph.D. in Managerial Economics from Rensselaer Polytechnic Institute in Troy, New York.

Linda Darling-Hammond is Charles E. Ducommun Professor of Education at Stanford University. Her research, teaching, and policy work focus on teaching quality, school restructuring, and educational equity. She is the author of 9 books and more than 200 journal articles on issues of education and policy. Her 1997 book, *The Right to Learn: A Blueprint for Creating Schools that Work,* received the American Educational Research Association's Outstanding Book Award.

Jennifer Imazeki is an Assistant Professor of Economics at San Diego State University where she teaches courses in public finance and applied microeconomics. She received her Ph.D. in economics from the University of Wisconsin-Madison, where she also worked as a researcher for the Consortium for Policy Research in Education. Her current research focuses on school finance reform and teacher labor markets.

Kieran M. Killeen is an assistant professor of educational leadership and policy studies at the University of Vermont. His areas of research include public school finance, planning, and institutional theory. He is a former special education teacher and participant of the Teach for America national teacher corps. Previously he was a lecturer at Pennsylvania State University. He received his Ph.D. from Cornell University.

Julia E. Koppich is President of Julia E. Koppich and Associates, a San Francisco-based education consulting firm. Dr. Koppich holds a Ph.D. in Educational Administration and Policy Analysis from the University of California, Berkeley. She has been a consultant to the National Conference of State Legislatures, National Governors' Association, AFT, NEA, and the National Alliance of Business. She has authored numerous articles and is co-author (with Charles Kerchner) of *A Union of Professionals* and *United Mind Workers: Unions and Teaching in the Knowledge Society.*

Sabrina W. M. Laine is Associate Director for Policy, Outreach, and Data Use at the North Central Regional Educational Laboratory. She leads the Lab's efforts to develop policy networks among its seven states, coordinates efforts to improve teacher quality in the Midwest, and has researched issues such as charter schools, the Third International Math and Science Study (TIMSS), comprehensive school reform, and professional development.

Hamilton Lankford is a faculty member (Economics and Public Policy) at the University at Albany, SUNY. His research focuses on issues relating to elementary and secondary education, including research regarding the allocation of educational resources and the determinants of school choices by families. He is currently collaborating with other researchers in an effort to better understand the functioning of teacher labor markets and, in particular, policies that can help in the recruitment and retention of more qualified teachers and administrators, especially in low performing schools.

Susanna Loeb is an assistant professor of education at Stanford University, specializing in the economics of education and the relationship between schools and federal, state and local policies. She studies resource allocation, looking specifically at how the structure of state finance systems affects the level and distribution of funds to districts and how teachers' preferences affect the distribution of teaching quality across schools. She is particularly interested in issues of equity. She also studies poverty policies including welfare reform and early-childhood education programs.

Tom Meyer is Assistant Professor of Secondary Education at the State University of New York at New Paltz. He received his Ph.D. in curriculum and teacher education from Stanford University. His research focuses on teacher learning and professional development. He teaches courses related to curriculum and assessment, teacher research, and English Education. He directs the Hudson Valley Writing Project, a local site of the National Writing Project. Previously, he taught public secondary school English in the San Francisco Bay Area.

Karen Hawley Miles, founder of Education Resource Strategies in Dallas, Texas, specializes in strategic planning, organization and resource allocation in urban public school districts. She has worked with districts and schools nationwide to develop long range strategic plans that create accountability, restructure district organizations and implement programs that focus more effectively on school redesign and quality teaching. Dr. Miles has worked intensively with urban districts like Chicago,

Albuquerque, Boston, Atlanta and Cincinnati and taught administrator seminars at Harvard University Graduate School of Education and across the country.

Allan Odden is Professor of Educational Administration at the University of Wisconsin-Madison and Co-Director of the Consortium for Policy Research in Education (CPRE). He formerly was professor of education policy and administration at the University of Southern California, Director of Policy Analysis for California Education (PACE), and held various positions at the Education Commission of the States. He was president of the American Educational Finance Association in 1979–80 and received AEFA's Distinguished Service Award in 1998. His research emphases include school finance redesign, resource reallocation in schools, the costs of instructional improvement, and teacher compensation.

Jennifer King Rice is an Associate Professor in the Department of Education Policy and Leadership at the University of Maryland. Her research draws on the discipline of economics to explore education policy questions concerning the efficiency and equity of U.S. public schools and school systems. Prior to joining the faculty at Maryland, Dr. Rice was a researcher at Mathematica Policy Research in Washington D.C. She earned her M.S. and Ph.D. degrees from Cornell University, and is a National Academy of Education/Spencer Foundation postdoctoral fellow.

Christopher Roellke is Assistant Professor of Education and Urban Studies at Vassar College where he teaches courses in educational policy and urban education reform. He earned M.S. and Ph.D. degrees from Cornell University. Previously, he taught public secondary school history in rural, suburban, and urban settings. In 1997, he was the recipient of the outstanding dissertation award of the American Education Finance Association, the Politics of Education Association, and Division A of the American Educational Research Association.

Jon Snyder is currently Dean of the Graduate School of Education at Bank Street College. He has worked as a researcher and a teacher educator at the University of California, Santa Barbara, Teachers College Columbia University, the National Center for the Restructuring of Education, Schools, and Teaching, and the National Commission on Teaching and America's Future. He remains engaged in researching teacher learning, conditions that support teacher learning, and the relationships between teacher and student learning.

Neil D. Theobald is Professor of education finance and Vice Chancellor for Budget and Administration at Indiana University-Bloomington. He is a Past-President of the American Education Finance Association, winning the Association's Jean Flanigan Award for the outstanding dissertation in the study of educational finance in 1990.

Jim Wyckoff is an Associate Professor in the Rockefeller College of Public Affairs and Policy at the University at Albany, SUNY. He is working with a research team to examine policies to recruit and retain more qualified teachers and administrators to urban schools, especially low performing schools. This work includes an examination of teacher preparation programs and pathways to determine the effect of specific program features on student achievement. He is president-elect of the American Education Finance Association and an associate editor of the *Economics of Education Review*.

Table of Contents

1

School Finance and Teacher Quality: Exploring the Connections

Margaret L. Plecki
University of Washington

David H. Monk
Pennsylvania State University

In recent years, attention has been focused on the quality of teachers and teaching as keys to improving student learning. Several studies point out that teacher quality is an important, perhaps the single most important, factor in raising student achievement. Consequently, policies at national, state, and local levels have increasingly called for strategies aimed at improving the quality of teachers and teaching. A specific example of the increased attention on teacher quality can be found in the recent federal legislation, No Child Left Behind, which requires states to ensure that every child has a highly qualified teacher.

This intensified focus on the quality of teachers and teaching is a predictable consequence of standards-based reform initiatives. For more than a decade, state after state has fashioned some version of an educational reform policy rooted in ambitious student learning standards that attempts to align higher expectations for all students with assessments, an accountability system, and other supporting policy features. Although much of the policy attention is focused on how states, districts, and schools perform in the aggregate, the weight of expectations created by standards-based reform efforts falls most heavily on the shoulders of classroom teachers. The standards-based movement asks a great deal of teachers and is dependent on teachers' knowledge, skill, and will to achieve results inside classrooms. These high expectations presume, at the very least, that a well-equipped and sustainable teacher workforce is available. They also presume that well-qualified teachers are appropriately and equitably assigned to teach the vast array of our nation's students.

Education finance policies and practices have direct bearing on the extent to which policies aimed at improving the quality of teachers and teaching are enacted. This yearbook provides research, information, and insights into the numerous connections between school finance policy and teacher and teaching quality. The goal of the yearbook is to stimulate thought, to inform debates, and to consider future research directions that will help us better understand the connections between school finance and our efforts to improve the quality of teachers and teaching.

The yearbook also provides a variety of theoretical and methodological perspectives on school finance and its relation to the quality of teachers and teaching. Consequently, the works contained in this volume represent a wide range of theoretical and methodological approaches. The contributions here draw on a variety of conceptual approaches and disciplinary constructs, and the forms of inquiry used by the contributors include quantitative, qualitative, and mixed method designs.

The yearbook is organized around four issues, each of which can be viewed as representing an important focal point to improve teacher and teaching quality and having important implications for school finance. The issues are (1) teacher recruitment, induction, and retention; (2) the ongoing professional development of teachers; (3) equity in the allocation of teaching resources; and (4) teacher compensation and workplace conditions.

The first section of the yearbook comprises issues related to teacher recruitment, retention, and induction. The first contribution in this section is the work of Roellke and Meyer. They conducted a longitudinal, qualitative examination of the early career experiences of "academically talented" teachers in New York City. Their work discusses the research, policy, and practice implications of what they learned from the experiences of novice teachers working under challenging circumstances. The second contribution, by Theobald and Laine, explores why teachers are leaving public school districts in four Midwestern states and provides suggestions about what districts and states can do to address the issue of teacher turnover. The final chapter in the first section features the work of Boyd, Lankford, Loeb, and Wyckoff. The authors offer a detailed analysis of teacher labor markets and connect their findings to key issues of educational equity.

The second section of the yearbook focuses on another important aspect of improving the quality of teachers and teaching: investment in the ongoing professional development of teachers. In this section, Miles offers a comparative analysis of spending on teacher professional development in five urban districts and explores the implications for research and practice that emerge from understanding the differences in spending levels and patterns. Rice offers another perspective on professional development. Using a national database, her work involved an examination of professional development for high school mathematics and science teachers and its impact on teaching practices and student achievement in these two subject areas. A third perspective on teacher professional development is found in the work of Plecki, Monk, and Killeen. They analyzed the issue of spending on teacher professional development by first examining state budgets to assess investment levels in four states (California, New York, North Carolina, and Washington) and then offer a conceptual approach for improving our accounting of the level and type of investment made in professional development at the local level.

The third topic in the yearbook focuses on the equity of the allocation of teaching resources. Imazeki's work provides an examination of the effects of class size reduction policies in California on the distribution of teacher quality across the state and the equity concerns emerging from the transfer of qualified teachers away from the highest-need districts. The contribution by Darling-Hammond and Snyder provides a school-level analysis of the reallocation of teaching resources when comparing restructured with traditionally structured schools.

The final section of the yearbook examines issues of teacher compensation and working conditions. Odden describes and offers an early assessment of alternatives to the traditional compensation structures for teachers, with a specific focus on three examples of comprehensive new structures in Cincinnati, Philadelphia, and Iowa. This section concludes with the work of Koppich. She draws on examples in Minneapolis, Denver, Seattle, and Montgomery County, Maryland as a context for discussing the interaction between labor-management agreements and decisions regarding the allocation of fiscal resources for purposes other than the improvement of salary levels.

In many ways, this volume provides an example of how school finance research is evolving, both in terms of the types of inquiry methods employed and the range of topics and issues emerging as worthy of the attention of school finance scholars. We are indebted to the contributors of this yearbook for their disciplined pursuit of important questions regarding the conditions that impact the teacher workforce, the policies and strategies that have been employed to address teacher quality, and the challenges that lie ahead to improve the quality of teachers and teaching, and—ultimately—the continuous improvement of student learning.

Section I

Teacher Recruitment, Induction, and Retention

2

Recruitment, Induction, and Retention of Academically Talented Urban School Teachers: Evidence from New York City

Christopher Roellke
Vassar College

Tom Meyer
State University of New York, New Paltz

The intent of this study is to better understand the challenges associated with recruiting, inducting, and retaining high-quality teachers in urban areas. Specifically, this chapter draws on longitudinal case study data and supplemental interview data (Appendix 1) to analyze the early career experiences of academically talented teachers in New York City public schools. The respondents in this study are graduates of most-selective undergraduate institutions and are currently within the first five years of a teaching career in the New York City Public Schools system. Each of these teachers was identified for excellence in urban teaching by teacher education faculty of the Consortium for Excellence in Teacher Education (CETE)[1]

---

1   CETE, consisting of 20 highly selective undergraduate teacher preparation programs, was formed in 1983 when the first of the national education reports began calling for improvements in both the caliber of individuals entering the teaching profession and the education they receive. See Appendix 2 (p. 31) for a more detailed description of CETE and a current list of member institutions.

The purposeful selection of teacher education graduates from most-selective colleges and universities is intended to shed light on the high attrition and mobility behaviors of this type of classroom teacher. Moreover, the selectivity and prestige of the institution attended by the teacher have a positive effect on student achievement.[2] A severe teacher quality gap, as measured by academic indicators such as college selectivity and college entrance examination scores, clearly exists between low-poverty and high-poverty (and often urban) schools.[3] Therefore, understanding the early career experiences of this talented pool of New York City teachers may be helpful for policymakers and school officials as they seek to address issues of teacher supply and quality in our central cities.

The following research questions guide the inquiry:

1. How are academically talented novice teachers prepared, recruited, and inducted into New York City Public Schools?

2. What are the professional challenges and rewards of academically talented novice teachers in New York City?

3. From the perspective of academically talented novice teachers, what preparation practices, school policies, and working conditions are likely to improve their recruitment and retention in New York City and other urban schools?

This chapter begins with a brief summary of the research on teacher supply and demand in urban areas. Attention then turns to the specific teacher supply and teacher quality challenges faced in New York State and New York City in particular. The next section describes the data and methods used for the longitudinal, case study, and supplemental interview components of the study. The findings are organized thematically into five distinct but overlapping areas: (1) preservice teacher preparation, (2) recruitment and hiring practices, (3) induction, support, and evaluation, (4) compensation, and (5) short- and long-term career forecast. The chapter concludes with an effort to synthesize what we have learned from these beginning teachers and to assess the implications for research, policy, and practice.

Teacher Supply and Demand in Urban Areas

Demographic fluctuations, shifts in curricular emphases, and alterations in policies related to teacher education and licensing create changes in teacher sup-

---

2   See, for examples, Ingersoll, R. (2001). Teacher turnover and teacher shortages: An organizational analysis. *American Educational Research Journal, 38*(3), 499–534; Lankford, H., Loeb S., & Wyckoff, J. (2002). Teacher sorting and the plight of urban schools: A descriptive analysis. *Educational Evaluation and Policy Analysis 24*(1), 37–62; and Ehrenberg, R. G., & Brewer, D. J. (1994). Do school and teacher characteristics matter? Evidence from high school and beyond. *Economics of Education Review 13*(1), 1–17.

3   Wayne, A. J. (2002). Teacher inequality: New evidence on disparities in teachers' academic skills. *Educational Policy Analysis Archives 10*(30) (2002).

ply and demand. Boe and Gilford (1992) identify seven trends that will increase teacher demand and decrease teacher supply in the next decade: (1) high teacher attrition, (2) increasing teacher retirement rates, (3) increasing student enrollments, (4) decreasing pupil–teacher ratios, (5) decreasing enrollments in teacher preparation programs, (6) decreasing interest among women in teaching, and (7) more stringent entry standards and teacher licensing for the profession.[4] Although these trends apply to all schools, it is important to recognize that problems associated with low supply and high demand vary considerably across regions, schools, and subject areas.

Earlier analyses of the Schools and Staffing Survey (SASS), for example, showed that an overall balance in the supply and demand of teachers may mask critical shortages in particular types of schools and/or within specific subject areas. Although evidence suggests that temporary substitutes were rarely used to fill vacancies in schools, central city public schools were three times as likely to engage in this practice than were schools in rural areas or small towns. Similarly, central city public schools with high minority enrollments were more than twice as likely to hire uncertified substitutes than their more racially homogeneous urban counterparts.[5] This use of temporary, noncertified teaching staff has led some states to pass legislation to eliminate the practice. New York State, for example, has eliminated temporary teaching licenses beginning in the 2003–2004 school year.

This type of policy reaction will inevitably have differential impact among school systems, with the greatest challenges anticipated for low-income, urban schools. It is these schools in which critical shortages and alarming attrition rates of certified teachers are well documented. The supply and quality problem is most acute in schools serving primarily low-income, low achieving, nonwhite students.[6]

Although shortages periodically affect all types of schools and districts, urban school systems consistently suffer from high demand and low supply of qualified teachers. In a recent survey completed by the Council of Great City Schools, for example, all 40 cities sampled had immediate shortages of qualified teachers. Shortages are reported across all grade levels and subject areas, particu-

4 Boe, E. E, & Gilford D. M. (Eds.) (1992). *Teacher supply, demand, and quality: Policy issues, models and databases.* Washington, D.C.: National Academy Press.

5 National Center for Education Statistics. (1996). *Schools and staffing in the United States: A statistical profile, 1993–94.* Washington, D. C.: U.S. Department of Education.

6 See, for examples, Imazeki J. (In press). Teacher attrition and mobility in urban districts: Evidence from Wisconsin, in Roellke C. F., & Rice, J. K. (Eds.), *Fiscal policy in urban schools.* Greenwich, CT: Information Age Publishing; Jones, D. L., & Sandidge, R. F. (1997). Recruiting and retaining teachers in urban schools. *Education and Urban Society, 29*(2), 192–203; and Theobald, N. D., & Gritz, R. M. (1996). The effects of school district spending priorities on the exit paths of beginning teachers leaving the district. *Economics of Education Review 15,* 11–22.

larly in special education, secondary school math and science, and bilingual education.[7]

Challenging working conditions further complicate the low supply and high demand of urban teachers. Urban teachers, for example, educate a disproportionate number of students with special needs and confront the highest percentages of students who are not proficient in English. Urban teachers are much more likely than suburban and rural teachers to report problems such as high absenteeism, serious student violence, and poor parental involvement.[8]

New York State's Articulation of the Urban Teacher Supply and Quality Problem

In a recent task force report on teaching, the New York State Board of Regents identified four key gaps in the State's teaching workforce:

1. New York does not attract and keep enough of the best teachers where they are needed most.
2. Not enough teachers leave college prepared to ensure that New York's students reach higher standards.
3. Not enough teachers maintain the knowledge and skills needed to teach to high standards throughout their careers.
4. Many school environments actively work against effective teaching and learning.[9]

In the same task force report, several indicators are provided to illustrate the teacher supply and quality problem in New York State. First, teachers in New York State are aging: Half of the teaching workforce will be eligible for retirement in within the next 10 years. Second, one sixth of prospective teachers fail the State's certification examinations, and failure rates are highest in urban testing centers. Third, despite issuing an estimated 20,000 teaching certificates annually, schools within the State hired only 6,000 newly certified teachers.

The supply and quality problem permeates low-income, minority, urban neighborhoods. More than 12% of teachers in schools with high percentages of minority students are *not* certified (compared with 5.4% in schools with low

---

7 Council of the Great City Schools. *The urban teacher challenge* (pp. 20–21). Council of the Great City Schools.

8 See Lippman, L, Burns S., & McArthur, E. (1996). Urban schools: The challenge of location and poverty. Washington, D. C.: U.S. Department of Education, National Center for Education Statistics; Imazeki J. (In press). Teacher attrition and mobility in urban districts: Evidence from Wisconsin. In Roellke C. F., & Rice J. K. (Eds.), *Fiscal Policy in Urban Schools*. Greenwich, CT: Information Age Publishing; and Van Horn, R. (1999). Inner-city schools: A multi-variable discussion. *Phi Delta Kappan 81*(4), 291–297.

9 New York State Board of Regents. (1998). *Teaching to higher standards: New York's commitment*. Albany, NY: Author.

minority populations). Teacher turnover rates exceed 20% in schools with high percentages of minority students (compared with 7% in schools with low percentages of minority students). It is safe to conclude that the large urban centers of the State—serving a large percentage of poor, minority pupils—are confronted with a different set of teacher recruitment and retention challenges than their suburban or rural counterparts.

Why Focus Specifically on New York City?

New York City public schools educate approximately 1.1 million pupils, accounting for nearly 40% of the public school students in the State. The largest urban school system in the country, the New York City Public Schools, employs more than 75,000 teachers. Arguably, the system is currently confronting the most challenging teacher recruitment and retention challenge in its history. Recent estimates project a need for as many as 30,000 to 50,000 new teachers in New York City during the next four to six years.[10] Although it is difficult to predict exactly how many teachers will be needed, it is widely accepted that the New York City teaching force is a veteran one, with more than 16,000 teachers currently eligible for retirement (22% of the New York City teaching workforce).[11]

New York State's teacher supply and quality problems, outlined earlier, are clearly most acute in New York City. Whereas 82% of current suburban schoolteachers in the State are permanently certified, only 66% of teachers in New York City are permanently certified. In Bronx District 7, one of the poorest school systems in the State, only 48% percent of teachers are permanently certified.[12] The New Board of Regents' policy to eliminate temporary licenses by the year 2003–2004 will certainly exacerbate this teacher supply problem in New York City.

Recent research on the New York teaching workforce found that quit rates in the State are highest in New York City. In addition to these high quit rates, evidence suggests that teachers who leave New York City schools generally possess better qualifications than those who remain. These attrition patterns are consis-

10 Estimates obtained from the Office of Educational Staff Recruitment, New York City Public Schools, and The Chancellor's Report, First Year in Review. See also, Brumberg, S. F. (2000). The teacher crisis and educational standards. In Ravitch, D., & Viteritti, J. P. (Eds.), *City Schools: Lessons from New York* (pp. 141–165). Baltimore, MD: Johns Hopkins Press.

11 It is also known that more than 40% of the State's teaching force will be older than 55 years in the next five years. See Lankford, H., Wyckoff, J., & Papa, F. (2000). The labor market for public school teachers: A descriptive analysis of New York State's teacher workforce. Condition report prepared for the New York State Educational Finance Research Consortium, University at Albany.

12 New York State Department of Education. (1998). *Annual school district profile report.* Albany, NY: Author.

tent with earlier claims made that one out of every five New York City teachers leave after the first year, and one of every three teachers leave after three years.[13]

New York is one of many states in the country attempting to recruit and retain teachers in New York City through compensation policies, including $2,500 signing bonuses for teachers willing to teach in hard-to-staff locations and $2,500 scholarships for uncertified staff to obtain teaching certification.[14] Many hard-to-staff locations are also categorized as schools under registration review (SURR), which are chronically low-performing schools that run the risk of being closed if significant improvements are not made. Schools with more than 60% of their students failing to meet specified State standards are considered for inclusion on the SURR list. In the 1998–1999 school year, 95% (112 of 118) of the SURR schools were located in New York City. Several of the respondents in this study are currently teaching in these types of high need schools. In addition to the monetary incentives, other policy efforts in New York State aimed at enhancing teacher quality include increased standards and accountability for both teacher education programs and teachers. One goal of this study is to begin to assess, from the perspective of beginning teachers, the likely effectiveness or ineffectiveness of these types of policies for the teacher workforce in New York City.

Data and Methods

Several researchers have made excellent use of the rich secondary data available at state and federal levels to better understand teacher sorting and career paths, particularly as they pertain to urban educators.[15] To complement these

13 Schwartz, F. (1996). Why many new teachers are unprepared to teach in most New York City schools. *Phi Delta Kappan, 78*(1), 82–84; and Lankford, H., Loeb, S., & Wyckoff J. (2002). Teacher sorting and the plight of urban schools: A descriptive analysis. *Educational Evaluation and Policy Analysis, 24*(1), 37–62.

14 Massachusetts has been experimenting with an even more aggressive recruitment strategy to fill teaching vacancies by offering up to $20,000 signing bonuses in exchange for a four-year teaching commitment from promising novice teachers ($8,000 awarded for year one and $4,000 in years two, three, and four). Early assessments of the Massachusetts program have produced mixed results. See, for example, Fowler, R. C. (2001). An analysis of the recruitment, attrition, and placement of the Massachusetts signing bonus teachers. [Working paper]. Salem, MA: Salem State College.

15 See, for examples, Theobald, N. D., & Michael, R. S. (In press). Reducing novice teacher attrition in urban districts: Focusing on the moving target. In Roellke, C. F., & Rice, J. K. (Eds.), *Fiscal policy in urban schools.* Greenwich, CT: Information Age Publishing; Manski, C. F. (1987). Academic ability, earnings and the decision to become a teacher: Evidence from the National Longitudinal Study of the High School Class of 1972. In Wise, D. A. (Ed.), *Public sector payrolls* (pp. 291–312). Chicago: University of Chicago Press; Ballou, D. (1996). Do public schools hire the best applicants? *The Quarterly Journal of Economics, 111*(1), 97–133; and Loeb, S. (2001). How teachers' choices affect what a dollar can buy:

statistical analyses, it is important that we gain a better understanding of new teachers' experiences at their school sites. Our hope is that this type of contextual analysis—which addresses the work norms, professional challenges, and rewards of beginning teachers—can be helpful to policy makers and school leaders as they seek to recruit and retain high-quality teachers.

Our data collection strategy consisted of two phases. In phase one, we identified a small number (n = 4) of novice New York City teachers who could be studied longitudinally. These teachers have been periodically observed and interviewed since their initial New York City teaching appointments in 1999. These four case study respondents are graduates of a most-selective[16] undergraduate institution in the Northeast, where they earned their New York State teacher certification in NK-6 education. The lead author's close affiliation with and knowledge of this certification program permitted a longitudinal perspective on the preparation, induction, and professional development of these beginning city teachers. Case study respondents were interviewed three to five times each since 1999, with each interview ranging from 45 to 90 minutes. Follow up and clarification questions were asked via telephone and e-mail.

In phase two, we conducted a series of supplemental interviews with eight additional academically talented novice teachers in New York City. Each of the supplemental interviewees was identified for urban teaching excellence by participating faculty of CETE. These academically talented classroom teachers are in their first five years of classroom teaching in New York City public schools. The supplemental interviews for phase two of the study were conducted during the 2001–2002 school year. The length of the supplemental interviews ranged from 45 minutes to 90 minutes, and each interview was taped and transcribed. Follow up and clarification questions were asked via telephone and e-mail.

The sampling strategy for both the longitudinal case studies and the supplemental interview data can be characterized as purposive and criterion-based. Purposive and criterion-based sampling for case study work and qualitative interviewing involves the identification of key informants who possess special knowledge, skill, status, or communication skills, who are willing to share their knowledge and skills with the researcher and who have access to perspectives or observations denied the researcher.[17]

Although we recognize that our overall sample is small, our motivation for studying this particular group of teachers was predicated on the fact that their experiences are uncommon in a number of different ways. First, several of the

Wages and quality in k-12 schooling. *Education Finance Research Consortium Symposium on the Teaching Workforce (pp. 51–80).* Albany, NY: The University of the State of New York.

16 College selectivity was determined by the rating system used in *Barron's Profiles of American Colleges.*

17 Crabtree, B, & Miller, W. L. (1992). *Doing qualitative research.* Newbury Park, CA: Sage Publications.

case study and supplemental interview respondents were prepared explicitly for teaching in urban settings through the Consortium's Institute for Urban Education (IUE) and/or the Venture/Bank Street College urban education semester. Second, all but 2 of the 12 respondents had considerable preservice field experience in urban schools, most often in New York City public schools. Third, contrary to what research would have us expect, i.e., that these highly qualified teachers would quit or migrate, 11 of the 12 respondents elected to remain in urban school settings. The large majority of the migration that has occurred has been *within* New York City public schools and to schools with similar student demographics and achievement results. The study of revelatory cases can help us better understand the experiences of novice teachers in similar circumstances.[18]

Participation in all interviews, observations, and subsequent research for this study was voluntary. Before participating in the study, teachers were informed of the purposes of the study, the methodology, and the intended use of the data. Participants were free at any time to withdraw from the study and could decline to answer any questions posed by the researcher. Participants were informed that their names would not be used on any of the study documents; therefore, pseudonyms or generic respondent numbers have been used in the reporting of the results. Earlier drafts of the analysis were sent to each of the participants in the study for comments and for clarification and confirmation of the findings. A descriptive overview of the longitudinal case study sample and the associated district and school affiliations is shown in Figure 2.1.

18 Yin, R. K. (1994). *Case study research: Design and methods* (2nd ed.). Newbury Park, CA: Sage Publications.

Figure 2.1. Overview of Longitudinal (1999–2002) Case Study Sample and Selected School District, School, and Classroom Characteristics

	Molly (yrs 1 & 2)	Molly (yr 3)	Sharon (yrs 1, 2)	Sharon (yr 3)	Rachel (yrs 1, 2, 3)	Lee (yr 1)	Lee (yrs 2 & 3)
District	CSD no. 14	CSD no. 3	CSD no. 14	Great Neck	CSD no. 22	CSD no. 2	CSD no. 3
Interviews to Date	5	5	4	4	3	5	5
Undergraduate Major	Psychology	Psychology	English	English	Psychology	Sociology	Sociology
School	PK-6 (638 students)	PK-5 (647 students)	PK-5 (706 students)	K-5 (490 students)	PK-5 (650 students)	PK-5 (235 students)	PK-5 (647 students)
Grade Level	3 & 4	3	2	2	5	K	K
Student Demographics (School-Level Statistics)	79% Latina/o, 18% black, 2% white, 99% FRPL	79.7% Latina/o, 15.2% black, 2.6% Asian, 2.6% white, 92% FRPL	66% Latina/o, 32% black, 1% Asian, 1% white, 95% FRPL	8.7 % Latino/a, 1.2% black, 11% Asian, 79 % white, 6% FRPL	68% white, 22% black, 7% Latino/a, 3% Asian, 34% FRPL	43% Latino/a, 31% black, 17% white, 9% Asian, 83% FRPL	79.7% Latino/a, 15.2% black, 2.6% Asian, 2.6% white, 92% FRPL
Class Size	18-25 (yr 1), 18 (yr 2)	24-33 (yr 3)*	26 (yr 1), 14 (yr 2)	16 (yr 3)	25 (yr 1), 25 (yr 2)	20 (yr 1)	22 (yr 2), 20 (yr 3)

CSD, city school district; FRPL,

*This respondent filed a grievance when given a class size of 33. Contractually, her class size should not have exceeded 28 students. After several months of appeals, this respondent's class size was reduced.

Three of the four case study respondents changed schools within their first three years of classroom teaching, and these moves are reflected in Figure 2.1. Currently, three of the four respondents are teaching where at least 90% of the students qualify for a free or reduced-price lunch. In addition, three of the four respondents teach in schools where the majority of students are Latino or Latina and black.

An overview of the sample of supplemental interviews (n = 8) used to complement the in-depth case study analyses is provided in Figure 2.2.

Figure 2. 2. Overview of Supplemental Interview Sample

	School District	High-Need School?	Grade Level	Ethnicity	Gender	Years Exp.
Respondent no. 1	CSD no. 2	No	9	African American	Female	3
Respondent no. 2	CSD no. 2	Yes	6	Asian American	Female	4
Respondent no. 3	CSD no. 4	No	9–12	Asian American	Female	4
Respondent no. 4	CSD no. 6	No	4	White	Female	3
Respondent no. 5	CSD no. 2	No	9	Hispanic American	Female	1
Respondent no. 6	CSD no. 2	Yes	6	White & Asian American	Female	2
Respondent no. 7	CSD no. 11	Yes	4	White	Female	5
Respondent no. 8	CSD no. 32	Yes	9	Jewish American	Male	4

The supplemental interviews are intended to diversify the sample of beginning teachers across several areas, including the following: (1) undergraduate institution and teacher preparation program; (2) race, ethnicity, and gender; (3) grade level; (4) years of experience; and (5) school and district affiliation.

Although our goal of gender diversity was not met (we had only one male respondent), the remaining sample objectives were met. Six different teacher preparation institutions are represented in the sample. In addition to representing racial and ethnic diversity, the respondents vary in their grade level and their years of experience (range, one to five years). Half of the respondents teach in high-need schools, and five different community school districts are represented.

Findings

Preparation

Universally, the respondents commented on the importance of the field experience components of their undergraduate teacher preparation. Each respondent felt adequately prepared in terms of the philosophy of teaching and the theoretical underpinnings of curriculum development and classroom instruction. All four case study respondents, as well as the majority of supplemental interview respondents, expressed that additional explicit preparation in managing an urban classroom was warranted. Developing effective classroom management and appropriate disciplinary strategies were by far the greatest challenges these beginning teachers faced in their first three years. They also noted that inevitably there would be on the job learning.

Molly, one of the case study respondents, describes her undergraduate preparation in this way:

> I feel as though I obtained a good understanding of how to run a whole language classroom. The field experiences as an undergraduate were critical. I think I was not prepared to teach in the setting that I am teaching in, especially in terms of discipline and managing a classroom… it is practically impossible to run a classroom unless you can control the kids. So, that was such an important part of my learning in my first year of teaching that I had to do on the job.

Sharon had similar comments regarding the need for urban classroom management skills:

> There was lots of theory taught to me, and nothing at all about management. I was adequately prepared for teaching the academics, but not for managing the urban classroom. I wasn't prepared to handle situations where kids threw chairs at each other. When you are 21 you don't know how to parent these kids and you don't know how to control them.

All of the respondents indicated that a primary solution to the classroom management preparation challenge is to provide additional opportunities for field experience in urban settings. These teachers also expressed a need for additional time to work with urban children independently without a college supervisor or cooperating teacher present. This was not to suggest that college faculty and cooperating teachers play a diminished role in field experiences; rather, it simply meant that they needed time to develop confidence in working with children alone.

Multicultural education was another preparation theme that consistently emerged across the respondents. These teachers expressed the need for additional attention to issues of diversity, identity construction, and the political dimensions of teaching. They argued that more explicit and in-depth attention to these topics, in both undergraduate course work and related field experience, would benefit the beginning urban teacher a great deal. One respondent stated:

> As a teacher of color working in a public school where the population reflects my same ethnic background, I am still very conscious of my own identity as a whole and what the implications are when I stand up and teach my students… I think our undergraduate programs, in an effort to encourage students to consider urban education, need to have courses that explore issues of identity and how that plays out in the urban classroom. Teachers going into urban education from schools such as ours need to be consciously aware and reflective of the variety of things—power, privileges, assumptions, socioeconomics, race, ethnicity, sexuality, gender—we bring into the classroom.

Again, the respondents pointed to the need for additional, independent field experience in urban settings to address these gaps in preparation. In addition to this independent work, these teachers also commented on the importance of observing a variety of urban settings with numerous opportunities to observe successful city teachers. This would provide beginning teachers with a better understanding of how the system worked and how colleagues in the building might facilitate a teacher's job. As one respondent put it:

> I didn't know how the system worked essentially and I couldn't work the system for my kids... What does the school psychologist do? What does an evaluator do? What can the SBST [school-based support team] or a guidance counselor or a social worker do for me in a crisis situation?

One conclusion that can be drawn from these interviews is that these beginning teachers felt adequately prepared for classroom teaching in general but not for urban teaching specifically. Although gaps in any teachers' preparation are inevitable, these respondents suggest that some of the challenges of the first few years could be alleviated through more direct and thorough linkages between educational theory and urban classroom practice.

Recruitment and Hiring Process

Generally, the case study and supplemental interview respondents describe the hiring process as ad hoc, bureaucratic, and somewhat regulatory. Many of the respondents gained entrance to their schools through field experiences, through summer school teaching, or through personal connections with the building principal or with a classroom teacher. Whereas several of the respondents did participate in system-wide job fairs, only 2 of the 12 teachers reported that this process had an impact on their hiring. These teachers also complained about the paper work and bureaucracy (e.g., finger printing and other licensing procedures) associated with getting a teaching job in New York City. One respondent commented:

> There is a lot of Board of Education bureaucracy, so I had a difficult time processing paperwork. They wouldn't process my paperwork because they had excessed out teachers in the district, and they had to offer the job to them first. So, I actually taught here for a month before getting put on the payroll.

Another respondents' licensing process was sufficiently delayed that her entry into the New York Public Schools was deferred for a year:

> When I applied for my city license they rejected me because I didn't receive notification of my oral interview... So, when September came around and I didn't have a job, I spent some time out-of-state... It took three or four months for my fingerprints to clear... I applied three of four times until finally they got rid of the oral interview and they sent me three or four licenses!

Interestingly, then Chancellor Rudy Crew and members of his administration facilitated the hiring process for three of the four case study respondents. This, of course, is highly unusual and was due to the timing of a campus lecture by Chancellor Crew at the respondents' undergraduate institution. At the request of Mr. Crew, these three respondents met briefly with an upper-level personnel director who arranged for interviews with building principals. In two of the three cases, the interviews were brief (in one case fewer than five minutes), and the respondents were hired on the spot. In the third case, the respondent visited and completed intensive interviews in three schools within District 2 and received offers from all three.

The fourth case study respondent went through a more traditional hiring route, which included participation in a New York City teacher recruitment fair and a series of building principal interviews. Through the persistence of the candidate, who continued to call the building principal of her first-choice school, she was able to get a second interview and was subsequently offered a position.

Rachel and Lee were excessed (not guaranteed a job in the same school or in the district due to budget cuts) after their first year. Rachel, however, was called in June and was able to return to her original school. Lee, on the other hand, seriously contemplated leaving teaching altogether and took a retail job at Bloomingdale's (additional details on her first year experience are included in the next section on teacher induction and support). She also was called in the summer and was hired in a different district within New York City (District 3).

All of the respondents complained about the lack of school and classroom-specific information they received at the time of their hiring. These candidates expressed a need to know not only what and where they would be teaching but what they could expect in terms of work norms, collegial support, and additional resources that could assist them in the classroom. One respondent described the ad hoc nature of the hiring process in this way:

> I went to a lot of different job fairs and was hired on the spot by District 10, but then I knew someone who was the principal here. After about a five-minute interview, I was hired into a position without checking my references or seeing a portfolio, or really getting to know me.

Sharon eventually migrated from New York City public schools to a suburban district on Long Island. Sharon noted the sharp contrast in her urban and suburban hiring experiences. The brevity and impersonality of the New York City school's hiring was disconcerting to Sharon, particularly in light of her more recent experience on Long Island. She describes the process in her second setting as follows:

> I sent out resumes in December… I got a call for an interview in January. There was an extensive writing sample that I had to do based on the standards. Had to talk about a year's worth of curriculum… I was interviewed by 8 to 10 people. They told me to do a third grade lesson on problem solving… they called me back to do a lesson on persuasive writing. After that lesson, they hired me.

Sharon welcomed this type of intensive interview process because it gave her the opportunity to understand school-specific expectations, to meet several of her potential colleagues, and to discuss substantive pedagogical and management issues.

Whereas Sharon depicts an urban–suburban difference in her hiring experience, Molly described dramatic differences between her two schools within the New York City Schools. Molly, professionally unfulfilled in her first teaching setting within New York City, was inspired by her second interview experience in her current school:

> When I came for an interview, I was very impressed first off because there were six people interviewing me, not just the principal. Class-room teachers were actually assigned a forum, with six different peo-ple from different disciplines, different grade levels, who were clearly interested in who were going to be the new teachers at this school. That was really great.

These beginning teachers seemed to view the interview and job application processes as the first forms of induction into the system. In other words, as teacher candidates, they are learning as much about the school as the school is learning about the candidate. We turn our attention in the next section to further discussion on the induction of these beginning teachers.

Induction, Support, and Evaluation

The type of induction, support, and evaluation that each of the case study respondents received in their first years of urban teaching is shown in Figure 2.3.

Figure 2.3. Induction Support and Evaluation Case Study Sample

	Molly (yrs 1 & 2)	Molly (yr 3)	Sharon (yrs 1 & 2)	Sharon (yr 3)	Rachel (yrs 1, 2, & 3)	Lee (yr 1)	Lee (yrs 2 & 3)
Assigned Mentor?	No	No	No	Yes	No	No	No
Class-room Aid?	None	Full-time para-professional	None	Provided on request	none	none	Full-time para-prof.
Staff Devel-oper Support?	None	2-3 vis-its/mo	2 visits/mo	1 visit/wk	2 visits/y	2-3 vis-its/wk	None
Number of Adminis-trator Observa-tions per Year?	1 formal/yr	0 formal 1 infor-mal/ mo	0-1 for-mal/yr	Informal visits made every dayPeriod ic formal observa-tions	3-4 for-mal/yr	3 formal Weekly informal	0 formal 1 infor-mal/mo
Other Support?	Self-initi-ated mentor relation-ship	Self-initi-ated peer evalua-tions, grade-leve l meetings, staff devel-opment assistance from Teachers College	Self-initi-ated mentor relation-ship	Self-initi-ated peer evalua-tions, buddy system	New Teacher Institute	New teacher support group	Self-initi-ated peer evalua-tions, buddy system, staff develop-ment assistance from Teachers College

Clearly, there is considerable variability in the level and nature of support these respondents were afforded as novice teachers. None of the case study respondents—with the exception of Sharon in her third-year, suburban experience—were formally assigned a mentor teacher. Most, however, initiated informal mentor relationships with more veteran teachers in the building. For some, formal evaluation and guidance came in the form of one or two monthly observations from a staff developer in the first year. Two of the case study respondents received only a single formal evaluation from a building principal in their three years of full-time teaching (based on a single 30-minute classroom observation).

Induction activities also varied in their scope and frequency. Rachel attended a monthly mandatory new teacher institute, which was established to provide support and professional development opportunities explicitly for first-year teachers in District 22. An even more formal and intensive support and evaluation system was in place during Lee's first year experience in District 2. A staff developer observed and critiqued her teaching two to three times per week in the first year. The building principal conducted three formal evaluations and weekly informal observations. First-year teacher meetings were conducted monthly for professional development purposes. On the surface, it appears as though this type of support and evaluation structure could benefit a beginning teacher. In Lee's case, however, the nature of the feedback she received nearly led her to quit:

> When I started to really interact with my principal and other supervisors, I was sure that I was not meant to teach… I hated everything about it. I was having such a hard time in the building, I went home crying all the time. I felt so hopeless and I felt I could not do anything right. It was a constant evaluation, and I was never told that anything I did was good… I never minded having people in the room, but without ever hearing anything positive it was the worst thing that could happen to me as a first-year teacher.

A stark contrast to Lee's professional experience in her first setting is the support and mentorship she has received in her current position (District 3):

> It is a complete '180.' My room is across from the principal's office, and all summer I just [feared] that I was going to be in another school where the principal is going to come into my school every single day. Well, she loves what I am doing. She invites outsiders to come into my class to see what I am doing… She and the assistant principal have my students work hanging all over this school. I can go to them with any questions or problems and not fear repercussions.

In contrast to her first setting where she was under constant supervision and critical scrutiny, her current building administrator has not formally evaluated Lee. She describes her second setting as "collegial," "professionally invigorating," and a "completely different atmosphere from my first setting." In fact, she joined a group of K-1 teachers who have established their own peer observation system. The K-1 teachers in the school rotate to observe each other on a regular basis and meet weekly as a study group to assess curriculum and teaching strategies.

The situation is so improved from the first year, Lee has actively recruited others to her new school. Notably, this recruitment included Molly who departed District 14 to teach at Lee's school. Molly concurs with Lee regarding the professional culture of her second setting:

> If I had a problem and I went to the appropriate person here, I would be pretty sure that it would be fixed. Compared with the other school, I would go with tears in my eyes, screaming, kicking… and they would be like, you're doing fine and put me back in my room. It's just a completely different environment… it's just knowing that here are a number of people I can go to. A large majority of the staff is on the same page, they have a common vision of what the school should look like, what the kids should learn… there is just a collaborative and supportive environment.

Molly and Lee have also taken advantage of their school's partnership with Teachers College at Columbia University. Both have agreed to supervise student teachers and fieldwork interns from Teachers College. In return, they are entitled to free graduate courses and substantial professional development opportunities. Both Molly and Lee view this partnership as a vital nonmonetary component of their compensation and benefits package.

The need for a collegial, supportive group of peers and administrators was a priority for all of the participants in this study. A supplemental interview respondent was actually ineligible for mentorship assistance because he had successfully completed a student teaching experience. (Only those teachers who were working with emergency credentials are eligible for mentors in this particular school.) He also commented on the poor quality of the new teacher support in his setting:

> They do have a mentor system here, but almost without exception the mentors are the worst teachers in the school, and they do it because its one less period to teach… they didn't have any concept of what education is, and they were extremely lazy. Yeah, the in-school support was tremendously lacking.

Although this particular respondent found little or no support within his school, he did establish an informal mentorship with another New York City public school teacher through the New York City Writing Project:

> He'd been teaching for 32 years… he's the one that helped me understand how I should deal with a kid that's reading at a fourth grade level and what are the activities that I can do to get that student comfortable with text… If it were not for this friend of mine from the NYC Writing Project, I would have absolutely no idea what to do about these literacy issues in the classroom.

Four of the 12 respondents have switched schools and/or districts in their first three years of teaching. It is noteworthy that for the three moves within New York City public schools, the primary reason given for the switch was the stronger, more collegial professional environment afforded in the second setting. Compensation, which was not a factor in the moves within New York City, because salaries are set centrally, was a primary factor in the move by Sharon to a suburban district on Long Island. These compensation issues are discussed in the next section.

Compensation

It is clear from the case study and interview data that these teachers are primarily motivated by the intrinsic rather than extrinsic rewards of teaching. This finding is consistent with previous work on this topic.[19] When asked about their motivation for teaching in New York City, these teachers commented on the desire to work with kids, wanting to give something back and do something fulfilling, and to see that light bulb go on. "The specific attraction to New York City, they claim, was wanting to work with the kids who need the best teachers." Others shared the attractive features of New York City itself:

> I LOVE living in New York... the museums, the social life, the excitement... I don't want to leave here, and I want to be a teacher in New York City.

Despite the promise of these intrinsic rewards and the lure of city life, these beginning teachers find it exceedingly difficult to live comfortably on a beginning teacher's salary in New York City. They clearly question whether or not they can afford to remain a New York City schoolteacher. At the time of the first set of interviews, case study respondents had identical base salaries ($31,910 annually) determined by an expired teachers' contract.[20] Most of their college classmates, they claim, often earn twice as much and don't work nearly as hard. All four case study respondents, for example, report the need to supplement their income with summer school teaching, before- or after-school teaching, or additional work in retail sales. Six of the eight remaining interviewees supplement their income in some way. The two respondents who do not supplement their teaching salary report substantial spousal income or other family income.

All of the respondents are acutely aware of the low teacher salaries in New York City relative to neighboring school districts (most notably Long Island and Westchester). As Figure 2.4 indicates, New York City teachers are paid an average of at least $19,000 less than teachers in neighboring suburbs.

---

19 See, for example, Johnson, S. M. (1990). *Teachers at work*. New York: HarperCollins Publishers; and Liu, E., & Kardos, S. (2002). Hiring and professional culture in New Jersey schools. Cambridge, MA: Harvard Project on the Next Generation of Teachers.

20 At the time of the final set of interviews, the respondents were still working without a contract because negotiations between the United Federation of Teachers and the City were ongoing. A tentative agreement was recently reached which includes a considerable pay increase for beginning teachers. This proposed salary increase, however, still falls short of teacher salaries in the surrounding suburbs of New York City.

**Figure 2.4. Average Teacher Salaries 1998-1999,
New York City and Selected Surrounding Suburbs**

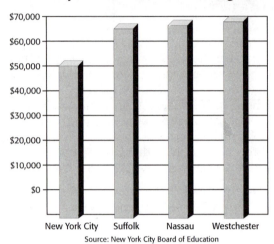

Source: New York City Board of Education

In an early interview, Sharon predicted her potential departure from New York City classroom teaching:

> I am actually looking for jobs outside the city now. Of course, the classroom management is a huge part of it, but the money is a huge part of it… the salary difference is ridiculous. I don't know if this is citywide or just my school, but there is no support at all. If I seek out support, I still don't get it. I would like to stay in education for the long-term… but I am not sure I can do it here.

After two years in District 14, she now earns an additional $15,000 per year as a result of her move to a suburban district on Long Island. She explains her decision to move:

> It wasn't so much the lack of a contract, but it was the lack of a pay increase. There were rallies and protests and all that, but the main issue for me was the money. I think if the contract with a pay increase was introduced when I was there, I might have stayed.

As Sharon's comments indicate, these beginning teachers are considering not only their current salary but also the prospects for future compensation and working conditions.

Several respondents shared specific details of the financial challenges, particularly in terms of housing costs, associated with teaching in New York City. Four of the respondents lived at home with their parents at one point of another because they could not afford to rent an apartment in New York City. Rachel, who has lived at home with her parents throughout her first three years, describes her housing challenge:

> I have lived at home with my parents these past three years to save money and pay for graduate school. I working on moving out, to a basement apartment, because it is the cheapest option to give me my

own space… I don't have supplemental income right now because I
am finding it challenging enough to be taking two classes a semester
in addition to teaching.

Lee illegally shared a one-bedroom apartment with two other teachers in her
first year (rent was $2,200 per month). She is now living in the same one-bedroom
apartment but with just a single roommate. Molly is living alone in a one-room
studio apartment that rents for $800 per month, but she needs to commute 60 to
75 minutes to her teaching job. She and other respondents have found it difficult
to find safe, affordable housing in and around their workplace. The New York
City Public Schools, in collaboration with a private real estate company, has
recently established a housing assistance program for city teachers. Although
this housing is not subsidized, there is no broker's fee associated with the placement service. Although this new program was not available to the respondents
during their first three years, all New York City Board of Education employees
are now eligible for this service.

Short-term and Long-Term Career Forecast

Previous research and recent evidence on teacher attrition, detailed earlier in
this chapter, would predict that this pool of academically talented beginning
teachers would not last long in the New York City public school system. At least
for the short-term, however, these teachers appear committed to a career in classroom teaching. Although it is difficult to predict migration or attrition that might
occur over the summer months and in subsequent school years, all but 1 of the 12
teachers studied plan to remain in their current schools. These teachers, it seems,
are beating the odds in terms of attrition and migration behavior that is typically
found among beginning urban teachers that possess strong academic credentials.

Although some migration has occurred among this group, only one subject
has moved from a low-income, urban setting to a higher-income, suburban setting. The intracity migration that has occurred is not a result of increased salary
or for a less challenging, higher achieving group of students. This suggests that
professional climate and other workplace conditions are important determinants
of a teacher's migration decisions.

Lee, for instance, appears strongly committed to a career in New York City
classroom teaching despite her highly negative first-year experience. She attributes this longer-term commitment to the collegial support and professionalism
she is experiencing in her second setting. Recall, again, that this was a first-year
teacher who was prepared to quit and enter retail sales. Lee's professional goals
are now more focused on specific programmatic changes she would like to make
in her classroom:

My goals are now much more focused on my own classroom. I am
feeling more confident about being able to run a classroom on my
own. I want to pursue things like developing my own math program,
not just these packaged programs we get. My goals are much more related to perfecting my kindergarten teaching.

Although all of the respondents plan to remain in New York City classrooms for the short-term, the longer-term forecast for these teachers is more variable. All 12 plan to remain in the field of education, but roughly half of the respondents are unsure about their future in urban classrooms. Two respondents, for example, have expressed an interest in pursuing graduate work in theater education. Three respondents plan an eventual move into educational administration, preferably within the New York City Schools. Another respondent has a longer-term goal of becoming a clinical psychologist, possibility to provide school-based counseling services.

It is interesting to note that when asked to generate a wish list for beginning urban teachers, the focus was not on compensation or other monetary incentives. Particularly as it applies to managing a classroom of high-needs students, the respondents' willingness to stay hinges primarily on strong, consistent administrative and collegial support, All of the respondents pointed to the need for beginning teachers to have a person or persons they can go to freely with questions and for constructive feedback on their teaching.

For at least one respondent, however, this support may not be sufficient to retain her on a longer-term basis as a New York City public school teacher:

> I don't know if I can be in New York City public education forever, or even for another five years. It's too much, the system is too big... you go home and like all of my friends are going to happy hour and I am grading papers. Every day you question yourself, even on the days where you feel like you have a really good support system, why I am doing this? I can't combat all of society's problems that are dumped onto my kids and dumped into the classroom.

In summary, the short-term forecast for this pool of academically talented teachers is bright. Although the field of education is in the longer-term forecast for these teachers, the specific roles they will play within the field remains unclear.

Conclusion

The Education Finance Research Consortium recently organized a symposium on the teaching workforce in New York State. A series of research papers, representing a diverse set of methodological and policy perspectives, was presented to the Board of Regents. Despite the divergent set of policy recommendations generated from that symposium, there appeared to be considerable agreement over at least the following:[21]

+ Teacher quality (how to get it and how to retain it) is *the* contemporary educational policy issue in the State.

[21] For commentary on the symposium's papers, see Roellke, C. F. (2001). Common threads and next steps: Comments on the symposium papers. *Education Finance Research Consortium Symposium on the Teaching Workforce* (pp. 168–173). Albany, NY: The University of the State of New York.

- Short-term urgent needs (e.g., teacher supply in hard-to-staff areas) must be balanced with longer-term objectives of sustaining high-quality teaching and improved student performance.

- The education policy environment in New York State can be described as top-down and regulatory, and the State should consider additional bottom-up, capacity-building strategies to add balance and coherence to the reform effort.

- Many seem to be talking *about* teachers instead of talking *with* them.

Based on the study reported here, we concur with these conclusions. This research effort is a preliminary attempt at talking *with* teachers about their preparation, recruitment, induction, and retention. We believe our discussion yielded some interesting and potentially useful results for both policymakers and school leaders. First, the professional experiences of classroom teachers are highly variable, particularly in terms of the support and guidance they receive. Second, it seems quite clear that the most pressing challenge confronted by beginning teachers is the ability to effectively manage a classroom of diverse students with high needs. Explicit attention to managing urban classrooms, including intensive preservice field experiences, might remedy this gap in preparation. According to the respondents, strong administrative and collegial supports are vital resources for meeting this challenge.

Although district-wide job fairs yielded a small number of these academically talented teachers, the majority of these candidates were hired through a seemingly ad hoc and insufficient process. All of these beginning teachers advocated removing the bureaucratic barriers to urban teaching and called for a more decentralized, informative, context-specific hiring process. For example, most of these beginning teachers expressed a need for a more thorough orientation to the work norms and teacher resources available within particular schools.

Many teachers, some more frequently than others, lack the opportunity to discuss and address classroom specific problems with colleagues and administrators in a nonthreatening, nonpunitive environment. This type of collegial, professional environment is equally as important, if not more important, than issues of compensation and other monetary, extrinsic incentives. According to these respondents, improved induction practices might be instrumental in facilitating the success of novice urban teachers.

Improved induction practices, however, may be too little to alter problems that may be endemic to the professional culture of schools. In spite of the best-designed induction plans, novice teachers will encounter many problems that cannot be fixed by a caring colleague. Induction, for example, may not be able to compensate for novices teaching outside their subject matter expertise, or teaching five classes in five separate classrooms, or working in relative isolation and privacy.[22]

---

22 Veenman, S. (1984). Perceived problems of beginning teachers. *Review of Educational Research, 54*(2), 143–178.

It should also be noted that the undergraduate institutions attended by these teachers prepare a very small percentage of the teachers currently employed in the public school system. The apparent retention success, at least initially, of this small pool of urban teachers may warrant a more prominent teacher preparation role for highly selective undergraduate institutions. Recall, also, that the majority of these respondents had considerable preservice field experience in urban settings. From the perspective of these beginning teachers, these opportunities were invaluable and should be expanded.

Living comfortably on a beginning teacher's salary in New York City is also proving to be a major hurdle for many of these beginning urban educators. Particularly troublesome is the challenge to find safe, affordable housing near their workplace. Whereas some of the respondents seem temporarily content living at home with their parents, this is not a realistic option for most beginning educators or for longer-term lodging for a career teacher. Our study confirms the need for additional housing assistance for beginning teachers in New York City. We suspect that this is a similar need in urban school systems throughout the country. New York City's recent development of a housing placement program appears to be an important step in the right direction.

As daunting as the urban teacher supply problem may be for New York City, it is our belief that the case studies and interviews conducted here give reason for optimism. All 12 respondents plan to remain in teaching, at least for the short-term. The longer they stay beyond the third through fifth year, research tells us, the more likely it is they will stay. Certainly, it is premature to make policy conclusions based on a study of this scope. The evidence presented here, however, does suggest that improved induction and professional support, coupled with competitive compensation, are likely to enhance both the recruitment and retention of qualified urban teachers.

Understanding the complex set of policy alternatives aimed at enhancing teacher quality, especially in a state as large and diverse as New York, is a major challenge. We certainly need to pay close attention to the monetary incentives we might structure to make teaching more responsive to labor markets. We also must remember that teachers do not enter the profession to become wealthy. Teachers enter the profession because they believe they can make a difference in the lives of young people. With this in mind, we must compensate and reward teachers creatively so that both the extrinsic rewards (compensation, monetary incentives) and intrinsic rewards (classroom success) can be realized.

Each of us is a former public school teacher as well as an author of this chapter. As we were examining the interview transcripts for this study, we were reminded of how our experiences as beginning middle school and high school teachers were dramatically different from our induction experiences in higher education. We do not pretend that higher-education models of faculty recruitment, induction, and retention are perfect—they most certainly are not. We would suggest, however, that the kind of signing incentives and professional support that are often afforded to junior faculty are rarely provided in K-12 education. Creative compensation packages—which might include low-interest loans, housing, childcare or tuition subsidies, and paid sabbatical leaves—are commonplace in higher education. Moreover, junior faculty in higher education are often shielded from committee assignments and may even benefit from a decreased course load as they adjust to their new professional surroundings. In our own public school teaching experience, and confirmed by the interviews conducted here, novice teachers in K-12 education are given the toughest assignments, often outside their content area or developmental expertise. They have multiple responsibilities outside the classroom, including graduate work, extra-curricular activities, committee assignments, etc.

Addressing concerns about the teacher workplace and professional climate requires moving beyond state-level and even district-level reform strategies. Because most recruitment and induction activities occur within local schools and even classrooms, it is important that policymakers at more centralized levels of the system be attentive to varying local capacities. Solutions to the teacher supply and quality problem in New York State (particularly in New York City) may require a more concerted effort to support creative, locally designed strategies to enhance the professional environment of emerging educators.

We have examined a critical but insufficient time period in the career of these academically talented classroom teachers. They teachers describe a current system of recruitment, induction, and retention that is flawed but that also has merit. Despite their criticisms, for example, these teachers were hired in hard-to-staff schools and plan to remain there for at least the short-term. Although their retention rates are near perfect at this point, it is important that we continue to track the professional progress of this talented pool of urban educators over a longer period of time. Our hope is that this type of longitudinal, case-study approach to analyzing retention and migration behavior of early career teachers can provide useful information to policy makers and school officials.

Acknowledgment

We gratefully acknowledge the research assistance of Nur-e-alam S. Chisty and Erica H. Zielewski as well as the generous support provided by the Ford Scholars program and the Faculty Research Committee at Vassar College. We also recognize Jennifer King Rice, David Monk, and Marge Plecki, each of whom provided helpful comments on earlier drafts of this chapter. We also wish to express our appreciation to participating faculty of the Consortium for Excellence in Teacher Education (CETE) for helping to identify respondents for this study. Last, we are especially indebted to the classroom teachers who volunteered their time to participate in this project.

Appendix 1. Sample Interview Instrument for Use with Novice[23] Teachers in Urban Schools

Note: Consistent with the interpretivist research methodology chosen for this portion of the study, this protocol should serve only as a

---

23 For the purposes of this study, novice is defined as a teacher with fewer than five years of full-time teaching experience.

general framework for organizing relevant topics. This general interview guide approach is described by Patton (1990) and presumes that there is common information to be obtained from each person interviewed. In addition to collecting information common to each respondent, the approach provides a degree of flexibility in the sequencing and wording of interview questions and also permits additional questions and probes as needed.

Introduction

Hello, I am Chris Roellke, an assistant professor at Vassar College. This interview will contribute to a study I am conducting on teacher preparation, recruitment, and retention in urban schools, and I am very grateful for your participation. I am going to ask you to reflect on your classroom teaching experiences as well as your preparation for teaching. Your responses in this interview will be kept confidential, and your name will not appear on any of the study documents or in the final report. To assure that I am accurate in capturing and understanding what you tell me in the interview, I would like to request your permission to tape record our discussion. I may also take a few notes. If there is anything you wish to say off the record, or if you have any questions or concerns along the way, please let me know. Your participation in this study is voluntary, and you may stop the interview at any point. Do you have any questions or concerns at this time?

Background Information

+ School and district information:
+ Undergraduate institution:
+ Undergraduate major:
+ Location and duration of student teaching assignment:
+ Other noteworthy field experiences that contributed to your preparation as a teacher:
+ Current class assignment and demographic makeup of class:

Sample Questions

+ Please describe your undergraduate preparation for teaching. In what ways do you feel you were adequately prepared? In what ways do you feel you were unprepared?
+ Please describe the process of being hired for a teaching position in this school. What were the particular features of this school that you found professionally appealing at the time that you were hired? What issues concerned you at the time you were hired?
+ Please describe how decisions are made about which class or classes you will teach?
+ Please describe a typical day in your classroom? Probe: How has this experience changed over the course of a school year? How about from one school year to the next (for those with more than one year of experience)?

♦ In addition to your teaching responsibilities, what other contractual and professional obligations do you have in this school?

♦ Describe the level of support you have received as a beginning teacher in this school. Probe: From other beginning teachers? From mentors and veteran teachers? From others?

♦ Please describe the opportunities for professional development within this school or school district.

♦ What are your professional plans and goals for next year? What are your longer-term professional plans and goals?

♦ What are the most rewarding aspects of your teaching experience? What are the least rewarding aspects of your teaching experience?

♦ If you could generate a wish list for beginning teachers in urban schools, what would be on that list?

♦ Please describe your living situation in or near New York City. Probe: What are the general monthly budget and managing expenses on a beginning teacher's salary?

♦ Is there any other information you would like to add regarding the preparation, recruitment, induction, or retention of beginning urban teachers?

Appendix 2.   The Consortium for Excellence in Teacher Education

The Consortium for Excellence in Teacher Education (CETE) was formed in 1983 when the first national education reports began calling for improvements in both the caliber of individuals entering the teaching profession and the education they receive. The initial goals of the Consortium were to create a support-and-exchange network for the teacher education programs at member colleges—which enjoyed many common possibilities, yet shared certain common concerns—and to explore ways to ensure that preparation to teach remained a compelling option for undergraduates at our institutions.

CETE students represent an especially talented pool of prospective teachers; they are individuals who respond resourcefully to the challenges of the classroom and who act effectively in the larger process of educational reform. They are also the beneficiaries of tremendous academic and institutional resources. For these reasons, we feel a strong sense of social responsibility to encourage and assist those who are interested in education and related human service fields.

The members of CETE view teaching as a moral craft and their role as one of helping to integrate theory and practice and to cultivate thoughtful analytical practitioners. It is a humanistic, inquiry-oriented approach to teacher education that is informed by two principles: development and integration. A third tenet of many CETE institutions is the working assumption that small is beautiful, especially in terms of the development and nurturance of a community of reflective practitioners. Because CETE members advocate high standards without standardization, they also endorse multiple pathways to teacher preparation, and each of their programs has a distinctive thematic emphasis. Like all good preparation programs, CETE programs are informed by best practice as articulated by the education research community and carried out by effective teachers in the schools. Finally, the various Consortium member institutions are influenced by and must be responsive to the regulation and mandates of their particular state department of education or state legislature. CETE member institutions include Barnard College, Bates College, Bowdoin College, Brandeis University, Brown University, Bryn Mawr and Haverford Colleges, Connecticut College, Dartmouth College, Harvard University, Middlebury College, Mount Holyoke College, University of Pennsylvania, Princeton University, Smith College, Swarthmore College, Vassar College, Wellesley College, Wheaton College, and Yale University.

3

The Impact of Teacher Turnover on Teacher Quality: Findings From Four States

Neil D. Theobald
Indiana University

Sabrina W.M. Laine
North Central Regional Educational Laboratory

Teachers constitute the basic manipulable input into the educational process as conducted in schools. Whether it is done in knowledge or in ignorance, the shaping of personnel policies is the shaping of school education. (Bowman, 1973)

Changing and improving schools has become, as Seymour Sarason observes, one of the largest cottage industries in 21st century America. Innumerable strategies for school improvement have been developed and are subject to ongoing experimentation. Yet, as Bowman so aptly notes, educating children is essentially a labor-dependent enterprise, and as such, school improvement efforts focus on placing qualified teachers in every elementary and secondary classroom.

This chapter summarizes briefly the results of a project that explored why teachers are leaving public school districts in four Midwest states (IL, IN, MN, WI), and what school districts and states can do to address these issues. This research project analyzed separately three types of novice teachers, specifically, (1) those who taught continuously in the same district all 5 years ("stayers"), (2) those who transferred to another school district(s) within a state but remained in the same state all 5 years ("movers"), and (3) those who left public school teaching in a state and did not return to teaching ("leavers"). To investigate the factors that contribute to retaining teachers in the profession, this study surveyed 392 5-year veteran teachers. In addition, the third component of the study reported on a survey of district superintendents' perspectives on effective strategies for recruiting and retaining teachers.

Our findings indicate that during the 5-year period, the cumulative losses of beginning teachers from the school district that hired them ranges from less than 40% in Minnesota and Wisconsin to nearly 60% in Illinois. "Leavers" comprise 20% of the entering cohorts in Minnesota and Wisconsin, 28% in Indiana, and 32% in Illinois. "Movers" comprise less than 20% of the cohort in every state except Illinois; in Illinois, movers comprise 26% of the cohort. Secondary teachers in low-wage districts are significantly more likely to leave teaching in three of four states. Teachers with graduate degrees, arts teachers, science teachers, and vocational education teachers are significantly more likely to leave teaching in three of four states. In every state except Indiana, special educators are significantly more likely to transfer to a position in another district than are other teachers.

Survey responses from "stayers" indicate that they are most dissatisfied with the amount of time required to do their job outside of the regular school day and are also very dissatisfied with their opportunities to teach small classes. In terms of the factors that are most important in their decision to continue teaching, survey responses focus on altruism; supportive colleagues, parents, and administrators; autonomy; and remuneration. These novice teachers cite opportunities to work with a mentor and opportunities to teach in a small school as the least important factors in their decision to continue teaching.

Survey responses from school administrators indicate that 75% to 100% of teachers who leave are regarded as "very effective" or "effective" in the classroom. This finding is supported by an analysis of federal survey data on teacher turnover conducted by Education Week (Edwards, 2000) that reported teachers who score in the top 25% nationally on the Scholastic Aptitude Test (SAT) or American College Test (ACT) assessments are more likely to leave teaching. The pressure is on, according to superintendents, to replace these teachers with equally effective recruits or to adopt strategies to retain effective teachers longer in the profession. Recruitment, retention, and mobility issues are closely related to one another, and policies to address these issues—especially as they relate to new teachers—need to be viewed systemically by schools, districts, and states. This chapter attempts to look at all three issues simultaneously by presenting the data, analyzing the implications of the data, and suggesting policy recommendations for both state and local education leaders. How teacher mobility, recruitment, and retention research fit into the larger picture of education reform will be discussed first.

The Role of Educational Reform

Lessons from previous reform experiences suggest that policymakers in the 21st century face a formidable task in devising strategies that will improve the quality of our teaching force. The last two decades of reform were set in motion by commission reports such as *A Nation at Risk*—which sought to rely primarily on state regulatory power and secondarily on additional financial resources—in a direct attack on schooling problems, including teacher quality. A key assumption underlying this first wave of reform was that teachers should continue to organize their classrooms as they always had done, only do so harder and faster and with stricter state scrutiny. Evidence quickly surfaced, though, that added bureaucracy and more centralized control did not improve teacher quality or lead to improved student achievement. Work by Darling-Hammond and Wise (1985) and Rosenholtz (1987) suggests that this first approach may actually have been counterproductive in addressing these issues.

A second reform approach ensued, seeking to decrease bureaucracy and decentralize decision making. Teaching was even more centrally the focus of this "second wave."

> Reforms began to focus on the structure of the teaching occupation and the overall structural features of schools. Thus, teachers' salaries in many states and districts were raised; teachers were often provided with some additional decision-making authority; and, to a lesser extent, opportunities were created that would allow teachers to advance professionally without leaving the classroom. (Hirsch, Koppich, & Knapp, 1998, p. 2)

The limited achievements resulting from these efforts to institute reforms, such as school-based management and teacher professionalism, spurred the current third wave of reform that seeks to increase the available supply of high-quality teachers. Programs such as Troops to Teachers and Teach for America were implemented nationwide to recruit new candidates into teaching. Additionally, many states have instituted alternative certification programs to decrease and postpone formal education training and place midcareer professionals into teaching immediately.

Yet, the payoff from such supply-side initiatives could be short-lived if state and local policymakers do not concurrently implement policies to improve the likelihood that these individuals remain in the profession. As John Goodlad observed, "Talk of securing and maintaining a stable corps of outstanding teachers is empty rhetoric unless serious efforts are made to study and remedy the conditions likely to drive out those already recruited" (1983, p. 173).

Teacher Quality at the Center of Education Reform

The issue of staffing all classrooms with qualified teachers has received increased attention in recent years because of accumulating research evidence showing that teacher quality (e.g., subject matter knowledge, cognitive ability, selectivity of college attended) is the single most important school factor affecting student achievement.[1]

Another reason teacher supply receives considerable attention is research showing that the career of teaching is characterized by high mobility (Ingersoll, 1995, 2001; Murnane, Singer, Willett, Kemple, & Olsen, 1991). Such high rates of teacher turnover thwart efforts to improve our schools in at least two significant ways. First, research shows that high-performing schools are distinguished by

---

1 Hanushek, Kain, and Rivkin (1999) reported that variations in teacher quality explain at least 7% of student test score differences. Although 7% may not seem like much, in these kinds of studies this is a large finding.

stability, continuity, and cohesion among employees (Bryk, Lee, & Smith, 1990; Coleman & Hoffer, 1987). High rates of teacher turnover obviously disrupt the stability, continuity, and cohesion of instructors, and thus student performance. Additionally, the ability of less-effective schools to institutionalize a successful reform effort depends crucially on the continued presence of large numbers of teachers who are knowledgeable about, and committed to, the change (Fullan, 1991). Although schools and districts undergoing reform often seek changes in staffing to align the skills and expertise of the faculty with a new vision and mission, veteran teachers play a vital role in providing continuing assistance to new teachers and administrators. Several studies point to high turnover in a school's teaching staff as one of the most powerful factors in stifling school improvement efforts (Berman & McLaughlin, 1977; Huberman & Miles, 1984).

Second, the art of teaching children is a developmental process involving a complex set of skills, many of which can be well honed only on the job. Although better preservice teacher education can begin the process of improving teacher quality, research clearly shows that inexperienced teachers continue to sharpen their skills and become more effective teachers during the first few years in the classroom. The continual need for school districts to hire new, inexperienced teachers to replace teachers who leave after a short teaching tenure "can only hinder these districts' efforts to improve the education they provide" (Murnane et al., 1991, p. 65).

Thus, state and local policymakers have come to recognize that efforts to improve elementary and secondary education will depend critically on our success in attracting, recruiting, and retaining capable people in the teaching profession. Simply put, we cannot have better schools until we have better teachers.

The Project

In 1999, the North Central Regional Educational Laboratory (NCREL) conducted a survey of state education policymakers in the Midwest to determine the most pressing policy questions related to teacher supply and demand. Teacher turnover and the effectiveness of teacher recruitment and retention strategies topped policymakers' list of concerns. With funding from NCREL, researchers at Indiana University, Ohio University, and the University of Minnesota began to study these issues.

Teacher Turnover

Previous research into teacher turnover tended to focus solely on those teachers who leave the profession altogether ie, the "leavers" or group 3 referenced in the opening paragraph of this article (Grissmer & Kirby, 1987; Heyns, 1988; Murnane, 1987; Murnane, Singer, & Willett, 1988). As long as an individual remains in teaching, that individual is not included in such studies. Thus, the traditional approach does not differentiate between a teacher who is employed by five different school districts in a state during the first 5 years in the profession (a "mover") and a teacher who works in the same district for all 5 years (a "stayer"). These two teacher career paths have vastly different effects on local school programs, though, because "movers" are indistinguishable—from the perspective of their former employers and former students—from "leavers." It is important to note that a limitation of this study is that it does not distinguish between teachers who transfer across schools in district and those who move from district to district. Such distinctions would help inform policy at the school level. For a school, any transfer—be it building-to-building or district-to-district—requires a teacher replacement. In this study, however, we concentrate on district-level impact and look at transfers out of district, out of state, and out of the teaching profession altogether.

This project follows the lead of Ingersoll (1995) and views teachers moving among school districts ("movers") to be as important for analysis as those teachers exiting from the profession ("leavers"). "The premise underlying this perspective is that, whether those departing are moving to a similar job in another organization or leaving the occupation altogether, their departures similarly impact and are impacted by the organization" (Ingersoll, 2001, p. 356). From the perspective of the school, whether a departing teacher is moving to another district or leaving the profession, that individual most likely must be replaced.

The focus on analyzing teacher attrition and retention at the school district level does not, of course, reflect a view that previous research into state-level attrition is unimportant. Instead, this focus is motivated by a judgment that the decisions most likely to influence teacher retention do not occur at the state level; they occur at the district level. Therefore, rather than investigating the behavior of a state's teachers, without accounting for movements among school districts, this study includes the movement of teachers across school districts in its analysis of teacher retention.

The dataset used for this study consisted of information on 11,787 teachers who began their teaching careers in four Midwest states during the 1995 to 1996 school year. The career of each teacher in the sample was followed up from the year of entry through the 2000 to 2001 school year. The dataset provides information on the characteristics of the teachers and their job assignments.

To investigate the factors that contribute to retaining teachers in the profession, this study surveyed 392 public school teachers who have continuously taught in the same districts for 5 years ("stayers"). This component will further our understanding of district characteristics that play a prominent role in teachers' decisions to continue teaching. In particular, this portion of the study examined the role of employee compensation, administrative support, and the degree of teacher input into and influence over school policies. In short, the first component of the teacher turnover study focused on determining which kinds of teachers are more prone to stay in teaching and the second component sought to answer why they chose to stay.

Teacher Recruitment and Retention

Another survey was sent to every school district superintendent in a seven-state region (IA, IL, IN, MI, MN, OH, WI) to begin to identify effective strategies for recruiting and retaining teachers in the profession, especially in the first 5 years. A one-page survey was designed to collect basic information about which strategies have been adopted and how effective they have been at recruiting and retaining teachers. The survey only included strategies that could be implemented at the school or district level. The purpose of the survey was to gauge district superintendents' perspectives about the effectiveness of the recruitment and retention strategies they have implemented. A total of 2,413 superintendents (69%) in the seven states responded to the survey. Survey results were largely representative of all districts based on the size of the districts, the poverty level of districts (as measured by free and reduced-price lunch rates), and the location of districts (urban, rural, or suburban).

With the exception of this survey, no single research study has looked broadly at the effectiveness of recruitment and retention strategies, incentives, and state policies. Although there are many evaluations of specific approaches to recruiting and retaining teachers—such as the New Teacher Project in Santa Cruz, CA—these studies do little to convince policymakers that these programs would be similarly effective if implemented on a larger scale. Much more data are needed, however, on the specific qualities of the recruitment and retention strategies rated as "very successful" by superintendents in this survey; nonetheless, it is a place to begin.

Findings

Tracking Teacher Turnover

Teaching is an occupation that loses many of its newly trained practitioners early in their careers. As shown in Figure 3.1, during the 5-year period, the cumulative losses of beginning teachers from the school district that hired them was slightly more than 50%, consisting of 23% who moved to different districts and 28% who left teaching altogether. These percentages are consistent with previous national findings (Ingersoll, 1995).

Figure 3.1 also provides information on the relationship between personal characteristics of teachers and the likelihood that they leave their district. In terms of over-all teacher turnover—the sum of the percent of teachers that move among districts and the percent that leave the profession—minority teachers and teachers who enter the profession at age 30 years or younger depart at significantly higher rates. Teachers who are 31 years or older when they enter the profession and teachers with graduate degrees are significantly less likely to depart. White teachers are also less likely to depart, but this relationship is not as strong as it is for those teachers who enter at an older age or who possess a graduate degree.

Figure 3.1. Percent Of Teacher Turnover by Personal Characteristics, In Five Years Among 11,787 Teachers

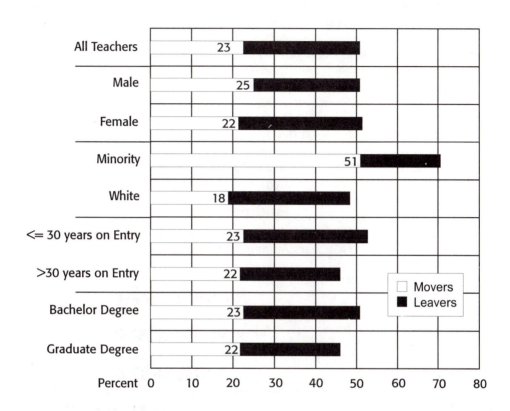

The results illustrated in Figure 3.1 emphasize the importance of clearly specifying how "teacher turnover" is to be defined. If we look at the traditional definition of "teacher turnover" (ie, those teachers who leave the profession altogether), minority teachers are significantly less likely to leave the profession. Researchers have concluded that minority teachers, because they tend to come from lower socioeconomic backgrounds, are less occupationally mobile than whites (Dworkin, 1980; Kemple, 1989). However, the results in Figure 3.1 show nuanced behavior. Although minority teachers are less likely to leave the profession altogether, they are much more likely to transfer among school districts. Theobald and Gritz (1996, p. 21) found that "teachers transfer from their first teaching position to another school district when they confront less desirable situations that are amenable to improvement by transferring to a different public school district," and they leave the profession when confronted with "less desirable situations that cannot be improved by moving to another school district." Thus, it appears that minority teachers are more able to improve their situation by transferring to another district than are other teachers. A possible explanation for this result is that high demand for minority teachers provides them with more job options than are available to other teachers.

Another interesting finding in Figure 3.1 is the lack of a significant difference by gender. Data from the 1960s and 1970s show that turnover rates among women entering teaching was approximately 30% higher than attrition among men entering at that time. Grissmer and Kirby (1987) explain this result by appealing to the differing "life-cycle priorities" of young women and young men and argue that women have been more likely to leave teaching because they do so to raise families. These data suggest that, in the late 1990s, this traditional pattern no longer exists in these four states.

The remaining results are consistent with previous research. Greenberg and McCall (1974) previously found that teachers with graduate degrees had lower turnover rates. Several previous studies have found that teachers' decisions whether to stay or leave the teaching profession are highly influenced by their age at entry (Bobbitt, Leich, Whitener, & Lynch, 1994; Boe, Bobbitt, Cook, Barkanic, & Maislin, 1998).

Figure 3.2. Percent Of Urban Teacher Turnover by Personal Characteristics, In Five Years Among 3,194 Teachers

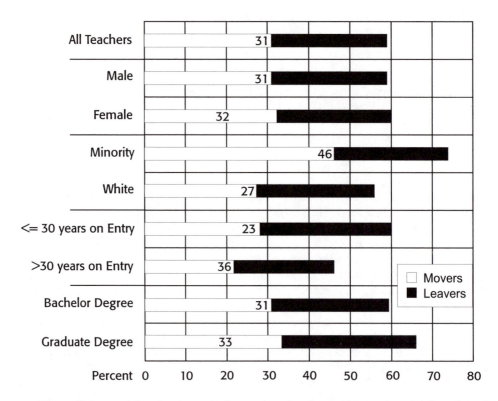

Figure 3.2 provides the same information for the 3,194 novice teachers hired by urban school districts during the period 1995 to 1996. Previous research (Darling-Hammond & Green, 1994; Kozol, 1991; Oakes, 1990; Rosenholtz, 1985) has

speculated that urban teachers have a higher turnover rate. These data clearly support this assumption. Urban teachers—regardless of their gender, race, age, or degree status—are significantly more likely to move out of their district than are novice teachers hired by nonurban districts. Yet, urban teachers are no more likely to leave teaching than are nonurban teachers.

This result highlights the importance of including "movers" in an analysis of teacher turnover. The more narrow definition of turnover (i.e., only those who leave the teaching profession) would lead us to conclude that turnover rates are no higher in urban than in nonurban districts. When we include "movers," though, the turnover rates for minority and older teachers are more than 20% higher in urban districts than they are in nonurban districts.

Figure 3.3. Percent Of Teacher Turnover by Selected Academic Field Among 11,787 Teachers

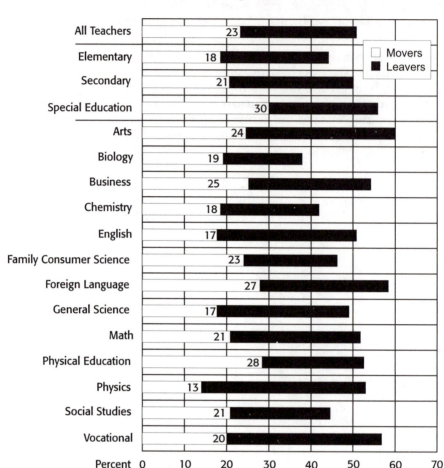

Percent of teacher turnover in five years among 11.787 teachers who entered the profession in four Midwestern states in 1995-96,

Among the most important findings in previous research is the influence of academic field on teacher turnover. Ingersoll (2001) reports "although both special education and math/science teachers were more likely to migrate [i.e., move] than other kinds of teachers, neither was more likely to leave teaching altogether" (pp. 519-520). The data in Figure 3.3 concur with this finding for special educators but differ substantially for math and science teachers. Novice special educators in these four states are more likely to transfer to another school district but are not any more likely to leave teaching altogether. As with minority teachers, it may be that high demand for special education teachers provides them with a greater ability to improve their situation by transferring than is available to other teachers.

Figure 3.3 shows, however, that math teachers—and all science teachers except those specializing in biology—are much more likely to leave teaching and are less likely to transfer among school districts. A variety of incentives influence the labor market decisions made by teachers. One set of incentives is the salary an individual can earn in teaching compared with a salary in an alternative occupation. Research has shown that math and science teachers can expect higher salaries in their alternative professions than can other teachers and, therefore, are more likely to leave (Murnane et al., 1991). Interestingly, in these four states in the late 1990s, biology teachers were the least likely to leave. Clearly, the alternative career paths available to individuals trained as high school biology teachers—as well as those teaching family consumer science, physical education, and social studies—differ substantially from those open to individuals trained in physics or chemistry.

The impact of academic field on being a "mover" is also quite striking. Physical education teachers are the most likely to move, and physics teachers are the least likely to move. To return to the reasoning discussed earlier for minority teachers and special educators, it appears that physical education teachers are able to improve their situation by transferring, although physics teachers cannot. Anecdotal evidence suggests that because physical education teachers are much more likely to be coaches, a transfer to another school district allows them to "move up the ladder" in a way that is not available to physics teachers—especially if the less desirable situation facing the physics teacher is relatively low pay compared to what he or she could earn outside the teaching profession. Few school districts pay teachers in high-wage academic fields more than they pay teachers in low-wage fields.

Understanding Teacher Turnover

The survey of 392 "stayers" asked them (1) to examine 21 characteristics of teaching and to indicate how important they considered each job characteristic to be in their decision to persist in teaching and (2) to rate their present level of satisfaction for each characteristic. Figure 3.4 identifies the seven characteristics that novice teachers judge important in their decision to continue their teaching career but with which they appear to be least satisfied, ie, the disincentives to continue teaching. From the perspective of these teachers, for each of the following characteristics, their current level of satisfaction lags behind the item's importance: (1) limited support from outside the school (parents and superintendent) for serving children as these novice teachers believe best, (2) too few opportunities to work individually with children in small classes, (3) a work schedule that is far more demanding than initially expected, and (4) limited financial rewards.

Figure 3.4. Job Characteristics: Perceived Importance and Satisfaction Indicating Significant Differences Reported by Novice Teachers (n = 392)

Characteristics	Indicate Important Job Characteristic (%)	Percentage Indicating Satisfaction With Job Characteristic (%)
Support Received From Parents of Your Students	99	72
Opportunities to Teach Small Classes	98	56
Amount of Time Required to Do Job Outside of Regular School Day	96	42
Potential Salary Level	95	57
Current Salary Level	94	55
Level of Fringe Benefits	96	69
Support Received from Superintendent	95	63

The relative dissatisfaction with the perceived support received from superintendents and parents is consistent with an environment in which novice teachers perceive themselves as professionals who best know how to educate the students in their classrooms. Thus, they look to outside entities for support in this mission. To the extent that parents and superintendents reflect priorities that are established outside the school, novice teachers may not perceive these parties as being supportive of their attempts to serve children as these novice teachers believe best.

The opportunity to work individually with children in small classes is consistent with these teachers' altruistic desire to impact the lives of children in a significant manner. One-on-one instruction can be customized, thus producing rapid and noticeable gains in student performance while providing the instructor with immediate, poignant rewards. In larger classes, the instruction is less tailored to each student, the gain in performance across all students may be less noticeable, and the ensuing emotional rewards may be diminished.

The role of teachers' salaries and benefits in making career decisions is one of the more intensely researched topics in education. Murnane and Olsen (1990) showed that K-12 teachers are at least as responsive as other workers to interoccupational wage differences when deciding to change occupations. Gritz and Theobald (1996) show that although teachers respond to interdistrict wage differentials within the teaching profession in deciding to change districts, this relationship is not as strong as the response to wage differentials between teaching and other occupations. Murnane and Olsen (1989) found that likely employment opportunities outside of teaching were powerful predictors of the length of teaching careers. The salary available in these likely alternative professions was negatively related to the amount of time a new teacher remained in a state's K-12 education system. Additionally, Murnane, Singer, Willett, Kemple, and Olsen (1991) concluded that the likelihood of returning to teaching after an interruption in a teaching career depends on the likely employment options outside of teaching.

Thus, novice teacher dissatisfaction with salary and benefit levels requires additional analysis. How do teachers' salaries affect career decisions? In what ways do these career decisions affect students? Most attention in many states has focused not on these questions but on the more general question of whether educational expenditures are associated with educational quality. A narrower focus that examines how these expenditures affect who teaches, and where, could provide useful information. Do educational expenditures impact districts' ability to hire skilled teachers?

Influencing Teacher Turnover

Strategies to recruit and retain teachers can have a tremendous influence on teacher turnover. The last several years have seen increasing attention being paid to the number of teachers retiring, the low numbers of teachers staying in the profession, and the increasing number of students in K-12 schools. Of course, issues of teacher supply and demand are primarily driven by geographic location and content area expertise. That is why the identification and implementation of strategies to address teacher turnover are so complex and varied. Most states in the Midwest reported knowing very little about the supply of teachers in the "pipeline," such as where teachers were educated or grew up and how this information might be used to attract teachers to high-need areas (Hare, Nathan, Darland & Laine, 2000). A study conducted by the Southern Regional Education Board reported that new graduates tend to take jobs in school districts close to the institution from which they graduated. "States might be able to use this pattern to their advantage, for example, by supporting school-college partnerships that promote quality teacher preparation" (Cornett, 2002, p. 5).

Although a variety of approaches to increase teacher recruitment and retention have been tried and used, one consistent theme emerged from the survey of district superintendents: New teacher support programs were reported as successful in both recruiting and retaining teachers (Figure 3.5). Although new teacher support programs exist at some level in every state in the region, they are not evenly distributed across all kinds of districts. New teacher support programs are most often found in urban and suburban districts with much smaller numbers being reported in rural and small districts.

Figure 3.5. Districts With New Teacher Support Programs by Location

State	No. Urban (%)	No. Suburban (%)	No. Rural (%)
Illinois	17 (68)	129 (73.3)	132 (44.6)
Indiana	19 (100)	30 (90.9)	128 (83.7)
Iowa	8 (87.5)	4 (66.7)	120 (41.8)
Michigan	8 (80)	65 (95.6)	232 (92.8)
Minnesota	4 (80)	40 (88.9)	127 (59.1)
Ohio	14 (82.4)	98 (87.5)	234 (92.1)
Wisconsin	10 (100)	31 (81.6)	124 (62.9)
Source: Hare, Heap, & Raack, 2001, p. 3			

Although a majority of superintendents providing new teachers with support programs reported that teacher attrition decreased by 50% or more, program implementation varied significantly. For example, programs rated as "very successful" were more likely to have adequate funding for all interested teachers, to provide additional training or professional development for new teachers, and to include training for administrators on how to support new teachers (Hare & Heap, 2001).

Other retention strategies that were rated "very successful" by a majority of the superintendents who have implemented them included the following: restructuring schools to make them smaller, recruiting from and training in the community, providing common planning time for teachers, and involving teachers in decision making. Although restructuring schools to make them smaller was a top-rated retention strategy, it had been implemented in only 14% of the districts responding to the survey. Similarly, recruiting from and training in the community had been adopted in only 28% of the districts responding, although the majority of districts making use of this retention strategy are either low-wealth or urban. What is important to note about all four of these strategies is that they can be adopted by districts seeking to stem teacher attrition for relatively low cost. Although they may require some change in how a school operates, the benefits—especially in rural and small school districts—appear substantial, according to survey respondents.

On the flip side of retention strategies are efforts by school districts to aggressively recruit new teachers (Figure 3.6). One recruitment strategy adopted by 58% of the districts in the Midwest is hiring under temporary licenses. Across the region, the largest districts and the poorest districts were most likely to report using this strategy (74% of districts with more than 10,000 students and 61% of the region's poorest districts as defined by the number of students receiving free or reduced-price lunches, respectively). Despite the number of districts hiring under temporary licenses, few of them rated this strategy as a "very successful" method of recruiting teachers. Some of the recruitment strategies that were rated "very successful" by superintendents included placing high-demand teachers above entry level on the salary scale, aggressively recruiting from teacher preparation institutions, retraining current staff, and providing flexibility in compensation in return for higher education and professional experiences outside of teaching.

**Figure 3.6. Most Successful Recruitment Strategies
As Rated by Districts Using a Strategy**

Recruitment Strategy	Rated "Very Successful" (%)
Placing High-Demand Teachers Above Entry on The Salary Scale	59
Aggressively Recruiting From Teacher-Preparation Institutions	49
Retraining Current Staff	47
Offering Support to Beginning Teachers	47
Providing Salary Schedule Credit for Higher Educational Experience	46
Providing Salary Schedule Credit for Nonteaching Experience	44
Source: Hare & Heap, 2001, p. 29.	

Three of the top-rated approaches to teacher recruitment require some form of flexible compensation strategy different from most traditional teacher contracts, which typically reward teachers for years of experience and degree level. Placing new teachers in high-demand subjects above the entry level on the salary scale allows superintendents to be more responsive to the marketplace. Minnesota, Wisconsin, and Michigan (35.4%, 33.7% and, 29.1%, respectively) were the most likely to report having adopted this strategy and found it to be successful in recruiting new teachers. Use of all three of these approaches varies significantly across the region, but where they were reported, they were found to be successful.

Policy Recommendations

The evidence presented in this report suggests that the current focus on addressing supply-and-demand issues through macro-level, statewide initiatives—such as Teach for America and generic alternative certification programs—may be misplaced.[2] Although each of these initiatives may be important for solving other problems facing the teaching profession, they are not well suited for addressing the micro-level, supply-and-demand issues facing urban school districts and all districts seeking to retain the services of teachers with skills that are in high demand in the general labor market. Thus, state policy must focus on those initiatives most likely to influence behavior of (1) teachers in specific subject areas in all districts and (2) all teachers in specific types of districts. Therefore, rather than outlining policy recommendations for a state's teachers, this section seeks to influence the behavior of teachers within school districts.

The findings in this report indicate that, during a 5-year period, the cumulative losses of beginning teachers from the school district that hired them ranged from less than 40% in Minnesota and Wisconsin to nearly 60% in Illinois. Secondary teachers in low-wage districts, though, are significantly more likely to leave teaching in each of the four states. How can states structure the profession to put these districts on a more level playing field with high-wage districts? Teachers with graduate degrees, arts teachers, science teachers, and vocational education teachers are also significantly more likely to leave teaching. How can states structure the teaching profession to stanch the outflow of individuals with other career options? Special educators are significantly more likely to transfer to a position in another district than are other teachers. This suggests there are may be qualitative differences in special education programs that may not exist in other parts of the school program. How do states make sure that special education students receive comparable services across a state?

Influencing Labor Market Behavior of Teachers in Specific Subject Areas in All Districts

Options include:

♦ Changing the current rigid teacher salary structure, which imposes costs to stay in teaching that vary considerably from field to field. State-level bonuses for novice teachers in high-attrition subject areas—such as arts, science, and vocational education—would lower the costs facing these teachers. Larger stipends for novice teachers with graduate degrees may better reflect the labor market value of these teachers. Discussions of differential teacher pay plans currently center on their effectiveness for enhancing performance. Yet, these plans founder because important attributes of teacher quality, such

---

2 The authors thank Ada Simmons of the Indiana Education Policy Center and William Driscoll of Levin & Driscoll for clarifying this point. Any errors or omissions, however, are the responsibility of the authors.

as the ability to convey knowledge or enthusiasm for class material, are difficult to measure and may not be related to more quantifiable characteristics. Unfortunately, though, even less evidence is available on the effects of differentiating pay at the individual level to pay for attributes that are highly correlated with student performance (e.g., teacher test scores, selectivity of college). Viewing the issue from a broader, labor market perspective might allow states to begin to allocate salary resources more effectively.

- Institute a retention bonus (ie, "golden handcuffs") for teachers in high attrition subject areas such as arts, science, and vocational education and for teachers with graduate degrees. Teachers that successfully complete 1 year of service would be eligible to participate in such a program. For each year of service, a teacher would have a bonus set aside in his or her name, and when he or she completed a fixed number of years (e.g., 5 years of continuous service), the first year's bonus would be distributed. Such a program could follow a 5-year vesting schedule for a set period. If a teacher leaves a district, unvested funds are forfeited.

- Lower barriers to entry for arts, science, and vocational education teachers to develop alternative routes into the profession for these subject areas only. These programs might target individuals older than 30 years who are more likely to remain in teaching and for whom high levels of off-the-job training may be particularly impractical.

- Work with the community and local institutions of higher education to retrain current staff to teach in high-attrition subject areas. Community institutions such as banks can help offset tuition costs to ensure greater retention of teachers who agree to continue to live and work in the local schools. Teacher preparation programs can work with local communities to provide access to classes and ongoing mentoring for home-grown teachers.

Influencing Labor Market Behavior of All Teachers in Specific Districts

Teachers in each state point to their altruism, a supportive teaching environment, autonomy in the classroom, and equitable remuneration as the most important factors in keeping them in teaching. Options for addressing these factors include:

- Provide higher funding to school districts with more disadvantaged students. What is most striking in the survey responses is the utter lack of comments about "difficult kids" or "discipline problems." What the surveys focus on instead is the difficulty in remaining altruistic in the face of a perceived lack of resources in some districts for providing smaller classes and the personal attention children need.

♦ Create an external context in all school districts that is supportive of novice teachers and their work. Survey results suggest that novice teachers find their colleagues and school-level principals very supportive. However, the next layer of interactions—those involving parents and superintendents—are much more varied. In a sizable number of school districts, there appears to be a mismatch between the goals and aspirations of those in the school and those most closely involved with, but outside, the school. States might review the superintendent and teacher preparation programs in their state universities to ensure that potential teachers and superintendents are well prepared to work in urban and poor rural districts. They might also launch education programs for parents in urban and poor rural districts that seek to provide them with tools to be supportive of their children's education.

♦ Support novice teachers through high-quality induction and mentoring programs that will have long-term benefits for both recruitment and retention. However, new teacher support programs without adequate training and funding for mentors, or enough access to mentors for novice teachers, are unlikely to have the desired effects.

♦ Specify desired learning outcomes with sufficient restraint for classroom teachers to have a reasonable say as well. The novice teachers surveyed in this report are well satisfied with the autonomy they currently have. As they move to implement new federal legislation, states must be cognizant of the extreme importance that teachers place on the freedom to make their own decisions regarding what is taught and what instructional approaches used.

♦ Restructure school size, the school day, and teacher' involvement in decision making to create a significant effect on teacher retention without significant costs to the school or district.

♦ Provide pay premiums for novice teachers in high attrition districts (ie, compensating differentials). The goal of this salary premium is to allow these districts to compete better for the best new teachers.

The evidence presented in this report suggests that the current focus on supply-side initiatives such as Teach for America and alternative certification may be misplaced. Consistent with prior empirical research (Gritz & Theobald, 1996; Ingersoll, 1995, 2001; Theobald & Gritz, 1996), the data show that Midwest schools face excess demand for new teachers caused by teacher turnover rates in the first five years that exceed 50%. The focus on increasing teacher supply is likely to prove inadequate—especially for poorer and more complex school districts that are rarely on the receiving end of teacher transfers—if new teachers brought into the profession continue to move and leave in such large numbers. Thus, state policies need also—if not primarily—to address this issue from the demand-side by decreasing turnover rather than focusing solely on the supply-side.

Demand-side options include:

- ◆ Increasing teacher salaries so that the general level of teacher salaries compares favorably to nonteaching salaries in the state.

- ◆ Changing the current rigid teacher salary structure, which imposes costs to stay in teaching that vary considerably from field-to-field and individual-to-individual. What are the alternatives? Currently, there is little evidence available on the effectiveness of performance-based incentive policies. One of the primary reasons is that important attributes of teacher quality, such as the ability to convey knowledge or enthusiasm for class material, are difficult to identify and may not be related to more identifiable characteristics. Unfortunately, though, even less evidence is available on differentiating pay at the individual level to pay for attributes that are highly correlated with student performance (e.g., teacher test scores, selectivity of college).

- ◆ Instituting a retention bonus (i.e., "golden handcuffs"). Teachers that successfully complete one year of service would be eligible to participate such a program. For each year of service a teacher would have a bonus placed aside and when they complete a fixed number of years (e.g., five years of continuous service) the first year's bonus would be distributed. Such a program could follow a five-year vesting schedule for a set period. If a teacher leaves a district, unvested funds are forfeited.

- ◆ Adopting policies that ensure equal access to high-quality teacher induction programs. Survey results cited by Hare and Heap (2001) indicate that such programs are very effective in decreasing the number of new teachers who leave.

Acknowledgment

The authors thank the North Central Regional Educational Laboratory for its generous support of this research and acknowledge Robert Michael, Deb Hare, and James Heap for their contributions to assembling and analyzing the data used in this study. We thank Michael J. Conkey, Donald P. Corrigan, and Connie Wise (Illinois); Dwayne James (Indiana); Richard Wassen (Minnesota); and Peter J. Burke (Wisconsin) for their assistance in providing data.

References

Berman, P., & McLaughlin, M. (1977). Federal programs supporting educational change. Vol. 7. Factors affecting implementation and continuation (Report No. R-1589/7-HEW). Santa Monica, CA: RAND Corporation.

Bobbitt, S., Leich, M., Whitener, S., & Lynch, H. (1994). *Characteristics of stayers, movers, and leavers: Results from the teacher follow up survey, 1991-92*. Washington, DC: National Center for Education Statistics.

Boe, E., Bobbitt, S., Cook, L., Barkanic, G., & Maislin, G. (1998). *Teacher turnover in eight cognate areas: National trends and predictors.* Philadelphia: University of Pennsylvania, Center for Research and Evaluation in Social Policy.

Bowman, M. J. (1973). Foreword. In K. G. Pedersen, (Ed.), *The itinerant schoolmaster: A socio-economic analysis of teacher turnover.* Chicago: Midwest Administration Center.

Bryk, A. S., Lee, V. E., & Smith, J. B. (1990). High school organization and its effect on teachers and students: An interpretive summary of the research. In W. J. Clune & J. F. Witte (Eds.), *Choice and control in American education: Vol. 1. The theory of choice and control in American education* (pp. 135-226). Philadelphia: Falmer.

Coleman, J. S., & Hoffer, T. (1987). *Public and private high schools: The impact of communities.* New York: Basic Books.

Cornett, L. (2002). *Quality teachers: Can incentive policies make a difference?* Atlanta, GA: Southern Regional Education Board.

Darling-Hammond, L., & Green, J. (1994). Teacher quality and equality. In P. Keating & J. I. Goodlad (Eds.), *Access to knowledge.* New York: College Entrance Examination Board.

Darling-Hammond, L., & Wise, A. E. (1985). *Beyond standardization: State standards and school improvement.* Elementary School Journal, 85, 315-336.

Dworkin, A. G. (1980). The changing demography of public school teachers: Some implications for faculty turnover in urban areas. *Sociology of Education*, 53, 65-73.

Edwards, V. B. (2000, January 13). Quality counts 2000: Who should teach? [special issue]. *Education Week*, 19(18).

Fullan, M. G. (1991). *The new meaning of educational change.* New York: Teachers College Press.

Goodlad, J. I. (1983). *A place called school.* New York: McGraw-Hill.

Greenberg, D. H., & McCall, J. J. (1974). *Analysis of the educational personnel system: VII. Teacher mobility in Michigan* (Report No. R-1343-HEW). Santa Monica, CA: RAND Corporation.

Grissmer, D. W., & Kirby, S. N. (1987). *Teacher attrition: The uphill climb to staff the nation's schools* (Report No. R-3512-CSTP). Santa Monica, CA: RAND Corporation.

Gritz, R. M., & Theobald, N. D. (1996). The effects of school district spending priorities on length of stay in teaching. *The Journal of Human Resources, 31,* 477-512.

Hanushek, E. A., Kain, J. F., & Rivkin, S. G. (1999, January). *Do higher salaries buy better teachers?* Paper presented to the meeting of the American Economics Association.

Hare, D., & Heap, J. (2001). *Effective teacher recruitment and retention strategies in the Midwest: Who is making use of them?* Naperville, IL: North Central Regional Educational Laboratory.

Hare, D., Heap, J., & Raack, L. (June, 2001). *Teacher recruitment and retention strategies in the Midwest: Where are they and do they work?* Naperville, IL: North Central Regional Educational Laboratory.

Hare, D., Nathan, J., Darland, J., & Laine, S. (2000). *Teacher shortages in the Midwest: Current trends and future issues.* Oak Brook, IL: North Central Regional Educational Laboratory.

Heyns, B. (1988). Educational defectors: A first look at teacher attrition in the NLS-72. *Educational Researcher, 17,* 24-32.

Hirsch, E., Koppich, J. E., & Knapp, M. S. (1998). *What states are doing to improve the quality of teaching.* CTP Working Paper. Seattle: University of Washington, Center for the Study of Teaching and Policy.

Huberman, M., & Miles, M. (1984). *Innovation up close.* New York: Plenum.

Ingersoll, R. (1995). *Teacher supply, teacher qualifications, and teacher turnover.* Washington, DC: National Center for Education Statistics.

Ingersoll, R. (2001). Teacher turnover and teacher shortages: An organizational analysis. *American Educational Research Journal, 38,* 499-534.

Kemple, J. J. (1989). *The career paths of black teachers: Evidence from North Carolina.* Paper presented at the meeting of the American Educational Research Association, San Francisco.

Kozol, J. (1991). *Savage inequalities.* New York: Harper-Collins.

Murnane, R. J. (1987). *Understanding teacher attrition.* Harvard Educational Review, 57, 177-182.

Murnane, R. J., & Olsen, R. J. (1989). The effects of salaries and opportunity costs on duration in teaching: Evidence from Michigan. *The Review of Economics and Statistics, 71,* 347-352.

Murnane, R. J., & Olsen, R. J. (1990). The effects of salaries and opportunity costs on length of stay in teaching: Evidence from North Carolina. *Journal of Human Resources, 25,* 106-124.

Murnane, R. J., Singer, J. D., & Willett, J. B. (1988). The career paths of teachers: Implications for teacher supply and methodological lessons for research. *Educational Researcher, 17*(5), 22-30.

Murnane, R. J., Singer, J. D., Willett, J. B., Kemple, J. J., & Olsen, R. J. (1991). *Who will teach?: Policies that matter.* Cambridge, MA: Harvard University Press.

Oakes, J. (1990). *Multiplying inequalities: The effects of race, social class, and tracking on opportunities to learn mathematics and science.* Santa Monica, CA: RAND Corporation.

Rosenholtz, S. J. (1985). Political myths about education reform: Lessons from research on teaching. *Phi Delta Kappan, 66,* 349-355.

Rosenholtz, S. J. (1987). Education reform strategies: Will they increase teacher commitment? *American Journal of Education, 95,* 534-562.

Theobald, N. D., & Gritz, R. M. (1996). The effects of school district spending priorities on the exit paths of beginning teachers leaving the district. *Economics of Education Review, 15,* 11-22.

4

Understanding Teacher Labor Markets: Implications for Educational Equity

Don Boyd, Hamp Lankford,
Susanna Loeb, and Jim Wycoff

Federal and state policy makers are struggling to improve the low student achievement of many students and to decrease the large differences in achievement that exist among racial, ethnic, and socioeconomic groups. Concern over low student performance has a long history, but has taken on urgency in an era marked by court cases that focus on adequacy, by dramatic increases in achievement information, and by widespread calls for accountability. Recent research on student achievement identifies the important link between teachers and student outcomes.[1] Yet, even with increases in spending equity within states (Evans, Murray, & Schwab, 2001), substantial differences remain across schools in the qualifications of teachers (Lankford, Loeb, & Wyckoff, 2002; Betts, Rueben, & Danenberg, 2000). Despite a rather large body of literature examining mobility decisions by teachers and the equity of education, we know relatively little about the distribution of teacher qualifications and how this relates to educational equity. This chapter examines the distribution of teacher qualifications, their relationship to educational equity, and the attributes of teacher labor markets

---

1 Rivkin, Hanushek, and Kain (2000) attribute at least 7% of the total variance in test-score gains to differences in teachers, and they argue that this is a lower bound. Sanders and Rivers (1996) found that the difference between attending classes taught by high-quality teachers (highest quartile grouping) and attending classes taught low-quality teachers (lowest quartile grouping) for 3 years in a row is huge, approximately 50 percentile points in the distribution of student achievement. They also find residual effects of teachers in latter years. That is, having a high-quality teacher in grade three increases learning not only in grade three but also in grades four and five.

that lead to the poor, nonwhite students being most likely to have teachers with the worst qualifications.

The connection between the distribution of teacher qualifications and educational equity already plays an important role in several aspects of public policy. First, the educational systems of some states are being challenged in court because they do not meet adequacy standards for student outcomes. Plaintiff's evidence in such cases is increasingly dominated by documenting the disparities in teacher qualifications across schools and districts and specifically the very low level of teacher qualifications for the teachers of children from nonwhite and low socioeconomic households (see, for example, Lankford [1999] and the text of Judge Leland DeGrasse's decision in *Campaign for Fiscal Equity v. New York State*, 2000). Second, federal, state, and district policies are focusing on attracting better-qualified teachers to schools that traditionally have been low-performing. These low-performing schools are overwhelming dominated by urban schools with high concentrations of poor, nonwhite students. Thus, identifying policies to address educational equity by improving the qualifications of teachers and to decrease interschool disparities in teacher qualifications does and will continue to play an important role in judicial, executive, and legislative policy development. As states focus on standards and accountability systems required by the No Child Left Behind Act, issues related to the equity of the distribution of teacher qualifications likely will grow. However, these efforts to improve educational equity are handicapped by an incomplete understanding of teacher labor markets.

Our results show striking differences in the qualifications of teachers across schools. Low-income, low-achieving, and nonwhite students, particularly those in urban areas, find themselves in classes with many of the least skilled teachers. Too often these teachers do not meet minimal thresholds for certification, not to mention the skills required to educate students to high standards. We believe that the lower qualifications often found in classrooms with poor, nonwhite, low-performing students result from a combination of factors that include district wealth, policies and practices of public schools, and the preferences of teachers for job attributes.

Background

Distribution of Teacher Qualifications

A number of studies have examined the distribution of teacher qualifications. Until recently, measures of these qualifications were typically limited to educational attainment and experience. More recently, researchers have employed state administrative data, which often have more detailed information describing the qualifications of teachers, e.g., teacher performance on certification examinations, identification of the undergraduate and graduate colleges from which degrees were obtained, and comparison of certification areas with current teaching assignments. These measures provide a much richer description of the qualifications of teachers, but little work has been done that connects these attributes with measures of student outcomes. In general, recent work finds that the qualifications of teachers are sorted such that poor and nonwhite students frequently have less qualified teachers. However, we know little about the factors that lead to this sorting.

Teachers differ fundamentally from other school resources. They have preferences about whether to teach, what to teach, and where to teach. Potential teachers prefer one type of district to another, and within districts they prefer one school to another. There has been much discussion about the role that compensation plays in the ability of schools to attract and retain high-quality teachers. A large body of literature suggests that teachers respond to wages. As a group, these studies show that individuals are more likely to choose to teach when starting teacher wages are high relative to wages in other occupations (Baugh & Stone, 1982; Brewer, 1996; Dolton 1990; Dolton & Makepeace, 1993; Dolton & van der Klaaw, 1999; Hanushek & Pace, 1995; Manski, 1987; Mont & Rees, 1996; Murnane, Singer, & Willett, 1989; Rickman & Parker, 1990; Stinebrickner, 1998, 1999, 2000; Theobald, 1990; Theobald & Gritz, 1996). Baugh and Stone (1982), for example, find that teachers are at least as responsive to wages in their decision to quit teaching as are workers in other occupations.[2]

Salaries are one element of employment that are likely to impact sorting, but nonpecuniary job characteristics appear important as well. These characteristics may include, among other things, class size, preparation time, facilities, or characteristics of the student body. For example, class size reduction in California resulted in an increase in demand for teachers across the state. Teachers in schools with low-achieving students chose to move to higher-achieving schools, leaving many high-poverty districts with vacancies and unqualified instruction (Betts, Rueben, & Danenberg, 2000; Bohrnstedt and Stecher, 1999). Similarly, in Texas, Hanushek, Kain, and Rivkin (1999) found that teachers moved to schools with high-achieving students and, in New York City, Lankford (1999) found that experienced teachers moved to high-socioeconomic status schools when positions became available.

2 These findings may appear to be contradictory to those of qualitative studies (such as Berliner, 1987; Feistritzer, 1992; Murphy, 1987; Wise, Darling-Hammond, & Praskac, 1987), which tend to find that ideology and the value individuals place on education for society are important factors in decisions about whether and where to teach. However, because individuals' answers to questions may not reflect their actions, factors less emphasized by respondents, such as wages and job stability, may still be relatively important to teachers.

Educational Equity

Research on the distributional equity of educational resources has a long and rich history. Numerous studies provide strong evidence of disparate student access to resources and the role that courts have played in addressing these issues. More recently, as policy became more concerned with student achievement, issues of resource disparity have been linked to student outcomes. In particular, high-stakes exit requirements for students have fueled the development of the "adequacy" of resources to reasonably attain these outcomes.[3] This discussion has generally occurred outside the black box, that is, expenditures have been tied to outcomes without an understanding of the mediating process. Researchers are focusing on how to translate definitions of adequate outcomes back to expenditure levels that would produce these outcomes. These researchers have made good progress on addressing a number of conceptual and empirical issues, but the still have some distance to go before results will withstand substantial scrutiny. For example, there is little agreement on the definition of adequacy let alone how to determine expenditures necessary to produce the outcome.

Teacher Labor Markets

Teacher labor markets are characterized by several institutions that enhance the likelihood of an inequitable distribution of qualified teachers. In theory, employer—in deciding to make job offers—consider an array of employee attributes and make offers to individuals who rank highest on the employers' weighted average of these attributes. Likewise, in evaluating which jobs to pursue and which offers to accept, prospective employees consider a bundle of attributes tied to specific jobs, preferring jobs that rank highest according to the individual's weighting of attributes. Typically, economists believe that wages adjust to equilibrate labor markets, allocating the most productive employees to their highest valued place of employment, ceteris paribus. Teacher labor markets are characterized by a number of institutions, a factor that likely inhibits market wages from functioning smoothly in the allocation of teachers.

Important among these institutions is the single-salary schedule, which operates in most school districts.[4] A common example of the single-salary schedule is one in which all teachers in a district are paid according to threshold levels of educational attainment and years of district experience. Thus, to the extent that the steps of the salary matrix do not highly correlate with teacher productivity, which is likely, wages will not allocate teachers to their most valued use. Moreover, use of the single-salary schedule makes it very difficult to increase salaries to attract more qualified teachers to hard-to-staff schools without also raising salaries in other schools in the district.

---

3 The chapters in Ladd, Chalk, & Hansen (1999) provide a good summary of the current state of research on educational equity.

4 Increasingly, school districts are altering teacher compensation away from the single-salary schedule. However, examples of such behavior remain rare. For examples, see Odden's chapter in this volume.

Another institution that inhibits teacher labor markets from freely allocating teachers is the post-and-fill, seniority-based, recruiting method employed in many districts. This practice requires districts to post vacancies within the district and give preference to within-district candidates based on their seniority. Thus, employers may be constrained from hiring the most productive applicant. One implication of this policy is that teachers working in hard-to-staff schools can easily transfer to other schools within the district after gaining some experience, taking their on-the-job training with them and leaving the hard-to-staff school to recruit again, most likely from the ranks of inexperienced teachers. This has the effect of encouraging higher turnover and systematically decreasing the qualifications of teachers in the hard-to-staff school relative to other schools within the district.

As is well known from the rich body of literature examining the equity of educational resources, reliance on local funding, in combination with geographically small school districts, is likely to encourage substantial differences in ability to pay for education across school districts. These differences are typically reflected in level of teacher salaries and other working conditions. When combined with the notion that working conditions are an important element in how teachers choose among jobs, likelihood of differences in the qualifications of teachers across districts within a job market increases.

Data

Our database links seven administrative data sets and various other information characterizing districts, communities, and local labor markets in New York State. It includes information for every teacher and administrator employed in a New York public school at any time from 1969 to 1970 through 1999 to 2000 (Appendix A, p. 79).

The core data come from the Personnel Master File (PMF), part of the Basic Education Data System of the New York State Education Department. In a typical year, there are at least 180,000 teachers identified in the PMF. We linked these annual records through time, yielding detailed data characterizing the career history of each individual.

Several other databases containing a range of information about the qualifications of prospective and actual teachers, as well as the environments in which these individuals make career decisions, substantially enrich this core data. For individual teachers, this information includes age, sex, race or ethnicity, salary, course subject and grade taught, experience (in the district, in New York State public schools, and total), years of education and degree attainment, and teacher certification examination scores of whether the teacher passed on the first attempt. In addition, we identified the institutions from which individual teachers earned their undergraduate degrees and combined it with the Barron's ranking of college selectivity to construct variables measuring the selectivity of the college from which each teacher graduated and the location of the institution. Measures of schools and districts include enrollment, student poverty, racial composition, limited English proficiency composition, student test results for recent years, dropout rates, district wealth, district salary schedules, crime, spending in numerous categories, number of employees in numerous categories, as well as many other measures. We were able to examine the geographic nature of labor markets by knowing an individual's ZIP code at various times as they moved from high school to their first and subsequent teaching jobs.[5]

To assess the distribution of teachers across the schools, we created multiple measures of average teacher characteristics at the school level. These measures include the following:

- ♦ percent of teachers with no previous teaching experience,
- ♦ percent with no more than a Bachelors degree,
- ♦ percent not certified in any current assignment,
- ♦ percent certified in all current assignments,
- ♦ percent of examination takers who failed the NTE General Knowledge Examination or the NYSTCE Liberal Arts and Science Examination on their first attempt,
- ♦ percent who attended Barron's College Guide's most competitive and highly competitive schools,
- ♦ percent who attended Barron's College Guide's competitive, less competitive, or least-competitive schools.

These data are a subset of the measures we have available but are illustrative of the trends we observed in all of our teacher attribute measures.

To simplify the discussion, we also created a composite measure using principal components analysis that combines a number of these characteristics. Appendix B (p. 80) describes the components of this measure.

It has a reliability of 0.86 and explains 52% of the variation in its component measures. The measure has a mean of zero and a standard deviation of one, indicating that a one-unit change in the composite corresponds to one–standard deviation change.[6]

---

5 This information is not uniformly available for all individuals, but it is available for a subsample and is known for all individuals when they applied for certification as well as subsequently.

6 Our measures of teacher qualifications reflect the performance of individual teachers and the attributes of the colleges and universities they attended. In addition to the measures presented, we also know the following: individual teacher certification examination scores and whether the individual passed each of three component tests in the general battery as well as scores on the content specialty tests; whether the individual is certified to teach each of the courses they teach; and the individual's tenure status, education level, experience teaching. For each of the higher educational institutions they attended we know the following: the identity of the college, the distribution of its math and verbal SAT scores, its ranking in the Barron's College Guide, and its admissions and attendance rate. There is remarkable consistency among most of the measures. The factor that we use is just one of many possible composite

Analysis of Teacher Labor Markets

We employed the New York State education workforce database described above to examine the distribution of teacher qualifications and to better understand the processes that resulted in the sorting we observed.

Distribution of Teacher Qualifications Among Schools[7]

We found substantial variation across schools in the qualifications of teachers. As shown in Figure 4.1, across a number of separate measures of teacher qualifications and a composite measure, there are schools with teachers whose qualifications are very strong and schools whose teachers have much weaker qualifications.

Figure 4.1. School Quantiles for New York State Teacher Qualification Attributes, 2000

Qualification Atrributes	Percentiles		
	10th	Median	90th
Overall Teacher Qualification Factor	-2.974	0.469	2.093
No Teaching Experience (%)	0.000	0.067	0.176
Bachelor's or Less (%)	0.029	0.125	0.262
Not Certified in Any Assignment (%)	0.000	0.038	0.243
ermanent Certification in All Assignments (%) or	0.449	0.731	0.889
Failed General KnowledgeP Liberal Arts (%)	0.000	0.077	0.308
Bachelor's from Most Competitive College (%)	0.000	0.088	0.234
Bachelor's from Least Competitive College (%)	0.000	0.097	0.300

For example, consider whether a teacher is uncertified to teach anything she currently teaches. The school at the 10th percentile of this distribution has no teachers uncertified to teach anything they currently teach (that is, they are all certified to teach at least some of their current teaching assignments). However, the school at the 90th percentile of this distribution has nearly a quarter of its teachers uncertified to teach anything they currently teach. Similar differences exist across the other teacher qualification measures. When these measures are

measures. We created numerous other factors to test the robustness of our results and found that the choice of factor made little difference.

7 Much of this analysis is drawn from Lankford, Loeb, and Wyckoff (2002).

combined into a composite measure, ie, the overall teacher qualification factor, substantial differences exist.[8]

These differences primarily represent differences within labor markets rather than differences across labor markets. We define labor markets as metropolitan statistical areas (MSAs), which in urban areas include a city school district and the districts in the surrounding suburban counties.[9] Figure 4.2 shows the distribution of the composite teacher qualification factor for each major metropolitan area of New York State (Albany-Schenectady-Troy, Buffalo, New York City, Rochester, Syracuse, and Utica-Rome counties) and for three rural regions (Mid-Hudson, Southern Tier, and North Country).

8 The school-level teacher qualification attributes are highly correlated. Schools that have lesser-qualified teachers as measured by one attribute are more likely to have lesser-qualified teachers based on all other measures. For example, schools with high proportions of teachers who failed examinations are more likely to have teachers from less competitive colleges (correlations of approximately 0.45); schools with a high proportion of teachers who are not certified to teach any of the courses that they currently teach are much more likely to have graduated from the less competitive colleges (correlation of .40). Thus, New York's schools are subject to substantial systematic sorting of teachers based on their qualifications.

9 The MSAs are defined by the Office of Budget and Management and used by the United States Census Bureau. The urban regions are Albany-Schenectady-Troy (including Albany, Montgomery, Rensselaer, Saratoga, Schenectady, ad Schoharie counties); Buffalo-Niagara Falls (including Erie and Niagra counties); New York City (including Putnam, Rockland, Westchester, Nassau, and Suffolk counties); Rochester (including Genesee, Livingston, Monroe, Ontario, Orleans, and Wayne counties); Syracuse (including Cayuga, Madison, Onondaga, and Oswego counties); and Utica-Rome (including Herkimer and Oneida counties). The rural regions are Mid-Hudson (including Columbia, Delaware, Dutchess, Greene, Orange, Otsego, Sullivan, and Ulster counties); North Country (including Clinton, Essex, Franklin, Fulton, Hamilton, Jefferson, Lewis, St. Lawrence, Warren, and Washington counties); and the Southern Tier (including Allegany, Broome, Cattaraugus, Chautauqua, Chemung, Chenango, Schuyler, Seneca, Tioga, Tompkins, Steuben, Wyoming, and Yates counties).

Figure 4.2

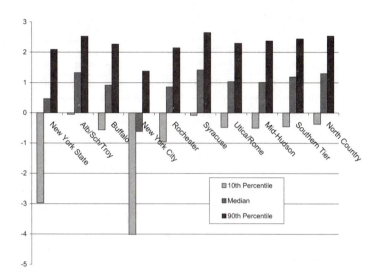

As shown, there is substantial variation within each region, and with the exception of New York City, this variation is very similar across regions. Figure 4.3 shows a similar picture when individual measures of teacher qualifications are examined.

Figure 4.3. School Quantiles for New York State Teacher Attributes by MSA and Urban Preference for All Teachers FTE > 0.5, 2000

		Buffalo		New York City		Rochester		Syracuse	
		Urban	Sub-urban	Urban	Sub-urban	Urban	Sub-urban	Urban	Sub-urban
Composite Qualification Factor	10th	NA	−0.56	−4.99	−1.47	−2.00	−0.55	−0.39	0.03
	Median	NA	0.92	−1.97	0.70	0.07	1.02	0.87	1.44
	90th	NA	2.27	0.15	1.93	1.45	2.30	2.10	2.70
No Teaching Experience (%)	10th	0.01	0.00	0.02	0.00	0.00	0.00	0.02	0.00
	Median	0.08	0.06	0.10	0.05	0.09	0.06	0.06	0.05
	90th	0.22	0.15	0.24	0.15	0.18	0.14	0.14	0.14
Not Certified in Any Assign-ment (%)	10th	NA	0.00	0.09	0.00	0.06	0.00	0.00	0.00
	Median	NA	0.00	0.20	0.03	0.14	0.02	0.05	0.02
	90th	NA	0.06	0.38	0.10	0.26	0.08	0.11	0.09
Failed NTE General Knowl-edge or NYS Liberal Arts Examination (%)	10th	0.00	0.00	0.00	0.00	0.00	0.00	0.00	0.00
	Median	0.10	0.04	0.27	0.09	0.13	0.00	0.10	0.00
	90th	0.33	0.20	0.53	0.32	0.25	0.17	0.24	0.19
Bachelor's From Most Competi-tive College (%)	10th	0.00	0.00	0.00	0.00	0.10	0.09	0.14	0.05
	Median	0.03	0.06	0.07	0.11	0.19	0.22	0.21	0.15
	90th	0.08	0.13	0.23	0.24	0.25	0.36	0.29	0.29
Bachelor's from Least Competitive College (%)	10th	0.00	0.00	0.11	0.06	0.00	0.00	0.00	0.00
	Median	0.06	0.03	0.24	0.15	0.10	0.03	0.05	0.03
	90th	0.14	0.09	0.42	0.28	0.16	0.09	0.09	0.07

For example, in the best 10% of schools in New York City, none of the teachers failed the general knowledge portion of the certification examination, whereas more than half of teachers failed the examination in the 10% of schools faring worst on this measure. Other measures show large but somewhat less striking differences across schools within the New York City. These results reflect substantial heterogeneity of teacher qualifications within New York City. Results from the other large cities show large differences in the qualifications across schools within districts. Figure 4.3 also highlights that although there is heterogeneity within suburban schools, they typically have teachers who are much more qualified than their urban counterparts within the same labor market. Seventy-five percent of the variation in the composite measure of teacher qualifications is roughly equally divided between differences between districts within a region and between schools within a district.[10] Thus, one lesson regarding educational equity of teacher qualifications is that important differences exist primarily within labor markets rather than across labor markets. This suggests that policy makers should focus on remedies that address within district and urban–suburban differences.

How is the variation in teacher qualifications distributed across schools and districts? In particular, are the qualifications of teachers sorted in ways that provide particular disadvantage to certain groups of students? We find that less well-qualified teachers are much more likely to teach in schools with higher proportions of poor, nonwhite, or low-performing students.

Figure 4.4 shows that the average nonwhite student in New York State has a teacher who is more than two standard deviations worse on the composite teacher qualification measure than her white counterpart (-1.48 versus 0.85, respectively).

[10] The remaining 25% of the variation reflects differences across regions. This figure decreases to 2% when New York City is omitted. Similar results hold when any of the individual measures of teacher qualification are examined.

**Figure 4.4. Teacher Attributes for the Average Student
With Given Characteristics**

New York State/School District	Composite Qualification Factor	No Teaching Experience	Not Certified in Any Subject Taught	Failed General Knowledge or Liberal Arts Examination	Bachelor's From Least Competitive College
New York State					
Nonwhite	−1.484	0.099	0.166	0.212	0.214
White	0.847	0.067	0.040	0.071	0.102
Poor	-2.393	0.118	0.207	0.279	0.250
Nonpoor	−1.223	0.098	0.159	0.202	0.239
New York City SD					
Nonwhite	−2.183	0.109	0.212	0.256	0.247
White	-0.726	0.078	0.150	0.161	0.254
Poor	-2.562	0.120	0.215	0.296	0.268
Nonpoor	−1.341	0.100	0.167	0.212	0.258
Rochester City SD					
Nonwhite	−0.302	0.105	0.148	0.107	0.103
White	0.051	0.089	0.147	0.099	0.107
Poor	-0.418	0.108	0.173	0.120	0.097
Nonpoor	−0.221	0.111	0.171	0.111	0.096
Syracuse City SD					
Nonwhite	1.029	0.080	0.058	0.100	0.045
White	1.254	0.063	0.054	0.095	0.043
Poor	0.970	0.081	0.056	0.109	0.046
Nonpoor	1.194	0.069	0.046	0.103	0.040

Nonwhite students are four times more likely to be taught by a teacher who is not certified to teach any of her current assignments, three times more likely to be taught by a teacher who failed the general knowledge portion of the certification examination the first time, and twice as likely to be taught by a teacher whose bachelor's degree is from the least competitive category of Barron's rankings of colleges than her white counterpart. Poor students are more often taught by less qualified teachers than are nonpoor students, but the differences are less dramatic. These differences reflect both the within- and across-district differences in teacher qualifications. When we consider only the differences within urban school districts, nonwhite and poor students are taught by less qualified teachers than are their white and nonpoor district colleagues, as shown in the bottom panels of Figure 4.4. In New York City, the average white or nonpoor student has a teacher with a composite teacher qualification factor that is more than one standard deviation better than that of their nonwhite or poor peer. Somewhat smaller differences exist in other urban areas and for other teacher qualification measures. Thus, even within an urban school system, nonwhite and poor students are systematically exposed to teachers with worse qualifications than white or nonpoor students.

Figure 4.5 shows that the lowest performing students are taught by the least qualified teachers.[11]

Figure 4.5. Average School Attributes of Teachers by Student Test Score: Fourth-Grade ELA Level 1, 2000

Teacher Quality Attributes	Students in Level 1 Fourth-Grade ELA (%)			
	0	0 to < 5	5 to < 20	> 20
Overall Teacher Quality Factor	0.98**	0.86**	-0.30**	-2.82
No Teaching Experience (%)	0.06**	0.07**	0.09**	0.14
Not Certified in any Assignment (%)	0.03**	0.04**	0.09**	0.22
Failed NTE General Knowledge or NYS Liberal Arts Examination (%)	0.09**	0.10**	0.19**	0.35
Bachelor's From Most Competitive College (%)	0.11**	0.11**	0.09	0.08
Bachelor's From Least Competitive College (%)	0.10**	0.11**	0.16**	0.26

ELA; NTE; NYS, New York State. Statistical significance refers to differences between other student performance levels and the > 20% level for each of the mean teacher attributes: ** $P < .01$.

Thirty-five percent of the teachers in schools where more than 20% of the students performed at the lowest level on the 4th grade ELA examination failed the general knowledge portion of the certification examination at least once. The comparable figure for teachers in schools in which none of the students scored at the lowest level is 9%. Similar relationships exist across all the teacher qualification measures. Correlations between school achievement and teacher characteristics tell the same story; the proportion of a school's students who achieved at level 1 has a 0.63 correlation with the proportion of that school's teachers who are

11 New York's student achievement data for fourth- and eighth-grade English, language arts, and math place each student's test results in one of four performance levels. The school data indicate the number of students in each level. To examine low-performing students, we employed the portion of the students tested whose results place them in the lowest performance group, level 1. Level 1 for fourth-grade ELA is described by the New York State Education Department as, "These students have serious academic deficiencies. They show no evidence of any proficiency in one or more of the elementary standards and incomplete proficiency in all three standards."

not certified to teach any of their current courses. The correlations for the proportion of teachers failing either the NTE General Knowledge or the NYSTCE Liberal Arts and Science examination are both 0.50, and the correlation of student achievement with teacher graduation from a less competitive college is 0.41. The results of these analyses are clear. Students in low-performing urban schools are taught by dramatically less-qualified teachers than their higher-performing, typically suburban counterparts. The results are similar if we use the fourth- grade mathematics examination or the eighth-grade ELA and math examinations. In summary, there is strong evidence that many of the least-qualified teachers are in schools with the lowest-performing students. Although these results provide powerful evidence of the sorting of teacher qualifications, they do not help us understand why this sorting has occurred. Some insights into this process result from a better understanding of the career paths of teachers, the geography of teacher labor markets, and the nature of teacher compensation.

Factors Related to the Sorting of Teacher Qualifications

Career Paths of Teachers[12]

Does the substantial sorting of teacher qualifications described above occur at the time of initial hiring decision, that is, are better-qualified teachers initially hired in predominately white, nonpoor, higher-achieving schools? Or does this result from the transfer-and-quit decisions of teachers so that a relatively equal distribution of teacher qualifications becomes skewed as better-qualified teachers systematically and disproportionately leave schools with higher proportions of nonwhite, poor, and low-achieving students? Our analysis suggests that the answer to this question depends on the nature of the school. For schools with relatively low percentages of poor, nonwhite, and low-achieving students, the qualifications of the teachers are predominately determined by the initial match and subsequent transfer-and-quit decisions leave these qualifications unchanged. However, for schools with relatively high concentrations of poor, nonwhite, and low-achieving students, the qualifications of teachers deteriorate substantially as a result of transfer-and-quit decisions.

Figure 4.6 shows, for the 1995 cohort of entering teachers, the proportion of teachers who failed the general knowledge portion of the certification examination at least once, separately for schools grouped by quartile of nonwhite student enrollment.

12 Much of this analysis is drawn from Boyd, Lankford, Loeb, and Wyckoff (2002a).

**Figure 4.6. New York City Teachers (%) from the 1995 Cohort
Who Failed a Teacher Certification Exam by Percent of Minority Students in
the Schools, 1995-2000**

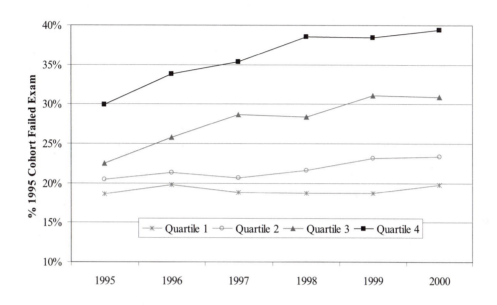

So, in 1995, schools in the lowest quartile of minority enrollment, 18% of newly employed teachers failed the examination. The comparable figure for schools in the highest quartile of minority enrollment is 30%. Thus, through their initial hiring decisions, these schools employed teachers who differed dramatically in this teacher qualification measure. Over time, the 12 percentage–point difference grew to 19 percentage points as the schools with high nonwhite enrollment increased the proportion of teachers in that 1995 cohort who failed the examination; there was no similar trend in the low–nonwhite enrollment schools. This results from relatively higher attrition in the high–nonwhite schools from that cohort of teachers who had not failed the examination. A similar pattern emerges when we perform the same analysis based on student performance quartiles rather than race, as shown in Figure 4.7.

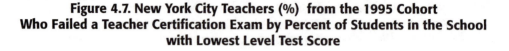

**Figure 4.7. New York City Teachers (%) from the 1995 Cohort
Who Failed a Teacher Certification Exam by Percent of Students in the School
with Lowest Level Test Score**

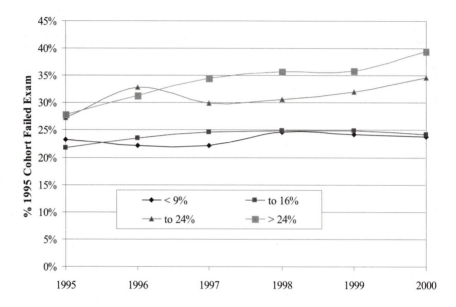

The 1995 cohort of teachers in schools where fewer of the students failed the fourth-grade ELA examination had roughly the same failure rate in 2000 as in 1995 (approximately 24%). However, the schools with the highest quartile of student failures on the 4th grade ELA examination experienced an increase in the proportion of teachers, from 28% to 40%, who failed the certification examination.

This suggests that both the initial match of teachers with schools and the subsequent career decisions of teachers contribute meaningfully to the sorting of teacher qualifications observed above. Thus, both recruitment and retention policies are important for improving the educational equity with respect to teachers. Can we further isolate the factors that influence these inequities in the qualifications of teachers?

Geography of Teacher Labor Markets[13]

What sustains the substantial differences in the qualifications of teachers at the time of initial match? These differences could result from a variety of job attributes, including compensation and working conditions. It is also possible that teachers have preferences regarding the location of their employment. Our analysis indicates that new teachers have strong preferences regarding the loca-

---

13 Much of this analysis is drawn from Boyd, Lankford, Loeb, and Wyckoff (2001).

tions in which they work, even after controlling for a variety of other attributes. In particular, new teachers much prefer to work close to their hometown and in a district with similar urban characteristics to the one where they attended high school.

Most teachers enter public school teaching close to their hometowns or where they attended college. Eighty-three percent of teachers entering the New York State public school workforce took jobs within 40 miles of their home (Figure 4.8).[14]

Figure 4.8. Distance From High School to First Job by MSA, 1997 to 2000

Region	0 to 15 Miles	15 to 40 Miles	40 to 100 Miles	100 or more Miles	All
Buffalo City	77.6	6.6	4.6	11.2	100.0
Buffalo Suburbs	71.8	19.3	3.9	5.0	100.0
New York City	62.4	27.3	6.5	3.8	100.0
New York Suburbs	69.6	23.5	3.3	3.5	100.0
Rochester City	48.7	10.8	21.4	19.1	100.0
Rochester Suburbs	42.3	27.0	18.4	12.3	100.0
Syracuse City	76.4	6.0	6.0	11.5	100.0
Syracuse Suburbs	51.4	22.9	15.3	10.4	100.0
Other	48.2	23.0	14.6	14.2	100.0
All	59.0	23.7	9.3	8.0	100.0

14 Distance from hometown is missing for many observations in our database, especially in New York City. However, distance from college of most recent degree to first job is available for 85% of the observations with missing hometown–first job distance data. Moreover, observations with missing hometown–first job distance data for which college–first job distance is available are more likely to take a job within 15 miles of the college where they received their most recent degree (47%) than observations for which hometown–first job distance is available (33%). Most New York City teachers come from one of the CUNY colleges or universities. CUNY students are overwhelmingly residents of New York City. As a result, the majority of the 78% of New York City teachers for whom we have no hometown–first job distance information likely have a New York City hometown. Thus, there is good reason to believe that our results would suggest that even more individuals would take a first job close to home if we knew the hometown–first job distance for all new teachers.

The relationship between hometown and first job varies across MSAs. In some regions, 90 of all teachers located within 40 miles of their hometowns (New York City, New York City suburbs, and the suburbs of Buffalo), whereas in other occupations the job search appears to be broader, e.g., in the city of Rochester, fewer than 60% of the teachers took a first job within 40 miles of home.

These relationships may involve more than just distance. For example, more than 90% of the individuals whose hometown is New York City and who entered public school teaching from 1997 to 2000 first taught in a New York City school (Figure 4.8, row percentage). Approximately 60% of those with hometowns in the New York City suburbs fist taught in those suburbs. Other major urban areas follow a similar pattern. Teachers with hometowns in urban locations are more likely to take a first job in that urban district relative to its suburbs, and those whose hometown is in the suburbs are much more likely to initially locate in those suburbs rather than the urban district. These patterns are summarized in Figure 4.9.

Figure 4.9. Urbanicity of Hometown by Urbanicity of First Job, 1997 to 2000

Region of High School		Region of Job			
		Urban	Suburban	Rural	All
Urban	Row Total (%)	84.6	12.8	2.6	100
	Column Total (%)	47.9	4.7	2.1	17.6
Suburban	Row Total (%)	23.6	67.4	9	100
	Column Total (%)	46.6	86.1	26.2	61.2
Rural	Row Total (%)	8	20.9	71.1	100
	Column Total (%)	5.5	9.3	71.7	21.3
All	Row Total (%)	31	47.9	21.1	100
	Column Total (%)	100	100	100	100

Eighty-five percent of teachers whose hometown is an urban district first teach in an urban district, although only 48% of urban teachers come from urban hometowns. Fully 47% of urban teachers originate in the suburbs, whereas only 5% of suburban teachers have hometowns in urban regions.[15] Although distance may clearly play a role in these results, it is also the case that apart from distance, the culture of schools or communities may play some role in the segmentation of teacher labor markets.

15 Again, these patterns are supported when location of most recent college is substituted for hometown location. Eighty-four percent of individuals who obtained their most recent degree in New York City first taught there.

Although these descriptive statistics are powerful, we are cautious about implying preferences of teachers based merely on these data. Accordingly, we estimate a multivariate model of the factors relevant to teachers' decisions about what regions in which to locate for their first job. These multivariate analyses confirmed the information in the descriptive statistics. Distance from hometown is very important in determining where a teacher would choose to initially look for employment, other things being equal.[16] After controlling for distance, teachers prefer regions similar to those of their hometown. For example, teachers whose hometown is in the suburbs are more likely to teach in the suburbs, whereas those whose hometown is in an urban area prefer to teach in urban areas. Taken together, this suggests that it is much easier to attract a teacher to an urban school when the candidate attended high school in that city. This is true primarily because of the importance of distance to hometown but also because teachers prefer to teach in schools similar to those they attended. As a result, teacher labor markets are quite local, and distance and preference for similar schools create a friction that make differential teacher qualifications more likely, other things being equal. For example, if urban areas produced proportionately fewer teachers with high qualifications—related perhaps to well-known correlations between many measures of teacher qualifications and socioeconomic status of individuals, which on average are higher in the suburbs—then the friction described above makes it less likely for teacher qualifications to be evenly distributed, even if other variables were equal. In many cases, other factors likely to influence teacher employment, e.g., the quality of the students themselves, safety, and building quality, work to the disadvantage of nonwhite, poor, and low-achieving students.

Teacher Salaries And Other Working Conditions[17]

Most models of labor markets posit that employees are responsive to real differences in compensation. To what extent might the differences in teacher qualifications be attributable to differences in teacher compensation? We now look at salary differences across schools to determine whether these differences are likely to be adding to the disparities that we see or perhaps decreasing additional inequities that would exist if salaries were the same across schools. Salary schedules generally do not vary within districts. That is, most teachers who remain within the same district would receive similar salaries regardless of in which school they taught. Thus, salary differentials are unlikely to be driving the substantial within district disparities in teacher characteristics across schools.

Although salary schedules are generally constant within districts, they do vary across regions and districts. Among districts in New York State, 72% of the variation in starting salaries for teachers with master's degrees is between regions, not between districts within regions. For teachers with 20 years of expe-

---

16 The results of the conditional logit estimation can be found in Boyd et al. (2001).

17 This section is drawn from Lankford et al. (2002).

rience, 79% of the variation is between regions (again, not between districts within regions). This suggests that the bulk of the variation in salaries does not contribute to the sorting of teachers across districts or schools within labor markets. It may contribute, however, to differences across regions or may simply reflect differences in the opportunity cost of teaching across labor markets.

Although less variation in salary exists within regions, this variation nonetheless appears to be large enough to impact teacher sorting.[18] To help assess whether these differences are likely to be contributing to teacher sorting, Figure 4.10 plots the 10th-, 50th-, and 90th-percentile starting salary for each region of the state. It shows that approximately 10% of districts have starting wages lower than $28,000, whereas another 10% have starting wages higher than $42,000.[19]

The New York City metropolitan area has the highest overall starting salaries, with Buffalo a close second. Within regions, the difference in starting salaries between districts at the 90th percentile and those at the 10th percentile ranges from $4,477 in the Utica and Rome region to $9,962 in the Mid-Hudson region. These differences are economically substantial and may contribute to sorting between districts within a region.[20]

---

[18] This is true nationally as well. Using the Schools and Staffing Surveys (1993-94), we found that although most of the variation was not between districts within the same region, the variation that did exist within regions was economically important. For example, in Pittsburgh, PA, the metropolitan area in our sample with the largest variation across districts (only MSAs for which at least 20 districts were represented in SASS), the lowest starting salary was $18,500, whereas the highest was $34,554. Chicago also showed substantial differences across districts, ranging from $19,891 to $31,621. The salaries for more experienced teachers showed even greater variation within regions. In Chicago there was a $36,978 difference in wages for teachers with 20 years of experience and a master's degree between the lowest and highest paying district. Only Dallas, Huston, and Tulsa showed ranges of less than $10,000 and even there the differences across districts were large enough to be economically important.

[19] These data are from the 1998 to 1999 academic year.

[20] As a check on the magnitude of salary differences across districts, we looked at the distribution of salaries for teachers with 20 years of experience. The variation across districts is even larger for experienced teachers. Approximately 10% of districts have salaries lower than $43,500 for these teachers, whereas another 10% have starting wages higher than $74,900.

Figure 4.10. The Distribution of Starting Salary in New York State, by MSA, 2000

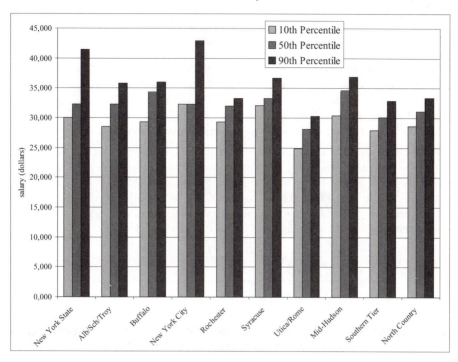

In 1970, in every major metropolitan region, salaries paid to urban teachers either matched or exceeded those paid to suburban teachers. In most of these regions, this pattern continued through 2000. In Buffalo and Syracuse, for example, there has been little difference over time between suburban and urban salaries either for starting teachers or more experienced teachers. They remain almost identical today. In Rochester, urban salaries have been higher on average than suburban salaries, although this difference has diminished in recent years, especially for new teachers. The pattern in the New York City region is quite different. During the 1970 to 2000 period, New York City urban salaries at both the entry level and the veteran level decreased substantially behind their suburban counterparts (Figures 4.11 and 4.12).[21]

In 2000, starting salaries for novice New York City school district teachers with a master's degree were approximately 15% lower than those for comparable suburban teachers; those for veteran teachers were more than 25% lower than salaries of their suburban counterparts.

---

21 We normalized all salaries over time using the Consumer Price Index for July of the relevant year. No adjustments were made to account for differences in costs across places at a given point in time.

Figure 4.11. Estimated Salaries for Teachers With MA and No Experience, New York Metropolitan Area, 1970-2000

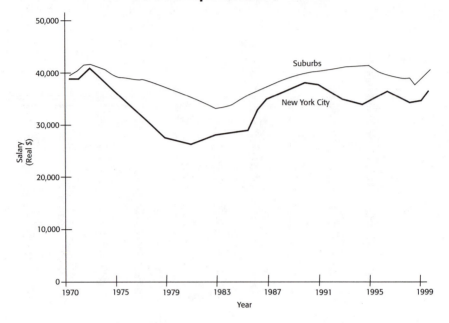

Figure 4.12. Estimated Salaries for Teachers With MA and 20 Years Experience, New York Metropolitan Area, 1970-2000

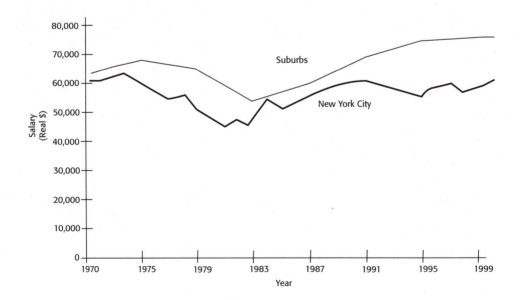

It is also the case that many other aspects of working conditions enhance inequities in the allocation of teacher qualifications. There is increasing evidence that student attributes affect the attractiveness of a school. For example, Boyd, Lankford, Loeb, and Wyckoff (2002b) found that both white and nonwhite teachers prefer to teach white, nonpoor, and higher-achieving students. These results may arise from the correlation of these student groups with unmeasured school attributes that prospective teachers care about. Whether a direct or indirect effect, teachers tend to prefer jobs in schools with fewer nonwhite, poor, and low-achieving students. As long as employers use teacher qualifications as attributes on which to select teachers, then schools with more nonwhite, poor, and low-achieving students will have teachers with weaker qualifications.

Summary

Teachers are sorted across New York State public schools such that the least-qualified teachers are much more likely to teach in schools with higher concentrations of nonwhite, poor, and low-achieving students than their more qualified peers. We believe that the preferences of teachers for better students and other student attributes that are correlated with higher student achievement (e.g., race and socioeconomic status) as well as attributes of the teacher labor market (e.g., districtwide single-salary schedules, post-and-fill seniority hiring, relatively heavy reliance on local property wealth for teacher salaries, and the geographically limited nature of the labor market) all contribute to this sorting. Our evidence on these points is circumstantial, but it accords with theory, common sense, and anecdotal reports.

Can the educational inequities that match the least well-qualified teachers to the most needy students be altered? Here the research evidence is particularly thin. A number of general policies conceptually could make a difference; however, little is known about how to specifically design these policies or their relative effectiveness. Moreover, frequently these policies pit the interests of key stakeholders against each other and make implementation difficult. For example, there is evidence that teachers respond to working conditions—including compensation, school culture, physical environment, and safety—but there is little information regarding the return from any particular investment or relative return in teacher qualifications across investments in these working conditions. What increase in teacher qualifications results from distributing a $100,000 salary increase among 100 teachers teaching in hard-to-staff schools? How does that increase compare with an increase due to spending the same $100,000 on improving supplies and the physical plant? We simply do not know. Additionally, attracting higher-quality teachers to hard-to-staff schools requires greater investment in these schools than in other schools in the district. Making such investments in teacher compensation violate the single-salary schedule compensation policies of most districts. Teachers' unions are likely to resist changing the single-salary schedule because doing so would create inequalities among their members.

The research required to make important progress on the issue of attracting and retaining highly qualified teachers to hard-to-staff schools needs to be much more sophisticated than that currently available. Two aspects are particularly important. First, much better measures of the qualifications of teachers, the environments in which they work, their classroom behaviors, and the outcomes they produce are needed to better understand the policies that would be most effective. Researchers will be required to go well beyond data typically available in national survey or state administrative databases, even those in data-rich states such as Florida, New York, North Carolina, and Texas. Second, researchers will likely need to develop conceptual models and empirical methods that account for the institutional structure of teacher labor markets. For example, most models currently employ situations in which wages continually adjust to equilibrate markets. That is clearly not the case for public school teacher labor markets.

Acknowledgments

We are grateful to the Smith Richardson Foundation, the Office of Educational Research and Improvement, the United States Department of Education, and the New York State Education Department for financial support. They do not necessarily support the views expressed in this paper. All errors are attributable to the authors.

Appendix A. Workforce Database

	Personnel Data	*Certification & Examination Data*	*SUNY Student Data*	School & District Data
Universe	All public school teachers, superintendents, principals, & other staff	All individuals taking certification examinations	All SUNY applicants (including nonteachers)	All public schools & districts
Elements	• Salary; • Course subject & grade; class size; • Experience (district & other); • Years of education & degree attainment; • Age; • Gender	• Scores on each taking of NTE & NYSTCE (general knowledge, pedagogy, & content specialty) examinations; • College of undergraduate & graduate degrees; • Degrees earned; • ZIP code of residence when certified; • Race	• High school attended; • High school courses; • High school GPA; • SAT examination scores; college attended & dates of attendance; • Intended college major; actual college major; • College GPA; • Degrees earned	• Enrollment; • Student poverty (free & reduced-cost lunch counts); • Enrollment by race; • Limited English proficiency; • Student test results; • Dropout rates; district wealth; • District salary schedule; • Support staff & aides
Time Period	1969 to 1970 to 1999 to 2000	1984 to 1985 to 1999 to 2000	1989 to 1990 to 1999to 2000	1969 to 1970 to 1999 to 2000
Source	New York State Education Department	New York State Education Department	The State University of New York	New York State Education Department

SUNY, Syracuse University New York; NTE; NYSTCE; GPA, grade point average; SAT, Scholastic Aptitude Test.

Appendix B. The Composite Measure of Teacher Quality

Components:	Scoring Coefficients
Teachers with less than or equal to 3 years of experience (%)	-0.36449
Teachers with tenure (%)	0.36032
Teachers with bachelor's or higher (%)	0.31576
Teachers certified in all courses taught (%)	0.39435
Teachers from less-competitive or noncompetitive colleges (%)	-0.27578
Average teacher score on the NTE communication skills examination	0.37538
Average teacher score on the NTE general knowledge examination	0.34601
Average teacher score on the NTE professional knowledge examination	0.38134
NTE,; Eigenvalue: 4.17 (52.14% of variation); Cronbach's alpha (reliability): 0.8641.	

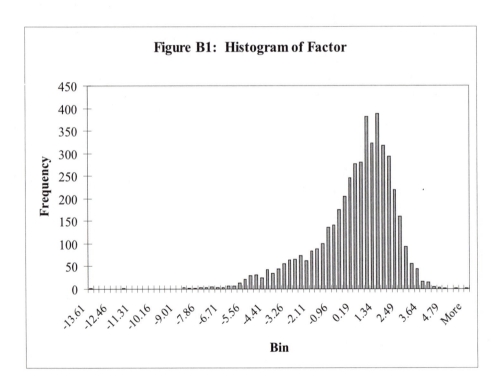

Figure B1: Histogram of Factor

Acknowledgments

We are grateful to the Smith Richardson Foundation, the Office of Educational Research and Improvement, the United States Department of Education, and the New York State Education Department for financial support. They do not necessarily support the views expressed in this paper. All errors are attributable to the authors.

References

Baugh, W.H., & Stone, J.A. (1982). Mobility and wage equilibration in the educator labor market. *Economics of Education Review,* 2(3), 253-274.

Berliner, D.C. (1987). Teacher selection in the Mesa Unified School District. In A. E. Wise, United States National Institute of Education and Center for the Study of the Teaching Profession, Rand Corporation (Eds.), *Effective teacher selection: From recruitment to retention—Case studies* (pp. 1-51). Santa Monica, CA: Rand Center for the Study of the Teaching Profession.

Betts, J.R., Rueben, K.S., & Danenberg, A. (2000). *Equal resources, equal outcomes? The distribution of school resources and student achievement in California.* San Francisco: Public Policy Institute of California.

Bohrnstedt, G.W., & Stecher, B.M. (Eds.) (1999). *Class size reduction in California: Early evaluation findings, 1996-1998.* Palo Alto, CA: CSR Research Consortium, Year 1 Evaluation Report, American Institutes for Research.

Boyd, D., Lankford, H., Loeb, S., & Wyckoff, J. (2001). Preliminary description of the geography of teacher labor markets (working paper).

Boyd, D., Lankford, H., Loeb, S., & Wyckoff, J. (2002a). Initial matches, transfers, and quits: The role of teachers' career decisions in the disparities in average teacher qualifications across schools (working paper).

Boyd, D., Lankford, H., Loeb, S., & Wyckoff, J. (2002b). Analyzing the determinants of the matching of public school teachers to jobs (working paper).

Brewer, D.J. (1996). Career paths and quit decisions: Evidence from teaching. *Journal of Labor Economics,* 14(2), 313-339.

Dolton, P.J. (1990). The economics of UK teacher supply: The graduate's decision. *The Economic Journal,* 100(400), 91-104.

Dolton, P.J., & Makepeace, G.H. (1993). Female labour force participation and the choice of occupation. *European Economic Review,* 37, 1393-1411.

Dolton, P.J., & van der Klaaw, W. (1999). The turnover of teachers: A competing risks explanation. *Review of Economics and Statistics,* 81(3), 543-552.

Evans, W.N., Murray S.E., & Schwab, R.M. (2001). The property tax and education finance: Uneasy compromises. In W.E. Oates (Ed.), *Property taxation and local government finance* (pp. 209-235). Cambridge, MA: Lincoln Institute of Land Policy.

Feistritzer, C.E. (1992). *Who wants to teach?* Washington, DC: National Center for Education Information.

Hanushek, E.A. (1986). The economics of schooling: Production and efficiency in public schools. *Journal of Economic Literature*, 24, 1141-1177.

Hanushek, E.A., Kain, J.F., & Rivkin, S.G. (1999). Do higher salaries buy better teachers? (working paper)

Hanushek, E.A., & Pace, R.R. (1995). Who chooses to teach, and why? *Economics of Education Review*, 14(2), 101-117.

Ladd, H.F., Chalk, R., & Hansen, J.S. (1999). *Equity and adequacy in educational finance*. Washington, DC: National Academy Press.

Lankford, H. (1999). *A descriptive analysis of the New York State and New York City teaching force*. Report prepared for the New York Supreme Court case Campaign for Fiscal Equity v. New York State.

Lankford, H., Loeb, S., & Wyckoff, J. (2002). Teacher sorting and the plight of urban schools: A descriptive analysis. *Educational Evaluation and Policy Analysis*, 24(1), 38-62.

Manski, C.F. (1987). Academic ability, earnings, and the decision to become a teacher: Evidence from the National Longitudinal Study of the High School Class of 1972. In D.A. Wise (Ed.), *Public sector payrolls* (pp. 291-312). Chicago: University of Chicago Press.

Mont, D., & Rees, D.I. (1996). The influence of classroom characteristics on high school teacher turnover. *Economic Inquiry*, 34, 152-167.

Murphy, J.T. (1987). Attracting talented students to teaching. *Harvard Educational Review*, 57(2), 177-182.

Murnane, R.J., Singer, J.D., Willett, J.B., Kemple, J.J., & Olsen, R.J. (1991). *Who will teach?* Cambridge, MA: Harvard University Press.

Murnane, R.J., Singer, J.D., & Willett, J.B. (1989). The influences of salaries and "opportunity costs" on teachers' career choices: Evidence from North Carolina. *Harvard Educational Review*, 59(3), 325-346.

Rickman, B.D., & Parker, C.D. (1990). Alternative wages and teacher mobility: A human capital approach. *Economics of Education Review*, 9(1), 73-79.

Rivkin, S., Hanushek, E., & Kain, J. (2000). Teachers, schools, and academic achievement. (National Bureau of Economic Research Working Paper No. 6691). National Bureau of Economic Research.

Sanders, W.L., & Rivers, J.C. (1996). *Research project report: Cumulative and residual effects of teachers on future student academic achievement*. University of Tennessee Value-Added Research and Assessment Center. Retrieved from http://www.mdk12.org/practices/ensure/tva/tva_2.html.

Stinebrickner, T.R. (2000). An analysis of occupational change and departure from the labor force: Evidence of the reasons that teachers quit (working paper).

Stinebrickner, T.R. (1999). Estimation of a duration model in the presence of missing data. *Review of Economics and Statistics*, 81(3), 529-542.

Stinebrickner, T.R. (1998). An empirical investigation of teacher attrition. *Economics of Education Review*, 17(2), 127-136.

Theobald, N.D. (1990). An examination of the influences of personal, professional, and school district characteristics on public school teacher retention. *Economics of Education Review*, 9(3), 241-250.

Theobald, N.D., & Gritz, R.M. (1996). The effects of school district spending priorities on the exit paths of beginning teachers leaving the district. *Economics of Education Review*, 15(1), 11-22.

Wise, A.E., Darling-Hammond, L., & Praskac, A. (1987). Teacher selection in the Hillsborough County public schools. In A. E. Wise, United States National Institute of Education, and Center for the Study of the Teaching Profession (Rand Corporation) (Eds.), *Effective teacher selection: From recruitment to retention—Case studies* (pp. 122-252). Santa Monica, CA: Rand Center for the Study of the Teaching Profession.

Section II

Professional Development

5

Rethinking District Professional Development Spending to Support School Improvement: Lessons From Comparative Spending Analysis

Karen Hawley Miles
Education Resource Management Strategies

Standards-based reform has entered a new phase that puts professional development of teachers at the center of the discussion. Even as many schools improve instruction to meet higher standards, concern is increasing regarding how to respond when school performance fails to imporve. One reform response focuses on changing the system to permit parents and their children to leave poorly performing schools. Unless there are large numbers of high-performing schools near these students, however, unsatisfied parents will have nowhere to go. So, the next step becomes finding ways to quickly increase the number of high-quality schools by creating new schools or improving existing ones. A large body of research tells us what good schools look like, but we know much less about what strategies and resources are needed to create and sustain large numbers of high-performing schools. Without this understanding, parents and reformers will be stuck demanding improvement without knowing whether schools or districts have the resources they need or whether they are making the changes necessary for improvement.

School districts across the country already invest significant sums of money each year in professional development to improve schools and teacher practice. The five districts studied here spent between 2.2% to 3.7% of total operating expenditures ($8.6 to $123 million dollars). No district, however, actively managed all of these dollars together, and none had a district level strategy to help focus and integrate professional development spending around improving student performance. To understand what districts will need to spend, they must first know what professional development they are currently providing, how much this costs, and which efforts improve school and teacher performance. With this information, they can organize more deliberately around a strategy for improving schools.

This chapter explores the lessons for research and practice that come out of comparing professional development spending across five urban districts. The findings presented here use an unusually intensive data collection effort and a collaboratively created standard for defining and coding professional development spending that can be replicated over time or in other districts. These five districts collected this spending information as part of their work to develop a district strategy for professional development. Because each district helped to collect and make sense of it, the data are uniquely detailed and have the potential to be more accurate than data gathered from secondary sources. Spending has been coded in ways that come out of the districts' own questions about how they spend their dollars. The framework for defining professional development cost elements was developed in collaboration with researchers from the Consortium for Policy Research in Education (CPRE) who were also working to develop and promote a replicable way to measure and describe professional development spending (Odden, Archibald, Fermanich, & Gallagher, 2002). The following two sections describe the methods and findings of this joint effort.

Approach and Methodology

The first step in supporting each district in creating its professional development strategy involved inventorying, describing, and quantifying their current efforts. With the complete set of activities identified, the districts then asked three questions:

1. How closely do the targets and purposes of these professional development activities align with our district priorities?

2. Is the district offering "high-quality" professional development opportunities that match research-based principles of effective efforts?

3. What can we learn from comparing our district with others?

Comparing professional development spending across districts is a difficult undertaking with little research available (Corcoran, 1995; Hertert, 1997; Killeen, Monk, & Plecki, 2000). Three main factors explain this dearth of information. First, districts often do not report all of their professional development spending in one place, looking only at certain departments or funding streams. Second, definitions of what to count as "professional development" vary significantly. Third, because professional development expenditures are not considered direct classroom instruction, some districts try to disguise them in other categories to protect them in tight budget times.

Responsibility for professional development spending and services is often spread across numerous district departments with multiple funding streams (Miles, Bouchard, Winner, Cohen, & Guiney 1999; Miles & Hornbeck, 2000). Each of these funding sources has different targets and reporting requirements. Frequently, even district administrators do not know how much they spend on professional development. One of the districts studied here reported professional development spending of only $460,000. When they included all funding sources and departments, they discovered they actually spent $8.9 million (Miles & Hornbeck, 2000). Similarly, a 1981 study of three urban districts found that actual professional development spending exceeded the districts' own estimates by a factor of 50 (Moore & Hyde, 1981).

Varying definitions of what to include as professional development expenditures also make comparison difficult. Most studies include activities such as workshops, conferences, and the "staff development" department. The more comprehensive studies include a wider range of investments aimed at building teacher capacity such as mentoring, teacher sabbaticals, student-free teacher preparation time during the school day, and salary scale increases resulting from additional training credits (Corcoran, 1995; Hertert, 1997; Miles et al., 1999; Miller, Lord, & Dorney, 1994). Studies vary on whether and how they include spending on intervention to support low-performing schools and school reform designs. The variations cause dramatic differences in spending estimates and make interpreting findings across studies complicated, at best.

District reluctance to clearly report professional development spending presents a final measurement challenge. In tight budget times, board members and other community members often insist that only "indirect" or nonclassroom costs be cut. In one district studied, the teacher-mentoring program was cut three times and then reinstated during a decade's time. Once the budget office stopped reporting this spending separately, it remained stable. This tendency reinforces the importance of having common definitions and measurement. If the need for higher levels of spending to build teaching capacity were widely understood, then districts might view this spending as an indication of their emphasis on teaching quality instead of as a target for budget cuts.

This study contributes to the available research by doing the following:

- Clearly defining the components of professional development cost by using the framework developed in collaboration with CPRE (Odden et al. 2002)
- Creating a coding scheme to describe the target, purpose, organization and funding of the professional development activities
- Collecting data directly from the district using a multistep interview and data analysis process
- Collecting detailed school-level data on professional development spending in two districts

Defining the Components of Cost

To create a standard definition for what to include as "professional development" and how to calculate its costs, CPRE researchers (Odden et al. 2002) collaborated with Jennifer King Rice of the Finance Project. The framework includes six core elements of professional development spending: (1) teacher time; (2) training and coaching; (3) administration; (4) materials, equipment, and facilities; (5)

travel and transportation; and (6) tuition and conference fees. The teacher time element of the framework provides a standard way to include district and school investments to provide teachers with time to participate in professional development. This is important because many districts pay teachers for extra workdays or hours scheduled for professional development. Because teacher compensation increases to pay for this time, it can represent considerable investment. The framework includes the cost of time added to teachers' work calendar when it is explicitly designated for professional development by contract or district policy. In addition, the framework includes the salaries of teachers on "sabbatical" if the district offers such time-off to pursue career development.

These calculations do not include the cost of teacher "planning time" during the school day. In most schools, teachers have regularly scheduled blocks of time, often known as "planning periods," that are free from instruction. Teachers use this time for a variety of activities including planning and preparing for lessons; working together with other teachers to improve or plan instruction; and, sometimes, participating in professional development activities. When this time is consistently scheduled for professional development or collaborative school improvement work, the cost of covering teachers' classes during this time might be considered a professional development expense. Capturing the use of this time, however, requires in-depth school-level analysis that is not included here.[1]

The framework includes the direct cost of training and coaching of all types, from the salaries of district trainers and consultant fees to the salary of full-time coaches at the school sites. It also attempts to capture the district's indirect cost. When staff members spend 20% or more of their time supporting or supervising professional development activities, the cost of this staff time is included. The cost of materials, equipment, and facilities is also included, as is the cost of travel to off-site professional development activities. Finally, the framework includes tuition and conference fees paid for teachers who obtain professional development on their own when the district reimburses teachers for it. It does not include the teacher's out-of-pocket expenses for training. More detailed information on the cost structure, the research supporting it, and the methods of calculation is available in Odden et al. (Odden et al. 2002; Miles, Miller, Hornbeck, & Fermanich, 2002).

Coding for Target, Purpose, and Delivery Strategy

The cost structure framework ensures that the same elements of cost are compared across districts. However, insuring inclusion of a full and common set of professional development activities requires clarity around the "targets," "purposes" and "delivery strategies" of the professional development investments.

Districts and schools balance professional development between two "targets": building individual skills and improving instructional capacity

---

[1] For an example of how the inclusion of this school-level expenditure affects spending levels, please see Archibald & Gallagher (in press); Fermanich (in press); and Gallagher (in press).

schoolwide or across certain content or program areas. The first category—individual professional development—refers to investments aimed at meeting the individual career needs of teachers or principals. This professional development is often triggered by the career stage or status of the individual, such as a beginning teacher or a teacher with an unsatisfactory rating. The teacher's or principal's individual initiative or need to gain specific skills, such as adding a special education certification or enhancing classroom management skills, can also drive the training.

Professional development aimed at the second target category—schools—builds individual capacity but in the context of a school-level or instructional program effort. These activities aim at teams of teachers, at all teachers in schools, or at building knowledge districtwide in program or subject areas. For example, schoolwide comprehensive school reform models would fit here as would any school-based coaching in content areas. Districtwide initiatives to build capacity in certain subjects or skills, such as required training to build science or student assessment skills, would be included here. However, subject training available to teachers on a voluntary basis would be coded as individually targeted spending.

Five categories of "purpose" for professional development aimed at individuals and four for training aimed at schools are shown in Figure 5.1.

Figure 5.1. Coding Categories for Target and Purpose

Target individual (teacher, principal and other subcategories)

- ♦ Preservice preparation
- ♦ Induction
- ♦ Remediation
- ♦ Teacher leadership

Target school

- ♦ Restructuring and transition costs
- ♦ Instructional improvement
- ♦ Program support (specialized schools or programs within schools)
- ♦ Support of special populations (special education, bilingual, Title I, gifted)

Once the purposes have been coded, additional coding tags provide further detail. For example, professional development aimed at continuing education would also be coded as to topic such as literacy, technology or math. Similarly, activities coded as "support to special student populations" would be tagged by the type of student such as bilingual or disabled and by the topic if appropriate.

Categorizing targets and purposes of professional development spending can help a district prioritize and focus its investment when analyzed further by subgroup. For example, the district could look to see how much it invested in professional development for certain categories of schools such as low-performing schools, elementary schools, or schools with high-poverty populations.

The final major coding step involved classifying activities into eight distinct delivery strategy categories. The term "delivery strategy" describes a particular way of organizing staff, consultants, and professional development content to improve individual or school capacity. This step helps ensure inclusion of all forms of professional development and later enables evaluation of various forms of providing professional development. For example, most districts would include spending organized as a "training academy," but they might not include spending on "comprehensive school reform designs." A comprehensive design would address school improvement by using a prescribed process and set of materials that address improved instruction across all grades in a school. These may include "off-the-shelf" whole school models such as Success for All or Co-Nect or locally developed models.

"Lead Teachers" is another category not always included as a professional development expense. This label refers to teachers who have a formal title of "Lead Teacher"—such as a "Literacy Lead" or "Team Leader" teacher—and who work within a school to lead improvement efforts. These teachers are paid an additional stipend and have defined responsibilities related to providing school-level coaching or professional development. Stipends for lead teachers not providing professional development or coaching would not be included here. A complete description of each delivery strategy category can be found in the Appendix (p. 107).

Collecting the Data

The data collection method for this five-district study helped ensure that all professional development investments would be considered and that sufficient detail on the target, purpose, and organization of the investment could be collected. The analysis began with the entire district budget. This included general funds as well as budgets from all other public and private sources of funding for the district. Researchers identified all line items that could contain expenses for "instructional support" defined as all district strategies, including professional development, used to support high-quality instruction in the district. Line items that were clearly unrelated to instructional improvement, such as transportation costs, were eliminated. Dollars allocated to school-level budgets were also excluded from this analysis.

District-level interviews clarified which expenditures were related to instructional and school support and allowed coding of department spending into seven categories: (1) professional development, (2) accountability, (3) curriculum development and support, (4) special program monitoring and compliance, (5) information systems, (6) district student services, and (7) community outreach. Interviews included department heads and fund managers in departments such as quality improvement, career in teaching, administration, curriculum and assessment, magnet, vocational education, accountability, professional development, Title I, Title II, and special education.

At this point, the focus narrowed to coding those expenditures within instructional and school support that had been defined as professional development using the framework and definitions described above. Perhaps the most challenging effort involved identifying the district staff time involved in professional development. Many district staff members devote a significant portion of their time to supervising or providing professional development activities. Interviewers asked each staff person to estimate the time spent on professional development-related activities.

Including School-Level Professional Development Spending

District-level spending on professional development represents only a piece of the total cost of improving school performance. School-level data on spending complete this picture. As for the district data, however, school budgets are not formatted to allow easy identification of these dollars. In fact, school-level interviews showed that school principals often do not quantify their total spending or record the use of dollars, time, and staff over the year. In two districts, Midwest and Mega, school case studies add to the district data presented here (Miles, Odden, Fermanich, Archibald, & Gallagher (in press); Fermanich, 2002). These data were collected through principal and teacher interviews as well as analysis of school-level budgets.

Findings

The five sample districts were at varying stages of reform efforts centered around building teaching capacity. Each used this research to integrate and focus their work. The Southwest, Northeast, and Mega districts were at the early stages of redefining the district role in supporting school improvement, and the Midwest district was three years into its strategy. The Southeast district, also beginning its restructuring effort, had recently received an infusion of new state and federal support, directly injected into whole school reform support for schools. The sample districts also vary in their level of decentralization. Midwest and Mega invest a greater portion of decisions and dollars in the school level than do the other three districts. As Figure 5.2 shows, the districts range in size from 50,000 to 500,000 students. They all have large proportions of poor and minority students.

Figure 5.2. Characteristics of Sample Districts

	Southwest District	Southeast District	Midwest District	Northeast District	Mega District
Location	Southwest	Southeast	Midwest	Northeast	Midwest
Enrollment	85,000	59,000	50,000	63,000	477,000
Teachers	5,200	3,900	3,100	4,600	26,350
Schools	120	103	75	130	500
Operating Budget (millions)*	$485.5	$626.1	$396.4	$526.3	3,500
Per-Pupil Expenditures	$5,700	$10,600	$7,900	$8,400	$7,500
Minority Enrollment (%)	60.9	93.6	75.3	85.0	85
Free or Reduced-Price Lunch (%)	43.3	75.4	65.6	74.0	84

*All expenditure numbers were adjusted for geographic differences in the costs of goods and services using the National Center for Education Statistics' Geographical Cost of Education Index.[2]

Five sets of lessons come out of comparing professional development spending across these districts. First, districts invested significant but widely varying resources in professional development. The numerous departments managing these professional development resources lacked a unifying strategy. Second, district spending to provide teacher time for professional development was the single largest investment in some districts, but investment levels varied widely. No district had strategies for holding schools or teachers accountable for effective use of professional development time. Third, most districts aimed the majority of professional development at building school-level capacity, but they used different, usually unplanned combinations of delivery strategies. Fourth, some schools supplement district resources with significant portions of their own dollars to support professional development, but these resources are often difficult to integrate with district support. Finally, districts rethinking their use of professional development spending can make dramatic changes that focus resources around a strategy for school improvement in a short period of time. The following paragraphs describe these findings in more detail:

♦ Districts invested significant but widely varying resources in professional development. The numerous departments managing these professional development resources lacked a unifying strategy.

2 National Center for Education Statistics, 2002.

The five districts examined here spent, on average, approximately 3% of the districts' total operating budgets and $3,600 per teacher. These estimates are in line with other research (Hertert 1997, Killeen et al. 2000). The methodology used here, however, allows more confident comparison of the differences across districts. As Figure 5.3 shows, the levels of investment ranged significantly, from slightly more than 2% of total operating expenditures in Southwest and Midwest to nearly 4% in Northeast and Mega.

Figure 5.3. Total Professional Development Expenditures with Contracted Professional Development Days: Five-District Comparison

	Southwest District	Southeast District	Midwest District	Northeast District	Mega District	Average
Total Expenditures (millions)	$11.2	$19.5	$8.6	$19.5	$123	NA
Percent of Operating Budget	2.3	3.1	2.2	3.7	3.4	2.9
Per Teacher	$2,100	$5,000	$2,700	$4,200	$3,900	$3,600
NA = not applicable.						

These investment levels are far larger than any professional development expenditures that the districts actively managed. For example, the Southwest district's professional development department spent $2 million, only one fifth of the total professional development investments. The remaining $9 million of expenditures was managed by others and was not part of an overall strategy for professional development. The most common departments included in professional development are curriculum development, Title I, special education, and instructional technology. The strategies and resources of these departments were not linked in any district at the beginning of this work. In addition to having departmentally organized professional development, both Midwest and Southeast districts maintained organized "intervention" support for low-performing schools that included significant professional development from staff and outside providers.

In three sample districts, outside providers, including nonprofit organizations and a university, administered a large portion of the professional development budget. As was true across district departments, the outside providers had their own approaches to professional development, and no district held outside providers accountable for demonstrating improved student performance or changes in teaching practice.

All five districts relied heavily on nonlocal revenue sources to fund their professional development programs, which contributed to the difficulty of creating a unifying strategy. As Figure 5.4 shows, on average, nearly half, 49%, of their revenue for professional development programming came from nonlocal sources or private, state and federal funds.[3] At one third of total revenue, federal funds provided the largest source of outside funding. Title I was the single largest source of federal funding, followed by the National Science Foundation, Individuals with Disabilities Education Act, and Title II Eisenhower Math and Science program grants.

**Figure 5.4. Sources of Funding for Professional Development:
Percent of Total Spending Not Including Professional Development Days**

	Southwest District	Southeast District	Northeast District	Midwest District	Mega District	Average
Federal (%)	28	36	50	24	28	33
State (%)	5	2	9	11	12	8
Local (%)	67	59	10	62	58	51
Private (%)	0	3	31	2	1	8
Total (%)	100	100	100	100	100	

Private sources, such as grants from foundations and corporations, accounted for an average of 8% of revenues but as much as 31% of total revenues in the Northeast district. The next closest district, Southeast, received only 3% of its revenue from private sources. At the time of this study, Northeast had just received significant private funding to implement a locally developed "whole-school improvement" model in approximately one quarter of its schools. State support for professional development that did not come from the general fund also varied across these districts, ranging from only 2% in the Southeast district to 12% in the Midwest district.

♦ District spending to provide teacher time for professional development varied widely in size and composition.

Districts pay for teacher stipends or substitutes to allow participation in professional development. Some districts also add days or hours to the teacher calendar to provide time for teams to work together. Northeast and Mega were the only two districts that designated such professional development time in its teacher contract. Northeast paid teachers for two full days of professional development plus an additional 18 hours scheduled during the year at each school. This adds nearly $7 million to the total spending and represents 35% of Northeast's total. Spending on eight days of contractual

---

3   As used here, "local sources" refers to the districts' general fund, which in most cases combined local property taxes and state per-pupil financing to be used at the districts' discretion.

time represented half of Mega's professional development investment. Including the cost of professional development days in
spending totals is necessary because providing this time reflects an
important district investment that is often not explicitly quantified
or managed but is so large that it distorts comparisons. As Figure 5.5
shows, when this spending is removed from the estimates, Northeast's spending levels decreases to 2.4 %, more similar to Southwest
and Midwest. Mega decreases to 1.9 %, the lowest level of any sample district. Because this adjustment changes spending level estimates so significantly, and because districts and policymakers address this investment in teacher time separately, cross-district
comparisons must explicitly account for this investment by stating
expenditure levels with and without this cost.

**Figure 5.5. Professional Development Expenditures With
and Without Contracted Professional Development Days**

	Southwest District	Southeast District	Midwest District	Northeast District	Mega District
Percent of Operating Budget With Contracted PD Time	2.3	3.2	3.3	3.7	3.4
Percent of Operating Budget Without Contracted PD Time	2.3	3.1	2.2	2.4	1.9
Dollar Amount per Teacher With Contracted PD Time	$450	$150	$100	$2,000	$2,000
Dollar Amount per Teacher Without Contracted PD Time	$450	$150	$100	$520	$200
PD, professional development.					

Districts devoted dramatically different portions of their dollars to providing
teacher time for professional development, ranging from 4% and 52% of all professional development spending. Even when dollars for contracted professional
development days are removed, spending on stipends and substitutes differs
greatly, e.g., from 4% to 21% (Figure 5.6). The districts that provided professional
development days, Mega and Northeast, also paid teachers more in substitutes
and stipends. Northeast invested 13 % of district dollars in stipends and substitutes for teachers to participate in professional development and the highest per
teacher amount at $520 per teacher. Southwest devoted the highest percent of its
professional development dollars to teacher stipends and substitutes.

Meanwhile, Southeast and Midwest spent only $150 and $100 per teacher
respectively at the district level to pay teachers for time to participate in addi-

tional professional development. While these numbers may indicate a low level of investment in teacher time, it would be dangerous to use these numbers alone to measure a district's commitment to providing teacher professional development time. Three kinds of information help complete the diagnosis.

Figure 5.6. Professional Development Cost Structure and Percent of Professional Development Spending: Five-District Comparison

Cost Structure Element	Southwest District	Southeast District	Midwest District	Northeast District	Northeast District (No Contract Time)	Mega District	Mega District (No Contract Time)
Teacher Time: Stipends and Substitutes (%)	21	4	4	13	19	6	9
Teacher Time: Contracted Days or Hours (%)	0	0	0	35	0	46	0
Training and Coaching ($)	70	87	84	45	69	35	70
Administration (%)	5	5	5	1	2	5	7
Materials, Equipment, and Facilities (%)	3	3	3	5	8	3	6
Travel and Transportation (%)	1	1	3	1	1	1	1
Tuition and Conference Fees (%)	0	0	1	0	0	4	7

First, school-level spending must be added. Especially in a decentralized district, such as Midwest, schools may use discretionary funds to pay teacher stipends and find substitutes to create professional development time. Second, school districts and schools can restructure the use of existing teacher time to create instruction-free time in ways that do not add cost (Miles & Hornbeck, 2000). Third, teacher compensation and job structure might create monetary incentives to devote additional time to professional development. For example, Midwest invests more than other districts to pay annual stipends to Lead Teachers who facilitate and prepare for teacher development. Midwest also provides a $5,000 incentive for teachers to obtain certification from the National Board for Professional Teaching Standards. Although this is not direct payment for time, it provides incentive to devote time to professional development. At the other end of the spectrum, Southwest's teacher salaries are so low, the district uses every opportunity for stipends to increase teacher income.

The process of quantifying the cost of teacher professional development days or hours spurred these districts to think more strategically about how to hold schools accountable for making more effective use of this time and to support them in doing so. It also highlighted situations in which extra time exists that could be used for improving school or teacher capacity, but where the district has no way of doing so. For example, in the Southeast district, the teacher contract includes 10 teacher workdays beyond the student calendar. However, these days are not explicitly designated for use as professional development, and no one is responsible for monitoring the effective use of this time.

- ◆ Most districts targeted the majority of professional development toward school-level capacity building, but no overarching strategy guides this support.

    Four of the five districts aimed the majority of their district spending at improving school-level capacity in some way and invested a much smaller portion in developing individual capacity apart from school or district programs and initiatives. Figure 5.7 shows that Midwest and Northeast districts both invested 1.8% of their operating budgets and approximately $2,000 per teacher in school-targeted professional development.

Southeast invested more heavily in professional development aimed at schools, spending $4,000 per teacher and 2.5% of the budget, in contrast to Southwest, which on the low end spent 1% and $970 per teacher. Interpreting these differences requires further detail in two areas. First, assessing the effectiveness of these investments, or even accurately describing them, demands more precision about which schools and teachers received resources for what purpose. The coding scheme presented here facilitates this analysis. Second, as discussed below, districts and policymakers need to know how this professional development is organized and delivered.

Figure 5.7. Professional Development Spending by Target and Percent of Operating Budget

	Southwest District	Southeast District	Midwest District	Northeast District
Percent of Operating Budget With Contracted PD Time	2.3	3.2	3.3	3.7
Percent of Operating Budget Without Contracted PD Time	2.3	3.1	2.2	2.4
Dollar Amount per Teacher With Contracted PD Time	$450	$150	$100	$2,000
Dollar Amount per Teacher Without Contracted PD Time	$450	$150	$100	$520
PD, professional development.				

Midwest provides a powerful example of how delving more deeply into which schools receive support can help target resources. More than 70% of all of Midwest's professional development resources are allocated to the school level, but the distribution of school-level resources is not planned across schools, and some schools have access to only a few sources of support. This means that total professional development resources for each school and teacher vary significantly. Figure 5.8 highlights a dramatic spread in the total professional development resources available to schools. It shows that the lowest elementary school receives approximately $545 per teacher in district support, whereas the highest school receives more than $8,000 per teacher in district resources for professional development and school improvement.

Figure 5.8. Professional Development Resources by School Performance

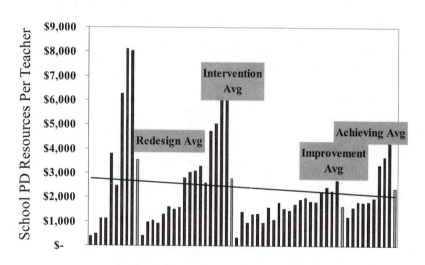

Despite the wide variance, Midwest's strategy lay behind some of the differences. The district rates schools at four levels depending on school performance and improvement over time, with the lowest level labeled "redesign" and the highest achieving schools labeled "achieving." The district organized to provide redesign and intervention schools with extra support and infusion of dollars along with intense supervision. The average numbers show that schools in the lowest performing category of "redesign" received an average of $3,500 not including the school's discretionary spending. Schools in the next-to-bottom category, "intervention," receive slightly less at $2,750 per teacher. However, Midwest discovered a deviation in the pattern with the schools in the "improvement" category. These schools received less per teacher on average than the schools in the highest "achievement" category.

Although school-level allocations followed a logical pattern, resources within performance categories varied significantly. Figure 5.8 shows the available resources per teacher for each "accountability" level along with the average for that level (the lightest bar at the end of each category). The analysis shows that the greatest variation in resource levels is in the bottom two performance categories. Some schools in the intervention category receive less than 25% of what the schools at the highest end receive. Because the district holds all schools to the same performance standards, leaders felt strongly that schools should have access to similar resources for transforming instructional practice.

Creating a powerful strategy also requires choosing how to organize the delivery of each kind of professional development. This analysis shows that districts use common delivery strategies for professional development but in very different mixes. Figure 5.9 shows professional development expenditures by district in terms of the percent of total expenditures by delivery strategy. The mix of strategies employed by a district reflects a blend of history, politics, and—to some degree—a deliberate strategy. The "range" calculated for each of the strategies highlights those strategies that represented significant commitments in one or more of the districts studied. Comprehensive school reform designs, school-based instructional facilitators, school-based lead teachers, and teacher mentors each represent more than one quarter of all professional development in at least one district and are not employed or used little in other districts. Often the difference between districts can be driven by heavy investment in one strategy. In the Southeast district, for example, if the dollars supporting "school-based instructional facilitators" were removed from spending estimates, it would drop to the same per-teacher level as the Midwest and Northeast districts. In the same way, if the resources devoted to Southwest's mentor program were removed, Southwest's investment in individual teachers would drop below the level of other districts.

Figure 5.9. District Delivery Strategies for Professional Development: Percent of Professional Development Spending (Not Including Contracted Professional Development Days)

Target and Delivery Strategy	Southwest District	Southeast District	Midwest District	Northeast District	Mega District	Range
School (%)	43	82	72	74	57	
CSRD and Other Models (%)	2	12	13	25	0	25
Department-Based Training (%)	23	12	13	28	12	16
School-Based Coaching (%)	16	13	17	17	40	37
School-Based Lead Teachers (%)	2	0	20	4	0	20
School-Based Instructional Facilitators (%)	0	25	0	0	0	25
Training Academy Coursework (%)	0	3	9	0	5	9
Individual (%)	57	18	28	26	43	
Department-Based Training (%)	22	12	6	12	18	16
Professional Development Schools (%)	0	0	2	0	4	4
Mentor (%)	34	3	10	4	8	31
Training Academy Coursework (%)	1	3	9	11	13	12

CSRD, comprehensive school reform design.

♦ Schools supplement district resources with significant but highly variable portions of their own dollars.

Two districts, Mega and Midwest, invested time in collecting school-level professional development data to complete their picture of district professional development spending. Because these districts both decentralized most of their federal dollars to the school level and had deliberate policies that allowed more school-level flexibility, this window on school activities was especially important. In each district, school-level spending on professional development varied widely across the sample schools. In Mega, spending in elementary schools ranged from a low of $885 per teacher to a maximum of more than $9,000 per teacher, a factor of more than 10. Average per-teacher spending was just under $3,800. Variation among the high schools was somewhat less, ranging from $2,354 to $7,541 per teacher, with average spending of $4,294 per teacher. Schools that had access to categorical funding sources, such as Title I or State Chapter I dollars, did spend more. However, higher-spending schools also seemed to dedicate more of their general fund dollars to professional development as well (Miles et al. 2002; Archibald and Gallagher (in press); Fermanich (in press); Gallagher (in press).

Even schools that fund at lower levels devote significant resources to professional development. At $900 per teacher, a typical elementary school with 40 teachers would have $36,000 to spend on professional development, an amount nearly sufficient to pay for the annual professional development costs of many established comprehensive school reform designs. Nevertheless, the disparity among schools is substantial enough to have a meaningful impact on teachers' access to professional development services. A school with 40 teachers spending $900 per teacher would have $116,000 less in professional development resources than a comparable school spending at the elementary average of $3,800 per teacher.

Combining district-provided school resources with school-level investments increases the resources available to promote deep instructional change as well as the disparities between schools. In the Midwest district, one-low performing school had $350,000, or $12,000 per teacher, in district- and school-level resources devoted to professional development, whereas another school in the same performance category had a total of $16,000 or fewer than $400 per teacher. This high level of investment and the inequities between schools create two challenges for districts. The first is to support schools in making effective use of large investments in professional development. In both Midwest and Mega, several schools had significant district resources for professional development that did not integrate well with, or even conflicted with, school-level professional development efforts. The second challenge involves finding ways to target more resources to underserved schools and to encourage them to spend more of their own dollars to build capacity.

♦ Districts that rethink their use of professional development spending can make dramatic changes that focus spending more clearly around school improvement in a short period of time.

One sample district, Southwest, conducted this professional development audit twice, once at the beginning of its efforts to develop a district-level reform strategy and again two years later. In the first year, Southwest was distressed, although not surprised, to find that they spent the lowest total amount and percent on professional development activities (Figure 5.2). District leaders aimed to "pool" professional development resources from across district departments, funding sources, and activities and redirect them to poorly performing schools in more integrated school-level activities that might impact the classroom more deeply. The district created "cluster support teams" that decentralized supervision, support, and professional development closer to the schools. These cluster teams combined resources that used to be organized in separate departments to provide integrated support to each school in developing a powerful school plan and then providing targeted support. The new organization allowed staff members who used to serve in compliance and monitoring kinds of roles to provide deeper support that also included ongoing professional development coaching. Next, they created a category of low-performing schools called "schools in need of improvement" (SINOI). Each of these schools was required to choose a specific literacy model and was provided with district resources to pay for technical assistance to implement it. In addition, each SINOI received professional development support from a specially trained district team and $10,000 to pay for teacher time to participate in professional development.

These and other changes showed up dramatically in spending numbers. As Figure 5.10 shows, only two years later total professional development spending had nearly doubled from $11.2 million dollars to $19.5 million dollars and from 2.3% of operating budget to 4.0%. Figure 5.11 shows that the percent of district professional development efforts targeted to school improvement went from 43%, the lowest in the sample, to 75% in the third year. This puts Southwest's percentage targeted toward schools in line with the Southeast, Midwest, and Northeast districts, each of which had significant school restructuring and improvement efforts underway. Fully 36% of all professional development resources were delivered as school-based coaching, the most of any district sampled here. District leaders now felt the pressure of ensuring that the investment generated improvements in classroom practice, but they were clearer about what activities they needed to evaluate.

Figure 5.10. Total Southwest Professional Development Expenditures With Contracted Professional Development Days: Changes in Spending on Professional Development During a Three-Year Period

	Southwest District 2000	Southwest District 2002
Total Expenditures (millions)	$11.2	$19.5
Percent of Operating Budget	2.3	4.0
Per Teacher	$2,100	$2,800

Figure 5.11. Professional Development Spending by Delivery Strategy: Percent of Professional Development Spending Not Including Contracted Professional Development Time

Target and Delivery Strategy	Southwest District Year 1	Southwest District Year 3	Southeast District	Midwest District	Northeast District	Mega District
School (%)	43	75	82	72	74	57
CSRD and Other Models (%)	2	14	12	13	25	0
Department-Based Training (%)	23	12	12	13	28	12
School-Based Coaching(%)	16	36	13	17	17	40
School-Based Lead Teachers (%)	2	0	0	20	4	0
School-Based Instructional Facilitators (%)	0	10	25	0	0	0
Training Academy Coursework (%)	0	3	3	9	0	5
Individual (%)	57	25	18	28	26	43
Department-Based Training (%)	22	1	12	6	12	18
Professional Development Schools (%)	0	0	0	2	0	4
Mentor (%)	34	21	3	10	4	8
Training Academy Coursework (%)	1	3	3	9	11	13
CSRD, comprehensive school reform design.						

Figure 5.12 shows the Southwest district having a much more focused and balanced professional development strategy. In the first year, Southwest devoted 40% of all professional development spending to preservice or induction training for teachers. Departmental teacher training on strategies for students with special needs was the second largest investment at 20%. Two years later, 50% of the dollars were aimed at school-level instructional improvement organized around literacy. The analysis also helped Southwest see how few resources they devoted toward developing strong principals and teacher leaders. By the third year, Southwest had already increased spending on principal development and made changes to increase spending on teacher leadership as well.

**Figure 5.12. Professional Development Spending by Target and Purpose:
Percent of Total Professional Development Spending
Not Including Contracted Professional Development Time**

Target and Purpose (%)	Southwest District Year 1	Southwest District Year 3
School (%)	43	75
Change Conditions and Restructuring (%)	2	10
Instructional Improvement (%)	10	50
Program Support (%)	11	5
Support of Special Populations (%)	20	10
Individual–Teacher Ratio (%)	57	23
Preservice and Induction (%)	40	12
Remediation (%)	0	0
Continuing Education (%)	14	8
Leadership Development (%)	3	3
Individual–Principal Ratio (%)	0	2

Southwest was able to use this information to define a strategy for professional development that seemed consistent with the research on effective professional development. The next step will be to test and refine this strategy by determining which efforts generate improved instruction and student performance, and by exploring the situations that foster such efforts. In some of the worst performing schools student performance increased in as little as one year. In schools where performance did not increase, however, Southwest had no way of knowing why or of targeting further support. To do this, Southwest realized they needed a systematic way of monitoring or measuring whether schools are using their new professional development resources effectively to improve instruction. They are currently engaged in developing an enhanced accountability system that systematically measures changes in instructional practice targeted by the school-based professional development.

Conclusion

The case of Southwest clearly illustrates the value of methodical quantification and coding of professional development. Once the district knows how much it is spending on what activities and for whom, it can begin to organize this spending into a deliberate strategy for improving schools and building teacher and principal capacity over their careers. Implementation of the district's strategy permits measurement of the strategie's impact on student performance. The comparisons presented here show that districts organize and invest differently in professional development. Collecting data from more districts that have deliberate professional development strategies and from more districts over time will provide important information for districts and policymakers. Districts can use this information immediately to craft more sensible, focused professional development strategies. However, until we can link these strategies to improvements in student performance, we will not be able to judge how much or what kind of investment is needed to sustain districtwide school improvement.

Acknowledgment

This article draws on some of the work conducted through a collaboration of the Consortium for Policy Research in Education at the University of Wisconsin and reported in Miles, Odden, Fermanich, & Archibald (in press).

Appendix: Delivery Strategies

♦ Comprehensive school reform design (CSRD, comprehensive, integrated designs for improving school performance)

A comprehensive design addresses school improvement by using a prescribed process and set of materials that address improve instruction across all grades in a school. These may include "off the shelf" whole school models such as Success for All, Co-Nect, or locally developed models.

♦ Department-based training

Department-based training is provided through various central office departments and offices and is not organized as "school-based coaching," which is defined below. This training is frequently more narrowly focused and less likely to be aligned with broader district priorities. Examples include training on special education regulations through a district's special education department or technology training sponsored by an instructional technology department.

♦ School-based coaching

Coaches are assigned by the district to work with instructional staff in the schools on either school improvement and organizational issues or on high-priority curricular areas. Examples may include literacy or math coaches or coaches working to facilitate staff review of student performance data and creation of a school improvement plan.

♦ School-based lead teachers

School-based lead teachers have a formal title of Lead Teacher and work within a school to lead improvement efforts in some way. Examples include the use of "Literacy Leader" or "Team Leader" teachers that are paid an additional stipend and have defined responsibilities related to providing school-level coaching or professional development.

- ◆ Mentors

  Mentors are master teachers who support and coach other teachers, generally either first-year teachers, struggling veteran teachers, or preservice teacher interns.

- ◆ School-based instructional facilitators

  School-based instructional facilitators are teachers who are members of their schools' instructional staff, who have an explicit role in leading instruction, and who do not handle a full class load. This position can be a district-sponsored position or a school-level decision. They generally are accomplished teachers who serve as the instructional leaders in their schools, frequently supporting specific strategies such as comprehensive school reform designs, curriculum standards, or literacy instruction.

- ◆ Training academy

  Training academy is a department or organization with a mission, mostly on a volunteer basis, of offering coursework and other training opportunities to teachers and principals. Many have an in-house professional development "academy" that offers a catalog of short-term workshops on a wide variety of topics. Alternatively, a district might contract with an outside organization to offer training programs.

- ◆ Professional development schools

  Professional development schools are demonstration schools staffed with master teachers and structured to allow apprenticeships. The additional costs of creating such schools would be included here but not the direct cost of providing instruction to students in these schools.

References

Archibald, S., & Gallagher, H. A. (2002). A case study of professional development expenditures at a restructured high school. *Education Policy Analysis Archives.* 10(29). Retrieved from http://epaa.asu.edu/epaa/v10n29.html.

Corcoran, T. B. (1995). Helping teachers teach well: Transforming professional development (Report RB-16-June 1995). Philadelphia: Consortium for Policy Research in Education.

Fermanich, M. (in press). School spending for professional development: A cross case analysis of seven schools in one urban district. *Elementary School Journal.*

Gallagher, H. A. (2002). Elm Street School: A case study of professional development expenditures. *Education Policy Analysis Archives.* 10(28). Retrieved from http://epaa.asu.edu/epaa/v10n28.html.

Hertert, L. (1997). Investing in teacher professional development: A look at 16 school districts. Denver, CO: Education Commission of the States.

Killeen, K. M., Monk, D. H., & Plecki, M. L. (2002). School district spending on professional development: Insights available from national data. *Journal of Education Finance,* 28(1), 25-49.

Miles, K. H., Bouchard, F., Winner, K., Cohen, M. A., & Guiney, E. (1999). *Professional development spending in the Boston Public Schools: A joint report of the Boston Plan for Excellence and the Boston Public Schools.* Boston, MA: Boston Plan for Excellence and the Boston Public Schools.

Miles, K. H., & Hornbeck, M. (2000). *Rethinking district professional development spending to support a district csr strategy* (Resource Reallocation, Issue no. 3). Arlington, VA: New American Schools.

Miles, K.H., Miller, B., Hornbeck, M., & Fermanich, M. (2002) *Chicago Public Schools Professional Development Project Final Report.* Chicago: Chicago Public Education Fund.

Miles, K.H., Odden, A., Fermanich M., Archibald, S., & Gallagher, A. (in press). Understanding and comparing district investment in professional development: Methods and lessons from four districts.

Miller, B., Lord, B., & Dorney, J. (1994). Staff development for teachers: A study of configurations and costs in four districts. Newton, MA: Educational Development Center.

Moore, D., & Hyde, A. (1981). *Making sense of staff development: An analysis of staff development programs and their costs in three urban districts.* Chicago: Designs for Change.

National Center for Education Statistics. (2002). Cost of education index dataset for 1993-94. Washington, D.C.: National Center for Education Statistics. Retrieved from http://nces.ed.gov/edfin/prodsurv/data.asp#cost_of_ed.

Odden, A., Archibald, S., Fermanich, M., & Gallagher, H. A. (2002). A cost framework for professional development. *Journal of Education Finance,* 28(1), 51-74.

6

The Incidence and Impact of Teacher Professional Development: Implications for Education Productivity

Jennifer King Rice
University of Maryland

Teachers are indisputably one of the central factors in the education instillation process. Teacher salaries alone constitute at least half of typical school district expenditures.[1] Given this high level of investment, much attention has been paid to understanding teacher quality and the implications of various measures of teacher knowledge and heir contribution to the attainment of desired educational goals, such as student achievement. For instance, research has focused on the impact of the specific types of courses teacher candidates take,[2]

---

1 Guthrie, J.W., & Rothstein, R. (1998). Enabling adequacy to achieve reality: Translating adequacy into state school finance distribution arrangements. In Ladd, H. F., Chalk, R., & Hansen, J. S. (Eds.), *Equity and adequacy issues in school finance* (pp. 209-259). Washington, D. C.: National Academy Press; Speakman, S. T., Cooper , B. S., Sampiere, R., May, J., Holsomback, H., & Glass, B. (1966). Bringing money to the classroom: A systemic resource allocations model applied to the New York City Public Schools. In Picus, L. O., & Wattenbarger, J. L. (Eds.), *Where does the money go? Resource allocation in elementary and secondary schools*. Thousand Oaks, CA: Corwin.

2 See, for examples, Ferguson, R. F., & Womack, S. T. (1993). The impact of subject matter and education coursework on teaching performance. *Journal of Teacher Education, 44*(1), 55-63; Hawk, P. P., Coble, C. R., & Swanson, M. (1985). Certification: It does matter. *Journal of Teacher Education, 36*(3), 13-15; Monk, D. H. (1994). Subject area preparation of secondary mathematics and science teachers and student achievement. *Economics of Education Review, 13*(2), the type and level of degree they have earned,[3] and the performance of teachers on various tests designed to measure their skills and abilities.[4] Because of the increasing number and sophistication of studies on teacher preparation, our understanding of this key input and its impact is improving.[5]

However, policymakers have also recognized that the skills of teachers are not fixed from the time that they are hired. Rather, their skills and knowledge presumably can be enhanced through ongoing professional development activities, and school systems invest considerable resources to do just that. A study by the Education Commission of the States estimated that district expenses for professional development were 3.6% of net district operations expenses.[6] Elmore's study of professional development in a New York City district found the figure to be 3%,[7] and Miller at al.'s estimate across four districts ranged from 1.8% to 2.8%

125-145; Monk, D. H., & King, J. A. (1994). Multilevel Teacher resource effects in pupil performance in secondary mathematics and science: The case of teacher subject-matter preparation. In Ehrenberg, R. G. (Ed.), *Choices and consequences: Contemporary policy issues in education* (pp. 29-58). Ithaca, New York: ILR Press; and Perkes, V. A. (1968). Junior high school science teacher preparation, teaching behavior, and student achievement. *Journal of Research in Science Teaching,* 121-126.

3   For examples, see Domas, S. J., & Brewer, D. V. (1950). Teacher competence: An annotated bibliography. *Journal of Experimental Education, 19*(2), 101-217; Goldhaber, D. D., & Brewer, D. J. (1997). Evaluating the effect of teacher degree level on educational performance. In Fowler, W. J. (Ed.), *Developments in school finance* (pp. 197-210). Washington, D.C.: United States Department of Education; and Turner, R., Camilli, G., Kroc, R., & Hoover, J. (1986). Policy strategies, teacher salary incentive, and student achievement: an explanatory model. *Educational Researcher, 15*(3), 5-11.

4   For examples, see Coleman, J. S., Campbell, E. Q., Hobson, S. C., McPartland, J., Mood, A. M., Weinfeld, F. D., & York, R. L. (1966). *Equality of educational opportunity.* Washington, D.C.: United States Department of Health, Education, and Welfare; Ehrenberg, R. G., & Brewer, D. J. Did teachers' verbal ability and race matter in the 1960s? Coleman revisited. *Economics of Education Review, 14*(1), 1-21; and Ferguson, R. F. (1991). Paying for public education: New evidence on how and why money matters. *Harvard Journal of Legislation, 28,* 465-498.

5   Monk, D. H., & Rice, J. K. (1999). Modern education productivity research: Emerging implications for the financing of education. In Fowler, B. (Ed.), *Selected papers in school finance* (pp. 111-139). Washington D.C.: United States Department of Education, Office of Educational Research and Improvement.

6   Education Commission of the States (1997). *Investing in teacher professional development: A look at 16 school districts.* Denver, CO: Author.

7   Elmore, R. F. (1997). *Investing in teacher learning: Staff development and instructional improvement in community school district #2, New York City,* Consortium for Policy Research in Education.

of district operating budgets.[8] Although these percentages may seem small, they translate into dollar values in the millions. To the degree that benefits outweigh the costs, teacher professional development can be seen as a path to realizing higher levels of productivity in the education sector. Unfortunately, empirical evidence documenting the impact of teacher professional development is limited.

This study draws on nationally representative data to profile the extent to which high school mathematics and science teachers participate in various forms of professional development, to explore factors related to their participation, and to examine the impact of various approaches on teachers' perceptions of the changes in their teaching practices and on student achievement. The following three research questions guide the analysis:

1. What is the incidence of high school mathematics and science teachers' participation in various forms of ongoing professional development?

2. What is the relationship between teachers' participation in professional development and teacher background (e.g., experience, educational background); teacher control in the school (e.g., grading policies or curriculum guidelines); recent policy changes in the school (e.g., teacher evaluation standards, student assessment); rewards and incentives for teaching (e.g., lighter teaching load, higher pay); and support for participating in professional development activities (e.g., stipends, professional growth credits)?

3. What is the impact of high school mathematics and science teacher participation in various forms of professional development on teachers' perceptions of changes in their teaching practices; and student achievement in mathematics and science?

The analysis is limited to the professional development experiences of high school mathematics and science teachers and the impact on teaching practices and student achievement in these subjects. This decision stems from the potential importance of linking professional development content with the subject taught.[9] The choice of math and science is based on the public attention given to

---

8   Miller, B., Lord, B., & Dorney, J. (1994). *Staff development for teachers: A study of configurations and costs in four districts*. Newton, MA: Education Development Center.

9   Several studies have documented the importance of aligning teacher preparation with teaching assignments. See Hawk, P. P., Coble, C. R., & Swanson, M. (1985). Certification: It does matter. *Journal of Teacher Education, 36*(3), 13-15; Monk, D. H., & Rice, J. K. Modern education productivity research: Emerging implications for the financing of education. In Fowler, B. (Ed.) *Selected papers in school finance* (pp. 111-139). Washington D.C.: United States Department of Education, Office of Educational Research and Improvement; Goldhaber, D. D., & Brewer, D. J. (1997). Evaluating the effect of teacher degree level on educational performance. In Fowler, W. J. (Ed.), *Developments in school finance* (pp. 197-210). Washington, D.C.: United States Department of Education; and

student proficiency in these subjects at the high school level. In addition, the concern about shortages of teachers trained in mathematics and science make professional development a particularly salient policy issue in these subject areas. Finally, the scope of the study is limited to in-service professional development and does not include preservice programs.

The next section of this chapter provides background on what is currently known about the incidence and impact of teacher professional development. The section that follows describes the data and methodology used in this study. Section four presents the findings, and the final section discusses the policy implications of those findings.

Literature on the Incidence and Impact of Teacher Professional Development

One recent effort to describe teacher professional development in United States schools drew on data from the Schools and Staffing Survey (SASS), a national survey that provides extensive data on the educational qualifications and working conditions of United States school teachers.[10] Researchers concluded that most teachers participate in some form of professional development, with workshops and in-service programs being the most common. Participation rates were highest among less-experienced teachers. Participation also appeared to be linked with recent reform efforts; approximately one half of all teachers had participated in professional development activities on education technology, student assessment, and/or cooperative learning. Support for professional development was also an issue raised in the study, which states,

> Effective professional development is dependent to a large extent upon institutional and financial support of teachers' professional development and a school climate that nurtures teacher learning.[11]

Approximately one fourth of teachers received no tangible support for their participation in professional development activities. The SASS study reads,

> for every dollar spent by districts and schools directly on formal staff development activities, individual teachers personally contribute 60

Goldhaber, D. D., & Brewer, D. J. (2000). Does teacher certification matter? High School teacher certification status and student achievement. *Educational Evaluation and Policy Analysis, 22*(2), 129-146.

10 National Center for Education Statistics (1998). *Toward better teaching: Professional development in 1993-94*. Washington, D.C.: United States Department of Education.

11 National Center for Education Statistics (1998). *Toward better teaching: Professional development in 1993-94* (p. vi). Washington, D.C.: United States Department of Education.

cents in volunteer time, with no present or future financial compensation.[12]

This finding is consistent with evidence from a study of the costs of professional development in California that recognized the considerable investment made by participants themselves.[13]

With respect to the impact of professional development, the study of SASS data relied on teachers' perceptions. Although most teachers expressed positive views of the impact of professional development on their teaching practices, 10% thought the programs had wasted their time.[14] Furthermore, teachers who reported higher levels of participation more were more likely to think that their participation had an impact.

The SASS study also raises issues about the forms of professional development to be studied. It specifies five broad categories of professional development: (1) district-sponsored workshops or in-service programs; (2) school-sponsored workshops or in-service programs; (3) university extension or adult education programs; (4) college courses in the teachers' subject fields; and (5) growth activities sponsored by professional associations. In addition to these more conventional approaches, newer conceptualizations of what counts as professional development have begun to emerge that involve shifts in use of time (e.g., to provide common planning time for teachers of the same subject) and collaborative structures for teachers to learn from one another (e.g., through teacher networks or mentor programs).

Little at al. defined professional development as

> ... any activity that is intended partly or primarily to prepare paid staff members for improved performance in present or future roles in the school district.[15]

Clearly, this definition includes an array of strategies involving conventional district-planned activities as well as innovative uses of time and teacher interac-

12 National Center for Education Statistics (1998). *Toward better teaching: Professional development in 1993-94* (p. 5). Washington, D.C.: United States Department of Education.

13 Little, J. W., Gerritz, W. H., Stern, D. S., Guthrie, J. W., Kirst, M. W., & Marsh, D. D. (1987). *Staff development in California: Public and personal investment, program patterns, and policy choices*. San Francisco: Far West Laboratory for Education Research and Development.

14 National Center for Education Statistics (1998). *Toward better teaching: Professional development in 1993-94*. Washington, D.C.: United States Department of Education.

15 Little, J. W., Gerritz, W. H., Stern, D. S., Guthrie, J. W., Kirst, M. W., & Marsh, D. D. (1987). *Staff development in California: Public and personal investment, program patterns, and policy choices* (p. 1). San Francisco: Far West Laboratory for Education Research and Development.

tion to promote teacher learning. The 1996 recommendations released by the National Commission on Teaching and America's Future called for a shift in thinking about professional development from conventional piecemeal approaches to more productive types, potentially requiring additional expenditures of greater than $1,000 per teacher annually (totaling more than $2 billion). These alternative approaches to professional development can be expected to utilize different configurations of resources (e.g., money, time) to support the improvement of teacher quality. Although this study recognizes the climate of change around notions of professional development, the data used in the study are limited to the more conventional categories and types of teacher professional development. This issue is revisited in the concluding discussion of implications for productivity and future research.

This study picks up where the SASS study left off. Specifically, it includes factors—such as teacher background, policy context, and institutional support—identified in the SASS study to be related to teacher professional development. Additionally, this work includes outcome measures to explore the impact of various types of professional development on teachers' perceptions of changes in their teaching practices and on student achievement. A final point of departure in this study is its focus on the professional development of high school mathematics and science teachers. The assumption here is that more focused studies of the impact of professional development can shed light on the extent to which such investments translate into improved outcomes.

Data and Methodology

This study draws on data from the National Education Longitudinal Study: 1988-1994 (NELS:88) to profile the extent to which teachers participate in various forms of professional development, to explore factors related to their participation, and to analyze the impact of participation in professional development on teachers' perceptions of changes in their teaching practices and on student achievement in high school mathematics and science courses. NELS:88 is a panel survey

> "designed to monitor the transition of a national sample of young adults as they progress from eighth grade to high school and then on to postsecondary education and/or the world of work."[16]

The primary purpose of the survey is to provide policy-relevant information on the effectiveness of schools and educational practices in bringing about educational achievement growth. The data collection began in 1988, and follow-up surveys were administered every two years thereafter through 1994. The base year of the survey included 24,599 randomly selected eighth grade students, and

16 Ingels, S. J., Scott, L. A., Lindmark, J. T., Frankel, M. R., & Myers, S. L. (1992)., *NELS:88 First follow-up data file user's manual: Teacher component* (NCES 92-085). Washington, D.C.: United States Department of Education, Office of Educational Research and Improvement.

a subsample was selected for follow-up in subsequent years. Panel test data were obtained from approximately 12,000 core sample individuals.

Public release data were collected from students and their teachers, parents, and school principals. In addition, subject-specific achievement tests were administered to the students every two years, corresponding with the years of the survey. All the data used in this study came from the second follow-up panel of data (i.e., the 1992 academic year when sampled students were seniors), except the pretest score, which was drawn from the first follow-up panel.

The data used in this study came primarily from the teacher and principal files.[17] Although specific variables are discussed below, it is important to recognize that this analysis is based on information that mathematics and science teachers reported about their participation in professional development activities, the availability of support for those activities, and the extent to which their participation affected their teaching practices. Likewise, school principals reported on a variety of school background variables, including teacher control in the school, recent policy changes in the school, and the availability of rewards or incentives for good teaching.

The study uses a three-tiered analytic approach. First, I relied on descriptive statistics to ascertain the extent to which sampled teachers reported participating in NELS:88 forms-of-professional development data set. The second tier of the analysis reviewed which school contexts and the types of teachers associated with higher levels of participation in professional development activities. This involved conducting a correlation analysis to observe the strength of the relationship between participation in various types of professional development activities and variables representing teacher background, teacher control in the school, recent policy changes in the school, the existence of rewards and incentives for good teaching, and the availability of support for participating in professional development activities. Hypotheses for these relationships are presented below in the description of the variables.

The third tier of the study relied on regression analysis to test the degree to which teacher participation in professional development affects teachers' perceptions of changes in their teaching and student achievement. Independent variables included multiple types of professional development as well as a number of control variables such as student pretest scores, teacher qualities (e.g., experience, certification status), and school factors expected to be related to professional development (e.g., support for participating in professional development).

This study's level of analysis in is the individual teacher. As described above, the NELS:88 data are organized around individual student records. The database often includes multiple students assigned to a particular teacher. To avoid counting a specific teacher's responses more than once, I aggregated the data to the

17 The only exceptions are student achievement test scores and student socioeconomic status, which are aggregated to the teacher level and used as control variables in the analysis.

teacher level so that the analysis is based on one record per teacher. All missing data were coded as such and excluded from the analysis. In addition, weights provided in the NELS:88 data set were used, so the analysis reflects the experiences of the mathematics and science teachers who instructed a nationally representative sample of United States high school seniors. The sample includes 5,658 mathematics and science teachers with sufficient data for the analysis.

Individual variables used in the analysis, including a statement of their scales, are described below. Because the scales for many of the variables are awkward to interpret in a regression context, these variables are normalized (mean = 0 and standard deviation = 1), and standardized regression coefficients are reported in the findings section. Other variables provided in more straightforward scales are analyzed in their natural metrics (i.e., left unstandardized) so that they can be interpreted in terms of a one-unit change. variable scales and descriptive statistics of the unstandardized data are provided in the Appendix (p. 135).

Professional Development Variables

Central to all three tiers of this analysis are professional development variables provided in the NELS:88 data set. The teacher survey asked respondents to report whether they participated in any of seven different types of professional development: (1) school system workshops attended during the school year or summer, (2) university extension courses, (3) college courses in education during the school year or summer, (4) college courses in subjects other than education during the school year or summer, (5) professional growth activities sponsored by a professional association, (6) teacher enrichment programs including "classroom techniques, advancements in technology, and applications of subjects," and (7) supervisors' observation of teaching. Each of these is coded as a dummy variable and standardized for the analyses. Additionally, I added the responses to these variables to construct a composite variable indicating the number of different types of professional development each teacher participated in during the school year.[18] This composite variable was standardized to facilitate easier interpretation of the regression analysis. The NELS:88 teacher survey also requested information on the extent to which professional development activities covered particular topics (e.g., student assessment, classroom management). However, nonresponse rates for these items exceed NCES standards; these items were not used in this analysis because of the potential for nonresponse bias.

Independent Variables

One goal of this study is to explore the degree to which teacher characteristics and school policies and conditions are associated with high school mathematics and science teacher participation in various types of professional development.

---

18 These dummy variables indicate whether a teacher responded that he or she participated in each of type of professional development. no information is available on the frequency of the participation for each individual or on the quality of the experience.

Five sets of variables are of particular interest: (1) teacher background, (2) teacher control over school matters, (3) recent policy changes in the school, (4) rewards for teaching, and (5) support for professional development. These variables were of central importance in identifying factors related to teacher participation in professional development. In addition, a number of these variables were independent variables in the regression analysis predicting the impact of participation in professional development on teacher perceptions of changes in their teaching practices and on student achievement.[19]

Teacher Background Variables

Several teacher background variables were included in the correlation analysis to study whether different types of teachers are more or less likely to participate in professional development activities. These teacher background variables include teacher sex (0 = female, 1 = male), years of experience teaching high school, whether the teacher has regular certification (0 = no, 1 = yes), whether the teacher is certified in mathematics (0 = no, 1 = yes), whether the teacher is certified in science (0 = no, 1 = yes), whether the teacher holds a bachelor's degree (0 = no, 1 = yes), whether the teacher majored in education (0 = no, 1 = yes), whether the teacher majored in mathematics (0 = no, 1 = yes), and whether the teacher majored in science (0 = no, 1 = yes). Of particular interest here is the experience and educational background of the teachers, and I hypothesized that more experience and stronger educational backgrounds would be associated with less involvement in professional development activities. In addition, teacher sex, experience level, and certification status were included as control variables in the regression analysis.

Teacher Control in the School

The NELS:88 data set includes several variables indicating the degree to which teachers have control over various matters in the school. A series of items in the principal file provided information on the amount of influence (three-point scale) teachers have on hiring and firing teachers, determining student grouping policies, deciding which courses will be offered, selecting books and instructional materials, setting curriculum guidelines, establishing grading policies, establishing discipline policies, and deciding how school funds are spent. I also created a composite by adding the values across these variables. One could hypothesize that because these responsibilities require expertise beyond traditional teaching skills, more professional development is needed (and occurs) in schools in which teachers have greater control over these matters. On the other hand, one might suspect that these additional responsibilities consume

---

19 As with any causal model and secondary data analysis, there are always questions of whether the control variables in the model are sufficient to warrant the description of the relationships being studied as causal. The model used here includes a variety of student, teacher, and school characteristics thought to be relevant in identifying a causal relationship between professional development and student achievement.

whatever discretionary time might have otherwise been available for teachers to participate in professional development activities.

Recent Policy Changes in the School

A third set of variables included in the correlation analysis was a series of items that indicated whether there have been changes in the school in the past three years with respect to a variety of policy issues. These include changes in teacher evaluation standards, new processes for making school policies, the addition of major new curriculum programs, changes in ability tracking and grouping policies, changes in schoolwide instructional methods, changes in staffing categories or roles for teaching and supervising staff, the establishment of interdisciplinary teacher teams, and the addition of new schoolwide procedures for student assessment. Each of these was coded as an indicator variable where 0 = no and 1 = yes. In addition, I summed these responses to construct a composite variable indicating the extent of different policy changes in the school during the past three years. Based on findings from previous research,[20] I hypothesized that changes in school policies, particularly new curriculum and instructional programs and student assessment practices, would be associated with greater levels of participation in professional development activities.

Rewards and Incentives for Good Teaching

An additional hypothesis was that teachers in schools that offer rewards and/or incentives for good teaching would have higher participation rates in professional development than those in schools without such rewards or incentives. This hypothesis assumes that teachers believe that professional development will improve their teaching and thereby qualify them for such rewards. Of course, this hypothesis also assumes that the rewards are desirable to the teachers. NELS:88 includes a series of items in the principal file regarding five possible rewards for teachers: (1) given special awards for good teaching, (2) assigned to teach the better students, (3) given a lighter teaching load, (4) given priority on requests for materials, and (5) given higher pay. Each of these was coded as a dummy variable where 0 = no and 1 = yes. In addition, I created a composite indicating the number of different types of rewards available to teachers by summing the values of these six variables.

Support for Professional Development Activities

A final set of variables included in both the correlation and regression analyses were various types of resources available in the school to support teacher participation in professional development activities. A series of items included in the teacher survey provided information on the availability of support for professional development. These included release time from teaching, travel or per diem expenses, stipend, and professional growth credits. Each of these was

---

20 National Center for Education Statistics (1998). *Toward better teaching: Professional development in 1993-94*. Washington, D.C.: United States Department of Education.

coded as a dummy variable where 0 = no and 1 = yes. I also created a composite, standardized for the regression analysis, indicating the number of different types of support available to teachers by summing the values of these four variables. I hypothesized that these variables would be correlated with participation levels in professional development activities, that the total level of support would have a positive effect on teachers' perceptions of the impact of professional development.

Other Control Variables

In addition to those listed above, three control variables were included in the regression model. These included two characteristics about the types of students taught by the teachers: the average subject-specific 10th-grade test score and the average student SES. In addition, the number of days that the teacher was absent for administrative reasons was included as a control. Presumably, more professional development can require more administrative absences on the part of the teacher, which can also have an impact on student achievement. Controlling for the number of administrative days absent helped to isolate the effect of teacher participation in professional development activities.

Outcome Variables

The impact of professional development was studied with respect to two types of outcome variables: (1) teachers' perceptions of changes in their teaching practices and (2) student achievement in mathematics and science. Each of these is described below.

Teachers' Perceptions

It is reasonable to assume that the impact of professional development on student achievement depends, at least in part, on the degree to which instructional practices change as a consequence of new teacher knowledge. This study relies on teachers' own reports of their perceptions of the degree to which professional development has changed their teaching practices. NELS:88 teachers were asked to indicate whether their teaching changed as a result of professional development in seven areas: (1) use of technology, (2) applications of science and math, (3) in-depth study of a specialized subject, (4) student assessment, (5) classroom management, (6) cooperative learning, and (7) improving higher-order thinking skills. Teachers were given the opportunity to indicate either "applies" or "does not apply." I coded these variables such that 1 = applies and 0 = does not apply and then added the responses to get a variable with values ranging from 0 to 7. This variable was standardized for the regression analysis.

Measures of Student Achievement

One of the central goals of this study was to estimate the effect of mathematics and science teachers' participation in professional development activities on the academic achievement of their students. The NELS:88 achievement test battery was designed to measure both individual status and growth in a number of achievement areas including mathematics; science; history, citizenship, and geography; and reading comprehension. The tests were developed to minimize floor and ceiling effects. Mathematics and science test scores, the focus of this study, were estimated using item response theory (IRT) scaling, which recognizes that some items on the testing instrument are more difficult than others. Students' response patterns were adjusted in light of these variable difficulty levels. Several transformations of the test scores are provided in the data set. The analyses in this study were based on the IRT-estimated number of correct answers, which reflects an estimate of the number of items that a person would have answered correctly if he or she had taken all of the items that appeared in any form of the test. To study the impact of teachers' participation in professional development on student achievement, I used the second follow-up (12th-grade) mathematics and science test scores as the outcome variables and controlled for the first follow-up (10th-grade) test scores in the regression equations.

Findings

Incidence and Correlates of Teacher Participation in Professional Development

Figure 6.1 presents the percentage of teachers participating in various types of professional development. The majority of NELS:88 teachers reported participating in some form of professional development, with more than 40% participating in three to four different types. According to the NELS:88 data, the most common form of professional development for high school mathematics and science teachers are school system workshops. more than 80% of teachers reported participating in this form of professional development. The second most common type of professional development was administrator observation of teaching, an activity reported by almost 65% of the NELS:88 teachers. Participation in enrichment and growth activities provided by professional associations were the next most common types of professional development, reported by 60% and 54%, respectively. College and university courses of all types were the least reported form of professional development reported by NELS:88 teachers. Lowest levels of participation are associated with university extension courses, with fewer than 12% of teachers reporting participation.

**Figure 6.1. Percentage of Teachers Participating
in Various Types of Professional Development**

Number of Different Types of Professional Development	Percent of Teachers Reporting Participation
0	2.84
1–2	26.53
3–4	41.20
5–6	21.89
7–8	6.92
9–10	0.62
Specific Professional Development Activities	
School System Workshop	80.85
University Extension Course	11.62
College Course in Education	21.54
College Course in Subject Other Than Education	26.51
Professional Association Growth Activity	53.83
Enrichment Activity	59.98
Administration-Observed Teaching	64.67

Figure 6.2 presents correlation coefficients showing the bivariate relationship between types of professional development and five sets of teacher and school variables hypothesized to be related to levels of participation in professional development: (1) teacher background, (2) teacher control over school matters, (3) recent policy changes in the school, (4) rewards and incentives for good teaching, and (5) support for professional development. Although many of the coefficients across all five categories are significant, the magnitudes of the coefficients are quite small. A few exceptions do exist, and these are worth noting.[21]

---

21 Relationships noted as exceptions were those with coefficients exceeding 0.10. Admittedly, this is generally recognized as a weak effect, but it provides a cut-off point for a discussion of the findings presented here.

Figure 6.2. Relationship Between Professional Development Practices and Teacher and School Attributes (Pearson Correlation Coefficients)

Figure 6.2	School System Workshops	Education Courses	Noneducation Courses	Professional Association Growth Activities	Teacher Enrichment Activities	Administrative Observation	Total Professional Development
Teacher Background							
Gender (1 = Male)	−0.08***	−0.03**	−0.02	−0.09***	−0.11***	−0.02	−0.09***
Experience	0.004	−0.20***	−0.11***	0.05***	0.005	−0.20***	−0.11***
Regular Certification	0.07***	−0.06***	0.008	0.01	−0.06***	−0.05***	0.01
Certified in Math	0.05***	−0.04***	−0.08***	−0.02	0.02	−0.04***	−0.05***
Certified in Science	−0.006	−0.04***	0.10***	0.05***	0.05***	0.008	0.05***
Bachelor's Degree Held	−0.01	0.02	0.01	−0.05***	−0.01	0.07***	−0.02
Education Major	0.01	0.08***	−0.02	0.006	0.02	0.005	0.03
Math Major	0.03**	−0.02	−0.10***	−0.02	−0.01	−0.03**	−0.05***
Science Major	−0.04***	−0.02	0.11***	0.04**	0.03**	0.004	0.04***
Teacher Control in School							
Hiring and Firing Teachers	−0.02	0.01	0.006	-0,006	0.01	−0.05***	−0.0004
Student Grouping Policies	−0.01	−0.02	−0.03**	0.002	−0.002	−0.03**	−0.02
Course Offerings	0.02	−0.002	−0.06***	−0.0005	0.02	−0.02	−0.02
Books and Materials	−0.06***	−0.02	−0.03**	0.003	−0.02	−0.008	−0.04
Curriculum Guidelines	0.03	−0.02	−0.05***	0.0003	0.001	−0.03	−0.03
Grading Policies	−0.002	0.02	0.003	−0.0005	−0.01	−0.05	0.007
Discipline Policies	−0.02	−0.02	0.004	−0.009	0.01	−0.03	0.003
Spending of Funds	0.06***	0.01	−0.02	0.009	0.01	−0.008	0.02
Total Control	0.007	−0.008	−0.03**	−0.002	0.005	−0.04	−0.01

Recent Policy Changes							
Teacher Evaluation Standards	0.05***	0.004	−0.009	0.02	0.04**	−0.10***	0.03
Policy-Making Process	0.02	0.0003	−0.002	0.003	0.02	0.02	0.01
Curriculum Programs	0.03**	0.05***	0.05***	0.02	0.03**	−0.006	0.06***
Student Group Policies	0.04***	0.01	−0.01	−0.04**	0.04**	0.03**	−0.0006
Instructional Methods	0.10***	0.03*	0.01	−0.002	0.08***	0.04**	0.06***
Staffin Categories	0.02	−0.003	0.001	−0.01	0.02	0.02	0.0007
Interdisciplinary Teams	0.06***	0.02	0.01	0.03**	0.04***	−0.02	0.05
Student Assessment	0.06***	0.04***	0.004	0.004	0.02	0.02	0.04
Total Policy Changes	0.08***	0.03	0.01	0.002	0.07***	0.05***	0.05
Rewards for Good Teaching							
Special Awards	0.06***	0.008	0.007	−0.01	0.01	0.02	0.02
Assigned to Best Students	−0.01	0.02	0.01	−0.03	−0.02	0.03**	0.003
Lighter Teaching Load	−0.004	0.02	0.005	−0.03	0.004	0.04**	−0.001
Priority for Materials	−0.01	−0.0003	0.01	−0.03**	−0.01	0.03	−0.01
Higher Pay	0.02	−0.07***	−0.04**	−0.01	0.04***	0.06***	−0.03**
Total Rewards	0.03	−0.004	−0.0007	−0.03**	0.01	0.05***	−0.003
Support for Professional Development Activities							
Release Time From Teaching	0.20***	0.06***	0.09***	0.22***	0.25***	−0.008	0.24***
Travel and Per Diem Expenses	0.18***	0.08***	0.09***	0.28***	0.29***	−0.02	0.26***
Stipend	0.19***	0.08***	0.13***	0.14***	0.16***	−0.0002	0.24***
Professional Growth Credits	0.25***	0.16***	0.17***	0.22***	0.24***	0.07***	0.34***
Total Support for Professional Development	0.32***	0.15***	0.18***	0.33***	0.37***	0.02	0.41***

$**P < .05$; $***P < .01$.

In the category of teacher background, experience seems to be a factor: more experienced teachers are less likely to take university courses or to be observed by administrators than their less-experienced colleagues. The certification and major variables also suggest that math teachers are less likely to take noneducation college courses, whereas science teachers are more likely to pursue this professional development activity. no other teacher background characteristics appeared to have any noteworthy association with participation in professional development.

Teacher control over school matters was hypothesized to be associated with higher levels of participation in professional development because these noninstructional responsibilities presumably require additional skills and knowledge. Correlations showed this not to be the case; there is no discernable relationship between teacher control over school matters and teacher participation in professional development activities.

Only two of the recent school policy changes were related to teacher participation in professional development activities. A change in teacher evaluation standards was inversely related to administrator supervision of teachers, suggesting that new teacher evaluation policies de-emphasize administrators' observation of teachers, perhaps in favor of other forms of evaluation. Additionally, a change in schoolwide instructional methods was associated with greater participation in school system workshops. This positive relationship suggests that systemic training is provided to teachers to support the implementation of new instructional methods in schools and school systems. Surprisingly, there was no apparent relationship between professional development participation and changes in student assessment because this was one of the policies found to be related to professional development in the study using SASS data.[22,23] This analysis provides no compelling evidence that rewards and incentives for good teaching are associated with teacher participation in professional development.

Variables indicating the availability of support for professional development stand out as the category with the strongest and most consistent relationship with teacher participation in professional development activities. All four types of support—release time from teaching, travel or per diem expenses, stipends, and professional growth credits—were positively related to teacher participation in all types of professional development, with the exception of administrator observation. In general, greater support for professional development was associated with greater participation in professional development activities, and, in

---

22 National Center for Education Statistics (1998). *Toward better teaching: Professional development in 1993-94.* Washington, D.C.: United States Department of Education.

23 This finding could be called into question as an endogeneity problem; that is, one might argue that better novice teachers may be more likely to engage in professional development. However, the correlation analysis did not find this to be the case, at least with respect to teacher qualities such as certification, major, and degree level.

most cases, the promise of professional development credits was the strongest correlate with participation.

The Impact of Professional Development on Teaching Practices

Figure 6.3 (page 128) presents the impact of teachers' participation in professional development activities on their perceptions of changes in their teaching practices. The first half of the table relates to mathematics teachers and the second half to science. For each subject, two specifications of the model are presented: the first column presents the model with the seven types of professional development, and the second column presents the model with the interaction between the amount of professional development and support for professional development.

Figure 6.3 shows that math teachers who teach higher SES students are more likely to perceive that their teaching has changed as a result of professional development. Perhaps it is easier to adopt new teaching strategies when teaching students from higher SES backgrounds. Conversely, a class of low SES students may make change difficult. This effect is not significant in science. Math and science teachers reported that neither gender nor experience level had a consistent impact on their teaching as a result of professional development.

Several types of professional development were related to teachers' perceptions of changes in teaching strategies, and these findings were strikingly similar among math and science teachers. Participation in school system workshops, professional association growth activities, and enrichment activities were all associated with teachers' perceptions of a change in teaching practice resulting from participation.

Furthermore, the availability of support for professional development was a positive predictor of teachers' perceptions of a change in their teaching practices. The interaction between participation in and support for professional development was positive and significant, indicating that more support enhances the positive impact that participation has on teachers' perceptions of a change in teaching practice. Again, this was the case for both math and science teachers.

The Impact of Professional Development on Student Achievement

Figures 6.4 (page 129) and 6.5 (page 130) present the findings with respect to the impact of professional development on student achievement in mathematics and science, respectively. The tables are divided into three sections: the first presents the results for all teachers, the second for less experienced teachers, and the third for more experienced teachers. The two columns within each of the stratifications are the same model specifications shown in Figure 6.3.

Figure 6.5 shows that both variables indicating student background, pretest and SES, were strong positive predictors of student achievement across all stratifications and specifications of the model. Turning to teacher background characteristics, although teacher gender did not affect student achievement, teacher experience and certification in mathematics were both positive predictors of student mathematics achievement. The number of days that teachers were absent for administrative reasons entered negatively, and this effect was limited to the less-experienced teachers.

Figure 6.3. Impact of Teacher Professional Development on Mathematics and Sciences Teachers' Perceptions of Changes in Their Teaching Practices (Regression Coefficients and Standard Errors)

	Mathematics		Science	
	(1)	**(2)**	**(1)**	**(2)**
Intercept	0.15*** (0.03)	0.15*** (0.03)	0.12*** (0.04)	0.10** (0.04)
Student SES	0.06*** (0.02)	0.06*** (0.02)	0.05 (0.02)	0.04 (0.03)
Teacher Gender	0.01 (0.04)	−0.02 (0.04)	−0.03 (0.05)	−0.04 (0.05)
Teacher Experience	−0.06** (0.02)	−0.02 (0.02)	−0.05 (0.03)	0.003 (0.03)
Days Absent for Administrative Reasons	0.14*** (0.02)	0.11*** (0.02)	0.01 (0.02)	−0.003 (0.03)
School System Workshops	0.07*** (0.02)		0.09*** (0.03)	
Extension Courses	0.04 (0.02)		0.04 (0.02)	
Education Courses	0.04* (0.02)		0.05 (0.03)	
Noneducation Courses	0.0004 (0.02)		0.01 (0.02)	
Professional Association Growth Activities	0.11*** (0.02)		0.12*** (0.03)	
Enrichment Activities	0.35*** (0.02)		0.32*** (0.03)	
Administration Observation	0.02 (0.02)		0.03 (0.02)	
Total Professional Development Activities		0.24*** (0.02)		0.25*** (0.03)
Total Support for Professional Development		0.24*** (0.03)		0.17*** (0.03)
Total Professional Development x Total Support		0.06*** (0.02)		0.06*** (0.02)
N	2453	2447	1810	1804
R^2 (adjusted)	0.18	0.16	0.15	0.12

$**P < .05$, $***P < .01$; (1) = model with types of professional development, (2) = model with interaction between amount of professional development and support for professional development.

SES, socioeconomic status.

Figure 6.4. Impact of the Amount and Type of Teacher Professional Development on Student Achievement in Mathematics (Regression Coefficients and Standard Errors)

	All Teachers		Less Experienced		More Experienced	
	(1)	(2)	(1)	(2)	(1)	(2)
Intercept	8.28*** (0.38)	8.40*** (0.38)	8.12*** (0.62)	8.54*** (0.63)	8.35*** (0.54)	8.35*** (0.55)
Pretest	0.92*** (0.01)	0.92*** (0.01)	0.93*** (0.01)	0.92*** (0.01)	0.92*** (0.01)	0.92*** (0.01)
Student SES	0.77*** (0.10)	0.84*** (0.10)	0.69*** (0.14)	0.85*** (0.14)	0.84*** (0.14)	0.84*** (0.14)
Teacher Gender	−0.15 (0.17)	−0.20 (0.17)	0.20 (0.26)	−0.32 (0.26)	−0.12 (0.24)	−0.13 (0.24)
Teacher Experience	0.36*** (0.09)	0.44*** (0.09)	0.36 (0.26)	0.60** (0.25)	0.56** (0.26)	0.58** (0.26)
Teacher Certification in Math	0.58*** (0.17)	0.55*** (0.17)	0.75*** (0.26)	0.69*** (0.26)	0.47** (0.23)	0.48** (0.23)
Days Absent for Administrative Reasons	−0.23*** (0.09)	−0.21** (0.09)	−0.39*** (0.13)	−0.31** (0.13)	−0.10 (0.11)	−0.13 (0.11)
School System Workshops	0.30*** (0.09)		0.35** (0.14)		(0.12)	0.24**
Extension Courses	0.14 (0.08)		0.13 (0.13)		0.15 (0.11)	
Education Courses	0.02 (0.08)		0.16 (0.11)		−0.20 (0.13)	
Noneducation Courses	0.08 (0.08)		−0.03 (0.12)		0.21 (0.12)	
Professional Association Growth Activities	−0.10 (0.09)		−0.05 (0.14)		−0.13 (0.12)	
Enrichment Activities	−0.01 (0.09)		0.16 (0.14)		−0.14 (0.12)	
Administrative Observation	−0.16 (0.08)		−0.26** (0.13)		−0.06 (0.11)	
Total Professional Development Activities		0.25*** (0.09)		0.45*** (0.14)		0.09 (0.12)
Total Support for Professional Development		−0.06 (0.10)		−0.09 (0.15)		−0.02 (0.13)
Intercept		0.09 (0.08)		0.01 (0.12)		0.17 (0.11)
Pretest	3696	3682	1584	1578	2111	2103
R2 (adjusted)	0.85	0.85	0.85	0.85	0.85	0.85

**P < .05, ***P < .01; (1) = model with types of professional development, (2) = model with interaction between amount of professional development and support for professional development.

SES, socioeconomic status.

Figure 6.5. The Impact of the Amount and Type of Teacher Professional Development on Student Achievement in Science (Regression Coefficients and Standard Errors)

	All Teachers		Less Experienced		More Experienced	
	(1)	(2)	(1)	(2)	(1)	(2)
Intercept	5.50*** (0.26)	5.37*** (026)	5.87*** (0.43)	5.74*** (0.44)	5.58*** (0.37)	5.40*** (0.37)
Pretest	0.82*** (0.01)	0.83*** (0.01)	0.81*** (0.02)	0.82*** (0.02)	0.83*** (0.02)	0.83*** (0.02)
Student SES	0.16*** (0.06)	0.16** (0.06)	−0.01 (0.09)	0.02 (0.09)	0.35*** (0.08)	0.34*** (0.08)
Teacher Gender	0.18 (0.11)	0.21 (0.11)	0.32 (0.17)	0.29 (0.17)	0.08 (0.15)	0.13 (0.15)
Teacher Experience	0.36*** (0.05)	0.34*** (0.05)	0.56*** (0.17)	0.57*** (0.16)	0.30 (0.17)	0.28 (0.17)
Teacher Certification in Science	0.35** (0.10)	0.37**** (0.10)	0.41** (0.17)	0.39** (0.17)	0.34** (0.14)	0.38*** (0.14)
Days Absent for Administrative Reasons	0.13*** (0.05)	0.12** (0.06)	0.05 (0.09)	0.04 (0.09)	0.17** (0.07)	0.15** (0.07)
School System Workshops	−0.09 (0.06)		−0.01 (0.09)		−0.18** (0.08)	
Extension Courses	0.04 (0.05)		−0.07 (0.08)		0.10 (0.07)	
Education Courses	0.04 (0.05)		0.009 (0.07)		0.06 (0.09)	
Noneducation Courses	0.03 (0.05)		0.009 (0.08)		0.05 (0.08)	
Professional Association Growth Activities	−0.12** (0.06)		−0.03 (0.09)		−0.21*** (0.08)	
Enrichment Activities	0.05 (0.06)		0.17 (0.09)		0.03 (0.08)	
Administrative Observation	−0.01 (0.05)		−0.07 (0.08)		0.06 (0.07)	
Total Professional Development Activities		0.006 (0.06)		0.07 (0.09)		−0.07 (0.08)
Total Support for Professional Development		−0.008 (0.06)		0.008 (0.10)		−0.03 (0.08)
Total Professional Development x Total Support		0.05 (0.05)		0.04 (0.08)		0.05 (0.07)
N	3674	3660	1575	1569	2098	2090
R^2 (adjusted)	0.67	0.67	0.65	0.65	0.68	0.68

**P < .05, ***P < .01; (1) = model with types of professional development, (2) = model with interaction between amount of professional development and support for professional development.

SES, socioeconomic status.

Few of the professional development variables were significant predictors of student achievement. Participation in school system workshops was a positive predictor of student achievement for all teachers. Being observed by administrators was inversely related to the math achievement of students having less-experienced teachers. This finding may have been caused by an endogeneity problem; less-effective teachers are more likely to be the target of administrative observation. No significant effect was observed for teacher participation in college or university courses, professional association growth activities, or enrichment activities. The sum of professional development activities was a positive predictor of student achievement in math for less-experienced teachers. In other words, math students assigned to less-experienced teachers appear to do better if their teachers participate in a variety of professional development activities.[24]

The availability of support for professional development had no discernable effect on student achievement in mathematics. In addition, the interaction between the amount of professional development and the availability of support was not significant in the models predicting mathematics achievement.

Figure 6.5 presents similar results for science. Again, average student pretest and SES were positive predictors of student achievement in science. As was the case for math, teacher sex was not a significant predictor of student achievement in science, but both teacher experience and certification in science entered as positive predictors, although the effect was significant only for less-experienced teachers. In contrast to the findings for math, more absences for administrative reasons was positively related to student achievement in science. Perhaps this reflects the policy of promoting the best and most experienced teachers to administrative posts and/or the assignment of stronger students to these teachers.

Turning to the impact of professional development, several findings surfaced that are different from those found in the analysis of mathematics. Two types of professional development activities surfaced as negative predictors of student achievement among the more-experienced science teachers: school system workshops and professional association growth activities. It could be that, among experienced science teachers, the least effective are more likely to participate in these forms of professional development. Recall, participation in school systems workshops was a positive predictor of mathematics achievement among both teacher stratifications. Participation in any other form of professional development has no significant effect on student science achievement. As reflected by the interaction variable, the level of support available for professional development did not affect the impact of professional development on student achievement. This was also the case for mathematics.

---

24 This finding could be called into question as an endogeneity problem; that is, one might argue that better novice teachers may be more likely to engage in professional development. However, the correlation analysis did not find this to be the case, at least with respect to teacher qualities such as certification, major, and degree level.

Summary and Implications

This study set out to profile the extent to which teachers participate in various forms of professional development, to explore factors related to their participation, and to analyze the impact of teacher participation in professional development activities on teachers' perceptions of changes in their teaching practices and on student achievement. Given the increasing emphasis on teacher quality as a key to improving schools, coupled with the considerable investments being made in professional development, the overall goal of the study was to provide information on the incidence and impact of teacher professional development so as to inform policy discussions, particularly those relating to education productivity. Several general findings from the study are as follows:

- The majority of teachers report participating in some form of professional development, with more than 40% reporting participation in three to four different types during the course of a year. The most common forms of professional development reported by high school mathematics and science teachers are school system workshops and administrator observation of teaching; the least common are college and university courses of all types.

- The only teacher characteristic related to levels of participation in professional development is experience; more experienced teachers participate less in some types of professional development.

- There is little evidence that school factors—such as level of teacher control in the school, recent policy changes in the school, and rewards for teaching—are related to teacher participation in professional development. Only two exceptions were found: Schoolwide changes in instructional methods are related to greater participation in workshops, and support for professional development is directly related to the level of participation in most forms of professional development.

- In terms of teachers' perceptions of changes in their teaching, both math and science teachers reported positive effects associated with several types of professional development activities: workshops, professional association activities, and enrichment activities. Greater support for professional development further enhances the perception of positive effects.

- School system workshops were the only form of professional development found to have a positive impact on student achievement, and this effect was limited to mathematics. Inverse relationships were found for administrator observation of math teachers as well as workshops and professional association activities for more-experienced science teachers.

The contribution of this work lies in the potential for more complete information on the education production process to inform decisions regarding how to direct scarce resources. As described in this first section of this chapter, considerable resources are devoted to the professional development of teachers. Furthermore, the number of alternatives for professional development is expanding to include more contemporary approaches, such as common planning time and networking, alongside more traditional forms such as workshops and conferences. These different approaches require different configurations of resources with the common goal of improving the quality of a given set of teachers. However, little empirical work exists to document the impact of these various forms of professional development. This study begins to fill that void by addressing questions about the incidence and impact of various types of investment in professional development on improve the quality of a key input in the education production process, ie, teachers.

Several specific findings from this study have implications for fiscal policy. First, this study sheds light on the importance of supporting teachers to participate in professional development. A variety of different kinds of support surfaced as significant correlates of teacher participation. This was not explored as a causal relationship; it may be that more participation leads to more support. nonetheless, the relationship is clear, suggesting that policymakers should pay close attention to how they allocate resources (both time and money) to support productive forms of professional development. This, like any investment, must be scrutinized.

Second, the lack of a relationship between levels of participation in professional development and changes in school policies or increases in responsibilities for teachers suggests a potential lack of alignment between investments and goals. Although there is evidence that teacher participation in professional development is widespread, it is not evident that the professional development is targeted to support new school policies or increased teacher responsibilities. To the degree that professional development could help with the successful implementation of new education policies and diffuse responsibilities for teachers, policymakers should better align investments in specific types of professional development to support their educational goals.

Third, the lack of a relationship between participation in professional development and rewards and incentives for good teaching may imply that teachers do not view professional development as a means to improvement that will help them earn these rewards. Alternatively, the rewards available to teachers may not be attractive enough to engage them in the professional development activities that might realize these rewards. Either way, the absence of a relationship between these two measures suggests another lack of alignment between investments, in this case between incentive structures and professional development opportunities.

Finally, the portion of this analysis examining the impact of teacher participation in professional development found an interesting discrepancy across the two types of outcome measures. Although teachers perceived a positive impact from their participation in professional development activities on their teaching practices, the analysis showed few significant effects on student achievement gains, and more of these were negative than positive. The disjuncture between teachers' perceptions of an impact on teaching practices and the lack of an observable impact on student achievement is a finding worthy of attention, particularly because many studies examining the impact of professional development rely on teacher perceptions as a primary outcome. The discrepancy between teacher perceptions and student achievement has important implications for how policymakers decide what types of professional development investments to make. This finding merits additional research.

Acknowledging several limitations of this study may hopefully guide future work in this area. The availability of data to conduct large-scale quasi-experimental studies of teacher professional development is one concern worth addressing. Although the results of the SASS study can provide in-depth descriptive information on teacher professional development, the lack of student test scores undermines study of impact. Consequently, I drew on NELS:88 data, which provide student test scores as well as teacher perceptions of the impact of professional development. The NELS:88 data, however, are limited in the quality of information available on teacher professional development as well as the kinds of teachers who engage in these activities.[25] More refined information on the number, duration, quality, content, and coherence of professional development activities would be most valuable. In addition, more attention to newer approaches to professional development that emphasize teacher collaboration and teacher learning in the context of the school day would help research keep pace with the emerging nature of the field. In addition, school-level information on professional development policies, practices, and participation rates would help to overcome some of the problems associated with the self-reported data currently available. Finally, research that examines actual changes in instructional practices as a result of participation in professional development could be an important contribution in understanding the link between professional development and student performance.

Acknowledgment

This work was supported by the National Center for Education Statistics/American Education Finance Association New Scholars Program. I am grateful to Bill Fowler, Susanna Loeb, Chris Roellke, and several anonymous reviewers for their helpful comments.

25 One concern with this study is the inability to detect the quality of teachers engaging in professional development. For instance, it may be that professional development has a positive effect on student achievement, but the worst teachers are the most likely to take advantage of professional development opportunities. To the degree that these teachers remain less effective than their colleagues, this could appear as a negative effect (as found in this study) even if these teachers are improving as a result of their participation in professional development. Controlling for typical teacher quality indicators—such as major, certification, and experience—was intended to help isolate the effect. However, this issue should be further explored in future research.

Appendix. Descriptive Statistics of Variables in the Study

Study Variables	Mean	Standard Deviation	n	Variable Description
Dependent Variables				
Twelfth-Grade Math Test Score	50.29	13.43	5311	Continuous NELS:88 variable
Twelfth-Grade Science Test Score	23.98	5.79	5055	Continuous NELS:88 variable
Professional Development Caused Change in Teaching*	0.33	0.89	5658	Range 0-7; sum of 7 dummy variables
Professional Development				
Workshop During Year*	1.03	0.65	4547	Range 0-2; sum of 2 dummy variables
University Extension Course*	0.10	0.30	4547	0 = no, 1 = yes
College Education Course*	0.27	0.58	4548	Range 0-2; sum of 2 dummy variables
College Noneducation Course*	0.31	0.61	4547	Range 0-2; sum of 2 dummy variables
Professional Association Growth Activity*	0.53	0.50	4547	0 = no, 1 = yes
Enrichment Activity*	0.58	0.49	4531	0 = no, 1 = yes
Administration-Observed Teaching*	2.95	0.85	4531	Range 1-6
Total Amount of Professional Development Activities*	2.23	1.48	4544	Range 0-8; sum of 8 dummy variables
Teacher Background				
Gender	0.58	0.49	5043	0 = female, 1 = male
Experience*	5.75	2.74	4641	Range 0-9: 0 = 0 years, 9 = 25 or more years
Regular Certification	0.76	0.42	5658	0 = no, 1 = yes
Certified in Math	0.53	0.50	5658	0 = no, 1 = yes
Certified in Science	0.39	0.49	5658	0 = no, 1 = yes
Bachelor's Degree Held	0.76	0.43	4617	0 = no, 1 = yes
Education major	0.25	0.43	4617	0 = no, 1 = yes
Math major	0.45	0.50	4617	0 = no, 1 = yes
Science major	0.35	0.48	4617	0 = no, 1 = yes
Teacher Control in School				
Hiring and Firing Teachers	0.52	0.59	5079	Range 0–2: 0 = no influence, 2 = major influence
Student Grouping Policies	1.34	0.61	5066	Range 0–2: 0 = no influence, 2 = major influence
Courses Offerings	1.29	0.58	5091	Range 0–2: 0 = no influence, 2 = major influence
Books and Materials	1.75	0.46	5108	Range 0–2: 0 = no influence, 2 = major influence
Curriculum Guidelines	1.44	0.57	5100	Range 0–2: 0 = no influence, 2 = major influence

Grading Policies	1.63	0.54	5107	Range 0–2: 0 = no influence, 2 = major influence
Discipline Policies	1.26	0.56	5109	Range 0–2: 0 = no influence, 2 = major influence
Spending of Funds	1.04	0.53	5086	Range 0–2: 0 = no influence, 2 = major influence
Total Teacher Control	10.26	2.59	4986	Range 0-16; sum of above
Recent Policy Changes				
Teacher Evaluation Standards	0.41	0.54	5092	Range -1 to 1: -1 = less rigor, 1 = more rigor
Policy-Making Process	0.55	0.50	5035	0 = no, 1 = yes
Curriculum Programs	0.73	0.44	5054	0 = no, 1 = yes
Student Group Policies	0.46	0.50	5024	0 = no, 1 = yes
Instructional Methods	0.44	0.50	5026	0 = no, 1 = yes
Staffing Categories	0.37	0.48	5052	0 = no, 1 = yes
Interdisciplinary Teams	0.39	0.49	5036	0 = no, 1 = yes
Student Assessment	0.33	0.47	5007	0 = no, 1 = yes
Total Policy Changes	3.73	2.13	4890	Range 0-8; sum of above
Rewards for Teaching				
Special Awards	0.55	0.50	5049	0 = no, 1 = yes
Assigned to Better Students	0.18	0.38	4995	0 = no, 1 = yes
Lighter Teaching Load	0.07	0.25	4990	0 = no, 1 = yes
Priority for Materials	0.08	0.27	4993	0 = no, 1 = yes
Higher Pay	0.16	0.37	4985	0 = no, 1 = yes
Total Rewards	1.11	1.13	4931	Range 0-5; sum of above
Support for Professional Development Activities				
Release Time From Teaching	0.41	0.49	4542	0 = no, 1 = yes
Travel or Per Diem Expenses	0.30	0.46	4542	0 = no, 1 = yes
Stipend	0.16	0.37	4542	0 = no, 1 = yes
Professional Growth Credits	0.32	0.47	4542	0 = no, 1 = yes
Total Support for Professional Development*	1.20	1.17	4542	Range 0-4; sum of above
Additional Control Variables				
Math Pretest (Tenth-Grade Score)	45.42	12.90	5311	Continuous NELS:88 variable
Science Pretest (Tenth-Grade Score)	22.22	5.55	5295	Continuous NELS:88 variable
Average Student SES*	0.10	0.75	5621	Composite NELS:88 variable
Number of Days Absent for Administrative Reasons*	1.64	0.90	4498	Range 1-6: 1 = 0 days, 2 = 1–2 days, 3 = 3–4 days, 4 = 5–7 days, 5 = 8–11 days, 6 = >12 days

Variables marked with "" are standardized for the regression analysis (mean = 0, standard deviation = 1).

NELS:88, National Education Longitudinal Study: 1988-1994.

7

Examining Investments in Teacher Professional Development: A Look at Current Practice and a Proposal for Improving the Research Base

David H. Monk
The Pennsylvania State University

Margaret L. Plecki
University of Washington

Kieran M. Killeen
University of Vermont

The extensive and growing interest in the use of staff development to improve the performance of educational organizations, such as schools, has prompted efforts to understand more about the underlying costs. Policymakers are seeking answers to questions about the likely budget implications, and there is perennial interest in learning more about the added value of different types of staff development. How valuable, for example, is professional development for administrators and others in leadership positions compared with the added value associated with enhancing the skills of those more directly involved in the delivery of instruction? Moreover, there are (or should be) questions about the balance between efforts to upgrade the skills of paraprofessional staff compared with efforts made to improve the skills of professional personnel.

Closely related questions exist regarding the merits of professional development aimed at enhancing the subject matter knowledge of teachers versus professional development intended to broaden teachers' knowledge about pedagogy and the interface between teaching and learning. In all these instances, metrics are needed to measure both the nature and extent of the various types of professional development and the ensuing consequences.

Our concern here is with developing measures of investments in professional development at different levels of the educational system, and the work we report is part of the federally supported Center for the Study of Teaching and Policy (CTP) at the University of Washington. The CTP research agenda has recognized the importance of the fiscal side of professional development, and it has been our responsibility to develop methods for measuring these investments and to generate point estimates of the actual magnitudes. In previous work (Killeen, Monk, & Plecki, 2002), we used national data collected by the National Center for Education Statistics (NCES) to generate global estimates of spending on professional development at the school district level. We calculated national- as well as state-level estimates and in general found that spending earmarked for this purpose in the period 1997 to 1998 amounted to 2.82% of school district spending nationwide and that the share has increased only modestly during the 1990s.

Here we turn to more detailed estimates of professional development spending within the four states that comprise one of CTP's major studies. The CTP research strategy has been to conduct in-depth analyses in four states that have been pursuing distinctive policies with respect to investment in teacher quality enhancement initiatives. The CTP work investigates both the policy and resource environment for the improvement of teacher and teaching quality. These four states are California, New York, North Carolina, and Washington, and reported here is the progress we have made both in terms of developing the necessary conceptualizations and the resulting measurement methods and results.

This work parallels efforts being made by others (most notably the work of Odden et al.) in the Consortium for Policy Research in Education (CPRE) (Odden, Archibald, Fermanich, & Gallagher, 2002) and the work of Rice (in press) and Cohen (2001). The National Center for Education Statistics has also been exploring ways to measure spending on professional development within school systems, and this is part of a larger effort to understand resource allocation at microlevels (Hartman, Bolton, and Monk, 2001).

There is an important multilevel nature to this work. At the more macrolevels of the system, say at the national or state levels, accounting methods have been developed to generate estimates of spending in various areas, including professional development. Although far from perfect, we used these accounting methods in our earlier work to estimate the national and state totals, and we continue to make use of these methods for each of the four states examined here. However, as the analysis moves away from national and state aggregates to a focus on what happens within districts and schools, we lack well-established and accepted accounting methods. Moreover, as the analysis moves toward these more microlevels, a number of thorny conceptual difficulties arise, and consensus has yet to emerge about the best resolution.

We use this article as an opportunity to report on what we have learned about what each of the four states in the CTP core study have been spending on professional development in the aggregate and to share where we are in our thinking about the best ways to approach the conceptualization and measurement of resource flows into professional development at more microlevels of the schooling system. We conclude with a recommendation that the NCES convene a panel charged with the development of new accounting guidelines that appropriately track professional development revenues and expenditures.

Estimates of Professional Development Investments in Four States

For purposes of this chapter, we describe state investments in teacher professional development at the point at which teachers are hired. We recognize that state investments are also made along a spectrum of preservice teacher preparation, but our focus is on state support for the improvement of the existing workforce. These investments are evidenced through a host of different state strategies that include beginning teacher support, additional time for professional development activities, instructional support in specific subject areas, and incentives to attain additional certification. We explain some exceptions to this approach; overall, however, these descriptions do not include those state resources designed to attract high school or postbaccalaureate students into teacher training programs as well as other recruitment strategies. We now turn our attention to brief descriptions of the types and levels of investment in teacher professional development in each of the four states under study.

Each of the states in our sample (California, New York, North Carolina, and Washington) varies in their attempts to address the quality of teaching. The four states differ in political, demographic, and fiscal context as well as size and capacity to mount a state-level strategy for improving teaching quality. However, each state has been actively engaged in standards-based reforms, and each views the improvement of teaching quality as an essential component in the effort to improve student learning. Our analysis focused on the period 1998-99 through 2000-01. The fiscal data for this inquiry were obtained by examining the state operating budgets for K-12 education for each year under consideration. During this time period, each of the four states experienced increases in their state budgets and each provided additional funding for policies aimed at improving teacher quality.

North Carolina

As part of the Excellent Schools Act of 1997, North Carolina funded a program that supports initially licensed teachers through a two-year mentoring program. Mentor teachers exist at each school and provide supervision and support for new teachers. Mentors are paid a stipend of $100 per month for 10 months. During the 2000-01 school year, this program was funded at $14.2 million, or approximately $11.40/pupil.

The North Carolina Teacher Fellows Program is an example of a program that mixes recruitment with mentoring strategies. The state uses multiple, statewide initiatives to recruit new teachers into the public schools. Key investments from North Carolina include a rapid increase in teachers salaries (salaries are governed centrally and supplemented locally), a centralized Center for Recruitment and Retention at the Department of Public Instruction, several innovative programs targeting high school students and midcareer professionals, and the use of revolving loan funds. Excluding expenses related to salary increases, North Carolina spent just a bit less than $11.00/pupil on teacher recruitment efforts during 2000-01. At $8.30/pupil, a key feature of North Carolina's recruitment efforts falls under its Teaching Fellows Program (TFP). The TFP provides expedited certification procedures, tuition remission, and comprehensive mentoring for second-career professionals to join the teaching ranks in conjunction with accredited teacher preparation programs.

North Carolina currently leads the nation in its number of teachers who have gained certification from the National Board for Professional Teaching Standards (NBPTS) and outspends most states in its support of NBPTS teachers. North Carolina pays for the NBPTS application fees as well as for three days of paid leave for application preparation. The state spent $2.9 million on application fees in the 2000-01 school year and $300,000 dollars on paid leave for preparation. This is equivalent to $2.55/pupil during 2000-01, up from $1.51/pupil during 1998-99. Reaching beyond the fee subsidies, North Carolina also distinguishes itself by adjusting the state salary schedule to reward teachers for their achievement of NBPTS certification. As the population of NBPTS certified teachers has increased, the additional salary credits have grown substantially, from $6 million during 1998-99 to $17.6 million during 2000-01. In per-pupil terms, the salary credits increased from $4.97 dollars during 1998-99 to $14.04 dollars during 2000-01.

The state legislature in North Carolina appropriates annual funding for general professional development activities at the local level. The state allocated $11.7 million during 2000-01 or approximately $9.37/pupil. This represents a 30% increase in expenditures between 1998-99 and 1999-00.

North Carolina recently transferred a series of teacher quality enhancement programs out from under the State Department of Public Instruction and consolidated their operations in an academic center housed at the University of North Carolina (UNC). Approximately 10 programs are housed under the UNC Center for School Leadership Development. Four of these programs target teacher quality improvement in various ways. The programs include short-term residential programs, focused seminars, a mathematics and science education network, and a model teacher education consortium. In total, state funding for these programs amounted to approximately $10.00/pupil during 2000-01.

New York

New York policy has supported teacher mentoring, particularly for newly licensed teachers. New York's mentor teacher program has been in place since 1986 and is administered through a competitive grant process. Funding has fluctuated markedly over the years and decreased by 50% between 1998 and 2001. Total grant funding was $5 million or $1.70/pupil during 2001-02. Recent changes in teacher licensing standards will require all initially licensed teachers to complete one year of supervised mentoring before receiving their permanent certification. By comparison, this heightened requirement was part of North Carolina's overall licensure reforms since 1997.[1]

New York modestly subsidizes the fees teachers incur as applicants for NBPTS certification. The state administers the Candidate Fee Subsidy Program based on federal funds as well as the Albert Shanker Grant Program, which is primarily funded by the legislature. The Shanker awards reimburses NBPTS applicants up to $2,000 toward the costs of their application fees and provides an additional $500 to LEAs to assist in paying for substitute teachers, travel, materials, and supplies for the candidate. The legislature appropriated $1 million dollars in funding during both 1999-00 and 2000-01 for this program, equaling $.35/per pupil.

Beginning in 1998-99, the state funded a new competitive grant program called Targeted Teacher Professional Development grants. The grant program targets efforts to improve student learning by aligning curricula with the state standards, comprehensive district educational planning, and the collaboration of professional development teams. Fifty per cent of the available funds are awarded to the five largest city districts. Funding levels increased from $1.5 million in 1998-99, to $5 million in 1999-00, to $10 million in 2000-01. A total of 54 grants, ranging from $80,000 to $300,000/district award, were awarded in 2000-01. The median award was $192,500.

Regional school district consortiums are used extensively among New York school districts to access professional development activities for teachers. Technology training centers provide a host of professional support services designed to diagnose professional development needs, provide training sites, and develop curricula toward the full integration of computers and technology in the classroom. Funding for the Teacher Resource and Computer Training Centers in New York increased from $20 million during 1998-99 and 1999-00 to $30 million during 2000-01. During 2000-01, New York spent $10.20/pupil on these centers. Historically, LEAs also contract with their local Boards of Cooperative Educational Services (BOCES) for professional development programming. It is common knowledge that BOCES are important source of professional development programming; however, there is no accurate means by which to determine how much total revenue BOCES receive from school district contracts, i.e., the amount the state reimburses districts for their relationships with BOCES. State support for BOCES increased from $394 million during 1998-99 to $458 million during 2000-01.

---

1 As part of a general teacher recruitment strategy, New York advocates on behalf of district-initiated alternative certification programs. These programs advertise expedited certification routes, tuition remission, and comprehensive mentoring (Opportunities for Teachers Brief, 2001) to second career professionals in conjunction with accredited teacher preparation programs. The most comprehensive program exists in New York City and is called the Teaching Fellows Program (see http://www.nycteachingfellows.org.) The Rochester and Utica City school districts also administer similar programs, which are funded at the local level.

Washington

During the period under study, state policy efforts and resources in Washington were focused primarily on the development and implementation of the Essential Academic Learning Requirements for students and the mandatory performance-based assessments. These priorities were accompanied by some investments in teacher professional learning focused on implementing standards and assessments (see Figure 7.1).

Mentoring of beginning teachers has been organized and funded by the state through the Teacher Assistance Program (TAP) since its pilot year with 100 teachers in 1985. For the next seven years, the amount of money paid to each beginning teacher–mentor team averaged approximately $1,780. Since that time, the remuneration steadily decreased. For example, during the 1996-97 school year, 1,527 teachers (84% of beginning teachers) participated in the program, and the stipend was $854. In 1997-98, the amount available was $782/team. The decrease in funding for TAP was reversed in 1999 when the state budget for TAP had more than doubled from previous levels, allowing for approximately $1,700/beginning teacher. However, during this time, approximately 20% of beginning teachers were not served by TAP, and observers of the program noted great variability from district to district regarding the type of mentoring that is provided for beginning teachers at the local level.

In addition to state support for mentoring new teachers, Washington also provided funds to support time for professional learning for all teachers. In 1999-00, the state provided funding for three Learning Improvement Days for all teachers. Funds for this program were acquired in part from the elimination of the state's Learning Improvement Grant program, which had been in existence from 1995 to 1998. In this case, the focus shifted from a program that supported the development of school-based strategies to improve the school's instructional capacity to the funding of three professional learning days, some of which are sometimes controlled at the district level. In addition to the Learning Improvement Days, the state provided for additional staff development resources under the Better Schools Program. This program provided an additional $18.52/pupil for two years (1999-00 and 2000-01).

Legislation passed in 1998 created a new program supporting the improvement of early reading instruction, called the K-2 Professional Development and Instructional Materials Program. This program provided $9 million for professional development and related classroom instructional materials for beginning reading instruction to teachers of K-2 students in targeted schools. Funding for this program was eliminated the next year, and the focus shifted to professional development in mathematics. During 1999, $1.5 million was allocated in the biennium budget to establish a training program for elementary, middle, and junior high school teachers to improve instruction in mathematics.

During the time period under study, Washington initiated state support for teachers pursuing NBPTS certification. The 1999 session allocated $327,000 for 15% salary increases for NBPTS teachers for two years. However, the limited funding allotment made it necessary for the state department to develop a competitive process to determine eligibility. Starting in 2000-01, the bonus for teachers achieving NBPTS certification was set at a flat \$3,500/year for two years. Figure 7.1 provides a summary of Washington's investments that were targeted for teacher professional development.

Figure 7.1. State Investments in Professional Development: Washington: 1998-99 through 2001-02

Budget Category	Per-Pupil Amounts (\$)			
	1998-99	1999-00	2000-01	2001-02
Learning Improvement Grants	49.52	0.00	0.00	0.00
Learning Improvement Days	0.00	74.29	79.73	80.17
Beginning Reading Pedagogy	9.00	0.00	0.00	0.00
NBPTS Certification	0.00	0.39	0.28	0.33
Better Schools Program: Staff Development	0.00	18.52	18.52	0.00
Excellence in Mathematics Training	0.00	0.00	0.79	0.00
Mentor and Beginning Teacher Assistance (TAP)	0.00	3.58	3.59	4.94
Totals	58.52	96.77	102.91	85.44

NBPTS, National Board for Professional Teaching Standards; TAP, Teacher Assistance Program.

California

Among the four states, California has invested most heavily in state support for mentoring beginning teachers. The state has funded the Beginning Teacher Support and Assistance Program (BTSA) since 1992. In 1998-99 and 1999-00, the program was funded at approximately \$12.00/pupil and increased to \$15.00/pupil during 2000-01. BTSA programs are locally designed and administered, and beginning teachers are supported through a variety of activities, including one-to-one support from experienced teachers. The program's funding level increased only incrementally during the first few years but experienced significant growth in the past few years. State officials estimated that BTSA was serving more than 20,000 beginning teachers in approximately 90% of the districts in the state in 1999-00.

The California Mentor Teacher Program was established in 1983 and continued through the 1998-99 school year. The Mentor Teacher Program was replaced with the Peer Assistance Review Program (PAR) in 1999 and funded at \$12.05/pupil. Funding for PAR increased in 2000-01 to \$15.00/pupil. The purpose of the PAR program is to assist teachers who are struggling with aspects of their performance evaluations through the provision of "consulting teachers." Districts are directed to set up a teacher–administrator peer review panel to select consulting teachers, to review reports, and to make recommendations to the school board about participants. In addition to the investments made in mentor teachers and PAR, the state provided additional funds through the Staff Development Buy-Out Program, funded at approximately $33.00/pupil in 1998-99 and increasing to $40.00/pupil in 2000-01.

During 1998, the state provided resources to deliver professional development in specific subject areas, known as the Subject Matter Projects. There are currently nine different Subject Matter Projects: writing, mathematics, science, history–social science, the arts, foreign language, international studies, and physical education–health. The delivery system consists of regional summer institutes, weekend workshops during the school year, and teacher networks. These projects were reported to involve more than 46,000 teachers each year—approximately one fifth of all teachers in the state. The 1998-99 budget provided these projects with $12.2 million. This amount increased somewhat in 1999-00, but funding was eliminated in 2000-01.

The Professional Development Institutes (PDIs) represent another state investment strategy. The institutes are focused on literacy and math, including institutes to provide support to teachers who serve English language learners. The institutes are conducted at higher education institutions and other regional sites throughout the state. School teams are offered initial instruction in intensive training segments of one to three weeks. Multiple follow-up sessions are provided throughout the school year. Participants receive stipends from $1,000 to $2,000 depending on the duration of the training. Funding for the PDIs remained constant at approximately $22.00/pupil during the period of this analysis.

In 1998-99, California offered teachers one-time awards of $10,000 for attaining NBPTS certification. Beginning in 2000-01, a new state initiative provided an additional $20,000 for NBPTS-certified teachers who commit to working in low-performing schools for four years. Figure 7.2 summarizes California's state investments in professional development initiatives from 1998-99 through 2000-01.

Figure 7.2. State Investments in Professional Development:
California: 1998-99 through 2000-01

Budget Category	Per-Pupil Amount ($)		
	1998-99	1999-00	2000-01
School Improvement Program	67.49	54.27	66.10
Staff Development Buy-Out Program	33.35	37.80	40.79
Mentor Teacher and Peer Assistance Review	13.79	21.00	22.62
Beginning Teacher Support and Assistance	12.00	12.05	15.00
National Board Certification	0.00	0.64	2.48
California Subject Matter Projects	2.09	2.52	0.00
California Professional Development Institutes	22.00	22.00	22.00
Education Technology Staff Development	0.00	0.04	1.07
Totals	150.72	150.32	170.06

Challenges in Specifying Investments in Teacher Professional Development

States use a variety of pathways to direct resources for professional development from state coffers to teachers. As is illustrated in the previous discussion, the four states in this analysis used a variable combination of direct support to local school districts or regional agencies, competitive grant processes, and specific incentives to individual teachers. Additionally, these pathways are often used to distribute federal grant funds, such as the Eisenhower Math and Science Education Funds. Each state's strategy also varied during the time period we examined, with some programs initiated in one year only to be eliminated in the next. The unique features of each state's overall education funding mechanisms, and the variation in the state share of total education revenues, further complicates any cross-state comparisons of relative investment levels.

However, the most perplexing challenge is to track how these state-level investments are organized and implemented at the district level and subsequently allocated to schools. It is to this issue of improving our ability to track expenditures for professional development at district and school levels that we next turn our attention.

Conceptual Issues at the Microlevel

At first glance, it would seem relatively easy to estimate the investment of resources into the kinds of professional development commonly provided by schools and school districts. Most people are familiar with teacher workshops, and it seems logical to equate the cost of teacher professional development with the cost of running workshops. However, modern professional development takes many different forms and goes well beyond the traditional practice of closing schools periodically for formal teacher workshops. In this discussion, we attempt to recognize the many different contemporary forms of professional development and to assess the resource allocation implications of each.

As we explore differences across the levels of educational systems, we are mindful of how resources for professional development can arise from many sources. We have already explored resources that enter the system at the state and federal levels. Here we will consider the disposition of these resources at the district and school levels. We must also be aware of how important slippage can be from one level to the next. For example, a district might earmark funds for professional development and allocate the needed resources into a school's budget. In turn, the school may choose to use these funds in a way that is different from what the district had in mind. Similarly, a school may take funds earmarked by the district for a use that is far removed from professional development and use the funds to provide professional development services. Such circumstances are commonplace as local decision-makers seek to reconcile the provisions of different pieces of legislation and as local officials are vested with certain degrees of discretion in the day-to-day administration of programs. These same points can also be made about districts in relation to the state.

The slippage question also surfaces in how we think about the difference between costs and expenditures. Ideally, we are interested in the costs of professional development because costs connect with results and provide insight into the minimum resource requirements for achieving particular results, e.g., improvement in teaching performance. Realistically, we are far from being able to assess the impact of professional development efforts, and this pushes us more in the direction of an expenditure analysis. Thus, the initial task is to figure out what resources are devoted to this activity called "professional development." For example, Allan Odden and his colleagues developed a list of attributes that they believe are characteristic of "high-quality" or "effective" professional development (Odden et al., 2002). Although the list is not unreasonable, it is problematic from a cost-analysis perspective because it is not based on independently verified connections between inputs and outcomes. Instead, it is driven by what is logically related to quality. A number of the ingredients of good or best practice have a circular nature. The stipulation that coherent programs are better than programs that are not coherent invites questions about how to assess coherence. Problems also arise when the criterion for good or best practice has a direct connection to resources. This point is especially relevant to the concept of duration, one of the criteria that Odden and his colleagues set forth as a determinant of quality. Duration is also directly connected to resources because, all else being equal, longer programs require more resources than shorter programs. Thus, there is a problematic sense in which costs and quality are being defined synonymously.

We are less inclined to draw explicit distinctions between good and bad types of professional development. Instead, we examine instances in which resources are directed explicitly into professional development. In these cases, we are interested in measuring the resulting flows of resources. We also focus our attention on resources that flow from school and school district sources. An interest in a more global assessment of resource flows would require the examination of external entities, such as universities, that sometimes collaborate with schools and districts.

Similarly, explicit distinctions in the timing of professional development activity can cloud the duplicative nature of services shared by multiple levels of government and agencies. For example, the traditional sharp distinction between preservice professional preparation and continuing professional development for practicing teachers is becoming increasingly difficult to maintain (Rice, in press). Even traditional student teacher programs blur the lines between preservice and in-service professional development because practicing teachers are directly involved. The advent of Professional Development Schools, which strengthen partnerships between schools and college- and university-based teacher preparation programs, makes it even more difficult to maintain this distinction, and this is also the case for the new induction programs that involve creating new partnerships between the schools and teacher preparation programs.

We use this chapter as an opportunity to think through the resource allocation and accounting implications of these new developments in the field. We do so by explicitly distinguishing between resources devoted to preservice and continuing professional development activities. In particular, we treat induction programs as initiatives that combine elements of both preservice and in-service professional development and provide explicitly for induction programs in our accounting framework. We remind readers that accounting efforts such as this inevitably involve making arbitrary decisions about what to include, what to exclude, and where to show what is included. We are less concerned about what is ultimately included or excluded and more concerned that agreement be reached about the method so that future work will be consistent. Consistency in this work is a high priority, and a national authority such as NCES can and should play a lead role in achieving this important goal.

We have organized our analysis around the different types of resources that are used to provide professional development. For each category, we examine the accounting issues and develop a worksheet (see Figure 7.3) that we believe can assist in the collection of the relevant data. These individual sections can be combined to create a master worksheet that is tied to a particular level of the educational system, e.g., a school or a district.

Figure 7.3. Data Collection Worksheet

Each worksheet pertains to a single expending unit (e.g., a school district or individual school). The goal is to capture all of the resources being expended by the schools and the district on behalf of professional development for teachers during one school year.

Elements of Expenditures for Professional Development

Human resources

- Deliverers of services
    - Staff developers
    - Administrators
    - Mentors
    - Workshop deliverers
    - Workshop helpers
    - Other support personnel
    - Volunteers
- Recipients of services
    - Current
        School year
        Nonschool year (e.g., summer)
        Replacement costs (e.g., substitute teachers)
    - Future
        Deferred compensation (in present value)
- Persons on whose behalf services are being rendered
    - Costs of foregone learning

Material resources and consumable supplies
Transportation
Facilities
Elements that cannot be allocated

- Comprehensive fees

Human Resources

Professional development involves different categories of human resources: those delivering services, those receiving services, and those on whose behalf the services are rendered. In addition, there are cases in which it is difficult to draw the distinction between who is the deliverer and who is the receiver, as is the case when teachers are collaborating with one another and assisting each other. Her we consider the resource accounting implications of these types of human resources.

Deliverers of Services

Those who lead workshops or who are employed formally as "staff developers" are appropriately thought of as deliverers of professional development services. Accounting for the dollar value of these resources is relatively straightforward. We need elements like the number of hours the person is engaged in this work along with a measure of the hourly wage. The worksheet in Figure 7.3 provides explicitly the resources directed toward those who are hired to deliver these services.

The broad class of "deliverers of services" can include administrators whose duties encompass but may extend beyond professional development–related of responsibilities. In these cases, the administrator's time needs to be divided across its various uses and the dollar value appropriately prorated. Grey areas abound here, and decisions need to be made about whether time administrators spend evaluating teachers is appropriately treated as a cost of professional development. When the evaluation is formative in the sense that it is part of an effort to provide useful feedback for subsequent improvements in performance, then a "professional development" charge seems appropriate. If the evaluation is purely summative, as might be the case when a teacher is being evaluated for a decision about tenure, the time is less obviously categorized as a professional development use.

A similar issue surrounds the question of how to treat the costs of NBPTS certification. The certification process itself is costly, and in some cases districts and states are bearing at least some of the cost. If going through the certification review is in itself instructive and enhances skills, then there is a clear sense in which the cost of the review is appropriately treated as a professional development expense. However, if the review serves exclusively to reveal pre-existing skills and capabilities, then the cost of the review is arguably not a relevant cost of professional development. It is also worth noting that not all observers are convinced that NBPTS certification truly reflects outstanding prowess as a teacher (see, for example, Ballou & Podgursky, 2001). Given the declared purpose of NBPTS certification to improve teacher quality, our inclination is to include BPTS-related expenditures as part of professional development when schools or districts make these payments.

Peer mentors, who may be accomplished teachers themselves, may also be assigned to provide assistance to teachers. If we think of mentoring as a one-way process through which the mentor provides services to the recipient, then the accounting is conceptually straightforward and parallels how we propose to treat administrators. If, however, we adopt a more sophisticated and accurate view that good mentoring involves a two-way exchange of information and insight such that both the mentor and the recipient realize benefits, then the accounting becomes more complex. We hold to this latter view, and this prompts us to move mentors into the class of "those who receive services," which we discuss in greater detail below.

Volunteers may also become involved in the delivery of these services, and the accounting conventions here are less straightforward. We can think in terms of the opportunity costs of volunteers' time, but these charges do not appear explicitly within the financial accounting systems of typical school districts (Brent, 2000). Our preference is to rely n a time rather than dollar metric for these resources. In this way, we can make it clear that these resources are real and can play a significant role without overstating the district's financial commitment to professional development.

Sometimes an external vendor delivers services, and a comprehensive fee or tuition is charged. A portion of the comprehensive fee or tuition covers the cost of the time of the deliverers of the services, but it can also cover other types of costs (e.g., materials, supplies, and transportation). For now, we will treat this as an unallocated expense. Depending on the question being asked, it may or may not be worth the effort to break down unallocated expenses such as a comprehensive fee into its pieces. These unallocated expenses appear at the bottom of Figure 7.3.

Unallocated expenses can vary with respect to whom makes the payment. An individual teacher might pay a tuition or fee, it might be shared with the school (or district), or the school (district) might make the complete payment. Given our interest in assessing spending by districts and schools, we will count only those tuitions and fees that are paid explicitly by the school or district.

Recipients of Services

Professional development endeavors are typically time intensive, and we need to think carefully about how to treat the time value of those who are receiving the services in question. In particular, three issues have emerged in the literature: the treatment of replacement costs, the treatment of time interdependencies, and the treatment of donated resources. We describe each of these issues and the disagreements that have emerged and then argue for a particular approach. Although our focus is on teachers, it is important to keep in mind that there can be many different recipients of professional development services, and these issues apply to each of the different categories of recipients.

Replacement Costs

We begin with the simplest case in which no one is proposing to count replacement costs. The example is a teachers participating in a summer workshop that operates outside their regular teacher contract. If the teachers are compensated for their time as participants, these charges are logically and straightforwardly included in the calculation of spending on professional development. If a teacher needs to hire child care services to participate, that is a matter in the private life of the teacher, and the costs of overcoming the resulting absence of the teacher in the home is not logically a part of the cost of the professional development program. The costs of providing the child care for the teacher's time correspond to what we are calling "replacement costs," and we are saying here that we would not include them.

Replacement costs can also be thought of in the context of a teacher taking a class outside of school hours during the school year (e.g., on weekends or after school). We do not see the relevance of charging for the cost of what a teacher is giving up by virtue of participating in these activities, even in cases where the teacher is under some pressure to do so (e.g., to maintain or to gain certification status). The tuition for such a program would be included if it is being paid for by the schooling unit and can be thought of as covering the costs of those who are delivering the service. It could show as an unallocated expense at the bottom of Figure 7.3. If the teacher is paying the tuition, it would not show in this accounting of what the school or district is investing, but it would count if the goal were to achieve a more global estimate of what the society is investing in professional development.

A second example, in which we do not propose including replacement costs, involves teacher time provided for in a teacher contract for professional development where no students are present. Districts often schedule teacher workshop days as part of the regular school year. Teachers devote time to these workshops, and the value of their time is logically included as a resource being invested in professional development. The teachers may have to engage the services of child care professionals to cover their absence in the home, but again we do not see these as relevant costs. Similarly, we do not propose to include the costs imposed on the parents of the students who must make plans and incur out-of-pocket costs for their children given the closure of the school for the workshops.

Let us shift now to a case at the opposite extreme in which there seems to be agreement about including replacement costs. Suppose a teacher is asked to participate in a workshop during the regular school day, and the district provides a substitute teacher to cover the class(es) the teacher otherwise would have taught. Here we have the direct cost of the teacher time, which is covered under the regular contract, plus the cost of the substitute teacher, which is incurred by the district to make the teacher available for the program. It seems reasonable to include the cost of the substitute teacher as a replacement cost, although there is an important question about how best to measure the cost of such a resource (see below).

A more ambiguous case arises when the teacher is engaged in professional development activities that are regularly scheduled as part of the school day and which may be provided for explicitly in the teacher contract. For example, suppose teachers are provided a one-period-per-day release for planning purposes, and let us suppose further that the planning is appropriately thought of as professional development. The question is this: Should we include the cost of covering the teacher's class while the teacher spends time in the planning center? Odden et al. (2002) argue that specialist teachers make it possible for teachers to engage in this kind of professional development, and thus the cost of the specialists' time are a relevant measure of the resources. They go on to note that these costs can be decreased if the school can find ways to deliver the specialist courses more cheaply (e.g., by combining classes and increasing the student–teacher ratio). We see the matter differently and think it would be cleaner to charge the direct cost of the time teachers devote to professional development planning time and to not include the replacement costs for this kind of regularly scheduled time. We think it is better to charge the cost of the specialists' time to the costs of offering the specialty rather than to use this as an indirect way to value the time of the teachers who are engaged in professional development. If a district is able to deliver its specialist offerings more cost effectively, it is not clear why this should show as a decrease in cost for teacher professional development.

In a case where no students are directly involved, as would happen if a school district added time to the school day with no students present and compensated the teachers accordingly, then the accounting would be similar to the case of an add-on summer workshop, and the direct cost of the teachers' time would be charged. A more interesting and complex case arises if a district decides to decrease the amount of time in the school day for students, earmarks the freed-up time for teachers to engage in professional development, and makes no change in teacher compensation. In a case like this, foregone learning costs are presumably being imposed on students, and a case can be made for including these opportunity costs in the calculation of the costs of professional development. See below for more on the foregone learning of students that may accompany professional development programs.

Our answer to the question about the inclusion of replacement costs is that the circumstances will dictate the best response. In the case of regularly scheduled activities that are part of the regular contract, or in cases where the services are being provided outside of the regular contract (e.g., a summer workshop), it is not appropriate to include replacement costs and is best to simply charge for the time of the receivers involved. In contrast, when the activity occurs outside the regularly assigned duties, and where explicit costs are being incurred by the schooling system (as is the case when substitute teachers are being hired), then it is reasonable to include the costs being incurred to make it possible for the teachers to participate.

Time Interdependencies

There is also an important and largely unresolved question about how best to handle resources that take the form of deferred compensation provided in exchange for a teacher's willingness to undergo training of some kind. Suppose a teacher earns graduate credits and thereby advances on the salary scale for the district. These benefits will be paid out over time, so the intertemporal nature of this resource flow needs to be handled. Technically, this is a relatively straightforward matter, and the dollar value of a stream of future benefits can be expressed in present-value terms. However, a larger conceptual question needs to be answered that goes beyond the technical matter of calculating a present value. Analysts have disagreed over whether or not to include subsequent compensation as part of the resource commitment of a school or district to professional development. Odden et al. (2002) argue against the inclusion, whereas Rice (in press) and Stern, Gerritz, & Little (1989) are more accepting.

The crux of the question is whether or not the extra salary payment constitutes an incentive that must be provided to induce participation. Incentives could take the form of tuition subsidies or future and incremental salary increases. In both instances, the reason for offering the discount has not changed, and it seems strange to be in a situation where only some forms of the discount are counted as an expense of the program

However, in some cases, salary increases are not directly tied to specific professional development activities. Their intent is to recognize the growing productivity of teachers over time, and this productivity growth is only partially and perhaps quite tangentially connected to particular professional development experiences. In this case, the higher salary is reflecting the benefits of ongoing investments in teachers' human capital and is less appropriately tied to individual professional development programs.

Actual practice is likely to include elements of both extremes, and this makes it difficult to make a principled decision about whether or not to include these expenditures as part of the calculation of the resources that are being devoted to professional development. Our approach is to recognize the potential legitimacy of this cost category, to keep the estimates separate, and to thereby provide policymakers with the option of including them or not as they see fit.

Donated Resources

This is really not so much a case of donate resources as a matter of how best to account for the resources that are invested. A teacher who spends his or her own time trying to improve as a teacher may or may not be compensated for this time explicitly by the schooling unit. From the school's perspective, these resources are donations. From a more global perspective, the resources are very real and costly, and their value is measured by the best opportunity the teacher foregoes as a consequence of spending the time in this way. There may also be indirect connections to resources. For example, Rice (in press) notes that performance incentives offered to teachers may prompt the supply of additional time and effort on part of teachers. In a sense, these are donated resources because they are not required, and the teacher may benefit from these additional investments to the extent that they translate into improved performance as a teacher, which in turn gives rise to additional student achievement gains, which in turn lead to salary bonuses. It is worth noting that foundation scholarships, university scholarships, and awards to teachers appear like donated resources but are more akin to resources provided by external organizations. They would be relevant, however, to a more global measure of professional development costs.

Persons on Whose Behalf Services Are Rendered

Recall our point about the relevance of including replacement costs when a teacher is removed from what he or she would ordinarily be teaching in the absence of the professional development activity. If we agree that we should include the replacement cost of the teacher's time, then the next question involves how best to estimate its value. Simply equating the cost of a substitute teacher's time to what needs to be spent to staff the classroom may seriously misrepresent the true cost of using this resource. Assuming a district is efficient in the sense that the best possible teacher resources are being allocated to classrooms, the use of a substitute teacher imposes a loss of teacher quality for the students who are involved. To the degree that the performance of students suffers because of the replacement of the regular teacher with a substitute, there is a level of foregone learning that constitutes a meaningful cost of professional development that is difficult to express in accounting terms. We can conceptualize the magnitude of this cost in two ways. First, what would be the extra resources required to hire a substitute who could perfectly substitute for the regular teacher in the sense that students would learn as much with the substitute as with the regular teacher? And second, what is the present value of the lost wages that can be traced to the learning that does not take place because of the use of the imperfect substitute teacher? Neither of these numbers will be easy to obtain, but it seems safe to presume that in most cases these numbers are greater than "0" (although we should at least acknowledge the possibility that the substitute could be more effective as a teacher than the actual teacher, in which case the numbers would be less than "0"). It also seems safe to presume that the size of the discrepancy between the actual cost of the substitute teacher and the real full cost will vary and will be largest in places where the substitute teachers are very poorly paid or where substitute teachers are not even available.

Lest this cost be dismissed as being too abstract to be real, there is considerable anecdotal evidence suggesting that teachers refuse to participate in professional development activities precisely because they are concerned about the disruption their absence would cause for their students' learning. The growing pressure on schools to be accountable for student performance gains may very well increase the reluctance of teachers to participate in this kind of professional development, an ironic result particularly if the professional development being foregone would actually have beneficial effects.

The fact that professional development for teachers can impose costs on current students also raises interesting equity issues. For example, days shortened for professional activity time among teachers may generate learning gains that more than justify the costs that are involved. These costs, however, are borne by today's students (in the form of missing their regular teacher), whereas the benefits mainly will accrue to future students. How can we justify imposing costs on one group so that another group can benefit? Do we not have some responsibility to minimize or at least offset these costs to some degree as part of the effort to promote professional development? For now, we show foregone student learning as a placeholder on the worksheet in Figure 7.3. Our purpose is to help sensitize policymakers to the fact that this issue is real and has impact.

Material Resources and Consumable Supplies

Expenses for materials and supplies are relevant and should be tracked and reported. In the case of consumable supplies, the accounting is relatively straightforward conceptually. It may be difficult to develop accurate estimates of how much is used for professional development, but it is largely a question of how much effort is devoted to keeping track. In cases of equipment and capital expenses, the matter becomes more complex particularly when the asset is put to multiple uses. Again, this is a matter of how much effort is devoted to maintaining an accurate record of what is used for what purpose. If this knowledge is accurate, the accounting problem becomes relatively straightforward.

Transportation and Travel

Transportation and travel costs become relevant in situations in which both recipients and deliverers of services incur explicit reimbursable costs. A staff developer who is hired as a regular employee by a school district might be reimbursed for his or her travel to different sites. In such a case the resources would be logically charged to the category of "transportation and travel."

Facilities

Comprehensive fees for professional development programs that are held off-site frequently include charges for the use of facilities. When professional development takes place within schools and districts, it is less customary to charge these fees explicitly; however, facilities are costly, particularly when costs such as utilities to heat a building for a Saturday workshop and janitorial and perhaps security costs become relevant. The unavailability of facility charges for "in-house" professional development is likely to impart a downward bias to the estimates obtained. In principle, the full costs of the facilities involved in professional development should be charged to professional development. We show these costs as a placeholder but recognize that it is not likely to be worth the extra effort required to gain precise estimates of the magnitudes. This is an area in which some simplifying assumptions could be helpful in generating sufficiently accurate estimates.

Elements That Cannot Be Allocated

We recognize two types of expenditures that are difficult to allocate into the categories we have defined. First, there are the comprehensive fees that external vendors sometimes charge. These fees mix human resources with travel and facilities costs. Although it may be possible to break these fees into their components, it may not be worth the effort, and in these cases they can be dealt with as an unallocated element of the professional development effort.

Second, partnerships that can exist that can be difficult to break into component parts. For example, suppose a school district provides a regularly scheduled planning time for its teachers. A case can be made for counting such time as "professional development," although there is no formally identified leader or deliverer of the service. The reasoning is that teachers can be resources for one another, and in a case like this the distinction between the deliverer and receiver of professional development breaks down. Pushing further, one could argue that an individual teacher can provide professional development to him or herself, but such a loose definition risks becoming unwieldy. Our inclination is to place bounds on what we mean by "professional development" to include instances in which two or more individuals (either a deliverer and a receiver or multiple receivers) meet on a regular and organized basis. It is useful to have a way to estimate the magnitude of this use of teacher time, and by maintaining it as a separate element in the accounting framework, policymakers have the option of using it as they see fit.

Because this use of time typically takes place during regular school hours and does not require the explicit use of substitute teachers, the cost accounting is relatively straightforward and involves totaling the hours spent in this way along with salary data expressed on an hourly basis. Mentoring programs that are part of induction efforts can be accounted for in this fashion.

Now that we have a conceptual framework that can be used to gather and interpret information about investments in professional development at the school and district levels, we are working at generating estimates using data from the core CTP study. As we move more deeply into the data, we will no doubt find that adjustments need to be made. Our plan is to assemble a careful record of how we proceed and to generate estimates of the spending magnitudes. Although these estimates will be of interest, we can anticipate difficulties in making sense of them in relation to other available estimates given the differences that exist in the methods being employed.

Conclusion

Numerous conceptual challenges arise in attempting to develop more refined measures to track spending on teacher professional development, especially when one desires to examine this issue at the district or school level. In this chapter, we have discussed numerous unresolved conceptual and methodological issues and have made some suggestions about how these issues might be clarified. However, these theoretical and technical questions require additional discussion among those interested in developing more refined measures of spending on teacher professional development. A number of school finance scholars have been making good progress in this arena, and we are optimistic that the collective knowledge base can be improved. We suggest that the NCES would be an appropriate convener for continued work and that the time is ripe for taking this step.

References

Ballou, D., and Podgursky, M. (2001). Defrocking the National Board for Professional Teaching Standards. *Education Matters*, 1(2).

Brent, B. O. (2000). Do schools really need more volunteers? *Educational Policy*, 14(4): 494-510.

Cohen, C. E. (2001). *Issues and challenges in financing professional development in education.* Washington, D.C.: The Finance Project

Hartman, W. T., Bolton, D. G., & Monk, D. H. (2001). A synthesis of two approaches to school-level financial data: The accounting and resource cost model approaches. In Fowler, W. J., Jr. (Ed.), *Selected Papers in School Finance, 2000-2001* (NCES 2001-378). Washington, D.C.: United States Department of Education, National Center for Education Statistics (2001).

Killeen, K, Monk, D. H., & Plecki, M. N. (2002). School district spending on professional development: Insights available from national data (1992-1998). *Journal of Education Finance*, 28(1), 25-49.

Odden, A., Archibald, S., Fermanich, M., & Gallagher, H. A. (2002). A cost framework for professional development. *Journal of Education Finance*, 28(1), 51-74.

Rice, J. K. (in press). Investing in teacher quality: A framework for estimating the cost of teacher professional development. In Hoy, W. & Miskel C. (Eds.), *Theory and research in educational administration* (Vol. 2). Greenwich, CT: Information Age Publishing.

Stern, D.S., Gerritz, W. & Little, J. W. (1989). Making the most of the district's two (or five) cents: Accounting for investment in teachers' professional development. *Journal of Education Finance*, 14(4), 19-26.

Section III

Finance, Equity and Teacher Quality

8

Class-Size Reduction and Teacher Quality: Evidence From California

Jennifer Imazeki
San Diego State University

Class-size reduction (CSR) is an enormously popular policy. With strong support from parents and teachers, policymakers in more then 20 states have instituted CSR programs in the last decade, often coordinated with federal funding and generally targeted at schools serving low-income students (U.S. Department of Education, 2000). At the same time, researchers still disagree about whether smaller classes significantly improve student learning and, even if they do, whether the gains are large enough to justify the cost. This conflict between political popularity and uncertain results has policymakers in the difficult position of deciding whether or not to adopt (or continue funding) CSR programs in the face of tighter budgets and an unstable economy.

The current trend to decrease class sizes gained much of its momentum with Tennessee's class-size experiment during the late 1980s. Project STAR (Student/Teacher Achievement Ratio) provided the most believable evidence to date that smaller classes significantly improve student learning (Finn & Achilles, 1999). SAGE (Student Achievement Guarantee in Education), a smaller program in Wisconsin, also produced similar results (Molnar, Smith, Zahorik, Palmer, Halbach, & Ehrle, 1999). However, these programs were relatively narrow in focus. In 1996, California became one of the first states to implement CSR statewide. Unfortunately, the adoption of CSR on such a large scale led to a substantial deterioration in teacher qualifications that likely mitigated the positive effects of smaller classes. Of particular concern was the realization that CSR may have contributed to educational inequities between students of different socioeconomic status because schools serving the most disadvantaged students were often the last to implement the program and had to hire the least-qualified teachers (Bohrnstedt & Stecher, 2000). Throughout the state, many districts did not see the expected gains, and a few are already abandoning the program (Hayasaki, 2002).

The lack of concrete results, the decrease in overall teacher quality, and the increasing disparities in teacher qualifications have been discouraging for CSR supporters. However, California's experience may contain valuable information about how other states can design and implement more successful CSR policies. For example, many of California's teacher labor market problems have been attributed to the speed and scale of implementation at a time when there was already a teacher shortage (see Bohrnstedt & Stecher, 2002a; Jepsen & Rivkin, 2002). In this chapter, I will also discuss the possibility that the way in which the policy was financed may have played a role, particularly in the distribution of teachers across schools. With a better understanding of what has happened in California, policymakers in other states may be able to avoid these pitfalls and design more effective CSR policies.

To further that understanding, this chapter examines the impact of California's CSR policy on the teacher labor market, with a particular focus on the distribution of teachers across schools serving different student populations. Section II reviews what we know about the effectiveness of teachers and smaller classes. Sections III and IV give a synopsis of California's experience with CSR and the changes in the teacher labor market. Using data from the California Department of Education, I reiterate the findings of other researchers (e.g., Bohrnstedt & Stecher, 2000, 2002a; Jepsen & Rivkin, 2002) that teacher quality, as measured by experience and education, did decrease significantly after implementation of CSR and that there are large inequities in how these measures are distributed across students of different socioeconomic background. However, the data also show that (1) these measures are slowly returning to pre-CSR levels and (2) there was substantial inequality in these measures even before the implementation of CSR. Although the gap in teacher quality between schools serving high- and low-income students did grow slightly wider after CSR, particularly the proportion of teachers lacking a full credential, the effect of CSR on the distribution of teachers should be kept in perspective. On the other hand, there is no doubt that low-income students were considerably worse off, in terms of teacher qualifications, after the program began and that the gaps have persisted over time. In section V, I discuss how the way in which CSR was funded may have contributed to the problems with the teacher labor market. I show that policies that do not account for differences in salary costs and hiring needs will exacerbate inequities. Section VI presents preliminary results of a simple simulation suggesting that more disadvantaged districts in California do indeed receive less CSR revenue per new teacher needed, making it more difficult to attract high-quality teachers.

The Effectiveness of Teachers and CSR

Deterioration in the preparation and qualifications of teachers, particularly in schools and districts with large concentrations of traditionally disadvantaged students, could have important implications for the success of CSR. If there is a negative impact on student performance because of lower teacher quality, this may offset the positive gains of smaller classes and greatly decrease the effectiveness of the original policy. In California, the media and policymakers have focused on the decrease in teacher experience, education, and credentials that came after CSR. Thus, throughout this chapter, these are the measures of teacher quality that will be discussed. However, it is important to point out that although several studies have found that teachers matter, in the sense that there are large and statistically significant differences in the performance of students with different teachers (e.g., Hanushek, Rivkin & Kain, 1998; Ehrenberg & Brewer, 1994), the production function literature has been somewhat inconsistent in measuring the effect of specific, observable variables (see Hanushek, 1986). It is possible that a decrease in characteristics such as education and experience will have relatively little impact on actual student learning.

On the other hand, the conflicting research may exist because the relationship between these variables and student performance is more complex than many studies reflect. For example, average teacher experience in a school may not appear to affect student learning because the effect of teacher experience may be highly nonlinear. Murnane (1975) found that the first few years of experience matter, at least for children in inner-city schools, and Murnane and Phillips (1981) found evidence that having more than 9 or 15 years of experience may matter, but the marginal effects of experience between these thresholds appears to be negligible. There may also be differential effects of teachers on different types of students; at least one article (Summers & Wolfe, 1977) reported that low-performing students do better with less-experienced teachers.

It is also important to point out that the impact of lower teacher education or experience on student performance need not be large to offset the positive impact of smaller classes. Tennessee's Project STAR, which randomly placed primary grade students in classes of either 13 to 17 or 22 to 25 students, is considered the most conclusive evidence on the effectiveness of CSR. Several studies of the STAR experiment have found that smaller classes do increase student performance, particularly for low-income and minority students (Finn & Achilles, 1999; Krueger, 1999), with student performance higher in the smaller classes by 0.15 to 0.4 standard deviations. At the same time, CSR is also one of the most expensive of education reforms and among the least cost-effective (Levin, 1988; Grissmer, 2002). Furthermore, these studies do not consider any impact on teacher labor markets;[1] any decreases in teacher qualifications resulting from CSR would further decrease the cost-effectiveness of the policy.

Early evaluations of California's experience are consistent with previous research in that gains from decreased class sizes appear to be small (Bohrnstedt & Stecher, 2002b). It can be difficult to isolate the effects of CSR given that California instituted numerous reforms during the same time period (for example, a highly-publicized accountability system and limits on bilingual education). However, early studies of the program suggest that the decrease in teacher qualifications is indeed offsetting the benefits of smaller classes (Jepsen & Rivkin, 2002). In the next sections, we take a closer look at what actually happened with the teacher labor market in California and whether the structure of the CSR policy might have contributed to the problems.

---

1   Such studies rarely consider the effect of smaller classes interacting with other inputs but instead calculate the effect of decreasing class size, all else being equal.

California's K-12 School System and CSR

California has long been in the spotlight for issues of school finance, beginning with the landmark *Serrano v. Priest* equalization case in 1971 and continuing with the passage of Proposition 13, which effectively eliminated all local control of the property tax. In response to Serrano, California's system of school finance was reformed to equalize per-pupil spending across districts, and it has been highly successful in doing so. However, this equality was largely achieved by decreasing spending in high-spending districts more than increasing spending in low-spending districts, so that during the 1980s and 1990s, average per-pupil spending in California decreased approximately 15% relative to that of the rest of the country (Sonstelie, Brunner & Ardon, 2000).

Districts responded to these decreasing revenues by increasing class sizes (Sonstelie et al., 2000). By 1993-94, California's average class size for grades K-6 was one of the highest in the country, at an average of 27.7 (U.S. Department of Education, 1996). At the same time, student achievement was decreasing: in 1994, California ranked second to last among all states for fourth-grade reading scores on the National Assessment of Educational Progress and in the bottom fifth in the nation for eighth-grade math (U.S. Department of Education, 1997b).

The dismal state of elementary and secondary education brought increasing pressure on California policymakers to accomplish reform. In 1996, with research emerging on the success of Tennessee's Project STAR CSR experiment, and with increasing state revenues from an economic upswing, California became one of the first states to adopt a statewide CSR program. Under the policy, schools receive a per-pupil grant for each K-3 student in a class of 20 students or fewer taught by a certificated teacher. In the first year of the policy, the grant was $650, or $325 for students in small classes for half a day. In 1997-98, this was increased to $800/$400, with a cost-of-living adjustment in each of the subsequent years.[2] Funding for capital and facilities is allocated separately. Schools are required to decrease class size for grade 1 first, then grade 2, and then may choose to decrease class size in either grade 3 or kindergarten.[3] To qualify for funding, schools must keep classes at or below an average of 20.4. students/class.

California's policy applies to any school serving K-3 students. Although, technically, the program is voluntary, 94% of eligible districts (839 of 895 districts) implemented the program at some level in the first year, although not in all schools or all grades. By the fourth year, all but 9 eligible districts were participating (California Department of Education, 2002). The size and speed of implementation led to several problems, some anticipated and some not. The two primary issues were the large quantities of physical and human capital required on rela-

---

2 The grant amounts were $832 and $416 in 1998-99; $844 and $422 in 1999-00; and $855 and $428 in 2000 to 2001 (California Department of Education, 2002).

3 Classes serving multiple grades are allowed under the program but second- or third-grade students in combined classes are only counted after all students in the previous grade (i.e., first or second, respectively) are in reduced classes.

tively short notice. Physically, districts needed space for the new classes. Some were able to buy or lease portable classrooms, if they had the land on which to put them, but many schools resorted to turning libraries, teacher lounges, and even cafeterias into classrooms (Bohrnstedt & Stecher, 2000). Districts also needed people to staff these new classes; in the first 2 years of the program, 23,000 new teachers[4] were added to California's K-3 teaching force (see Figure 8.1). Some of these new hires were experienced teachers (e.g., teachers who had left the profession and were enticed to return or who were hired from other states); however, a large number had never taught before. The shortage of certified teachers willing to teach led many districts to seek emergency waivers for new hires, thus allowing inexperienced teachers into the classroom while working toward their full teaching credential.

Figure 8.1. Teacher Characteristics in California Public Elementary Schools

	1995-96	1996-97	1997-98	2000-01
K-3 schools	4461	4503	4535	4692
K-3 teachers (total FTEs)	53,637	64,277	76,569	82,071
K-3 enrollment	1,571,774	1,610,435	1,619,035	1,635,556
School Characteristics:				
Average K-3 FTEs	14.81	17.55	20.65	21.93
Average K-3 enrollment	352.10	357.16	356.69	348.29
Percent of students in free and reduced price lunch	48.75%	50.05%	50.28%	49.28%
Teacher Characteristics:				
Average teacher experience	13.97	12.55	11.91	12.33
Bachelor's degree or less	13.0%	15.8%	18.2%	18.0%
Master's degree or more	25.0%	23.4%	22.8%	25.1%
Lacking a full credential	4.6%	7.7%	12.1%	10.6%
New Hire (first year in district)	8.4%	19.2%	17.2%	9.7%
Inexperienced teachers (less than three years experience)	11.3%	19.3%	23.0%	12.8%
Experienced teachers (ten or more years)	57.6%	51.3%	48.4%	49.3%

Figure 8.1 shows summary statistics for key variables in 4 years. The year just preceding the adoption of CSR was 1995-96; 1996-97 and 1997-98 were the first 2 years of implementation and the years with the greatest hiring activity; 2000-01, the fifth year of the program, is included to give some idea of whether the

---

4 Throughout this chapter, one "teacher" refers to one full-time equivalent.

changes brought about by CSR are long-run outcomes or primarily transitional problems. All of the data come from databases collected annually by the California Department of Education. Characteristics of teachers come from the Professional Assignment Information Form (PAIF), which contains information on the characteristics and assignments of individual teachers. For much of the analysis that follows, the PAIF data have been aggregated to create school-level variables. The teacher characteristics of interest include years of experience, level of education, and whether or not a teacher has a full teaching credential.[5] Although CSR had some impact on teacher qualifications at all levels, the analysis here is limited to K-3 teachers only.[6] Data on school and district characteristics are from the School Information Form and Aid to Families with Dependent Children. Because of problems with the PAIF data, all schools in the Los Angeles Unified School District are excluded from the analysis. The largest district in the state, Los Angeles, educates more than 235,000 K-3 students and employs approximately 12% of the K-3 teaching force. Because of its size, diverse student population, and the urban environment of many of its schools, Los Angeles faced the toughest challenges in implementing CSR. All of the trends discussed below are similar whether or not Los Angeles is part of the analysis, but the gaps between high- and low-poverty schools tend to be larger when Los Angeles is included.

The averages for the teacher characteristics in Figure 8.1 are over all K-3 teachers (excepting those in Los Angeles Unified). Both 1996-97 and 1997-98 are included throughout the analysis because although the policy began in 1996-97, many schools were not able to implement the policy beyond first grade until the second year or later. Thus, the increase in the total teaching force was just as large in 1997-98 as in the first year and the decrease in teacher qualifications just as sharp.

Figure 8.1 shows that teacher qualifications—such as experience, education, and credentials—all decreased dramatically in the wake of CSR. The proportion of teachers with fewer than 3 years of experience doubled, and those lacking a full credential tripled. These decreases have already been well documented by other evaluations of CSR (Borhnstedt & Stecher, 2000, 2002a; Jepsen & Rivkin, 2002).[7] However, the data from 2000-01 also suggest that some of these character-

---

5   In response to CSR, many teachers began teaching K-3 who had previously taught in other subject areas. These teachers may have already had a credential for their previous subject area but also needed a waiver or emergency credential to teach K-3. Therefore, rather than focusing on teachers with waivers, some of whom may be quite experienced and highly qualified, I use the percent of teachers who lack a full credential of any kind.

6   The movement of teachers within and between districts led to openings in all grades, not just those grades affected directly by CSR. The patterns of teacher qualifications for all teachers in all grades are similar to the patterns for K-3 teachers alone, although the changes are smaller.

7   Minor differences exist between the numbers in the analysis presented here and those in the CSR Consortium reports and in Jepsen and Rivkin, primarily

istics are slowly returning to their pre-CSR levels. The passage of time will accomplish part of this; by 2000-01, teachers hired in the first years of the program would have 4 or 5 years of experience and would have acquired their credential, which would also require them to have additional units beyond a bachelor's degree. To the extent that experience and training increase teacher quality, the teaching force appears to be slowly improving.

On the other hand, the proportion of teachers lacking a full credential in 2000-01 was still double the level it was in 1995-96, suggesting that schools were continuing to struggle to find experienced, qualified teachers. This may have been caused partly by the high turnover rate for new teachers. Teachers are most likely to leave a position in their first few years of teaching (U.S. Department of Education, 1997a), so by 2000-01, districts may already have needed to replace teachers hired in the early years of the CSR program. It could also reflect the fact that although the greatest hiring activity occurred in the first 2 years of the program, many schools did not fully implement CSR, in all eligible grades, until the third, fourth or fifth years (California Department of Education, 2002), and these teachers may still be working toward their credentials. Additionally, California has only recently adopted policies to address the teacher shortage (such as incentives for recruitment and retention in low-performing schools). Thus, it may still take a few more years before the teacher labor market settles into its long-run equilibrium.

It is also important to point out that experience, education, and certification, per se, may not fully reflect teacher "quality." With the enormous increase in the teacher labor force during the first few years of CSR, surely many teachers were employed who might not have been hired otherwise. If teachers hired during the first years of implementation are of lower quality overall (e.g., in immeasurable characteristics such motivation and creativity), they may continue to be of lower quality even after acquiring additional experience, education, or credentials.

Distribution of Teacher Characteristics

Clearly, the qualifications of K-3 teachers, in terms of education and experience, decreased for the state overall in the years after CSR. But much attention has also been directed at the distribution of the problem. Evaluations of the project have repeatedly pointed out that it was primarily large urban schools and those with more disadvantaged student populations (e.g., low-income, limited English proficiency, disabled) that had the hardest time filling new teaching positions and these schools saw the largest decreases in teacher qualifications

because of differences in how socioeconomic groups are defined and how averages are weighted (e.g., Jepson and Rivkin weighed averages by student enrollment).

(Bohrnstedt & Stecher, 2000; Jepsen & Rivkin, 2002[8] I therefore turn to the distribution of teacher qualifications across different types of schools. Schools were divided into five groups based on the socioeconomic status (SES) of the students where SES is measured by the percent of students in the federal free and reduced-price lunch program.[9] Figure 8.2 shows the poverty ranges and number of schools, teachers, and students in each quintile group.

Figure 8.2. Socioeconomic Status Quintiles

SES Qunitile	1995-96	1996-97	1997-98	2000-01
		K-3 Enrollment		
1	288,177	296,382	297,438	303,132
2	285,834	293,504	293,583	299,671
3	302,716	300,784	302,416	298,253
4	325,167	332,415	331,440	345,858
5	369,313	385,368	393,152	387,657
		K-3 FTEs		
1	10283.8	12522.4	14659.5	15834.7
2	10065.9	12311.5	14307.4	15612.5
3	10575.0	12282.8	14529.6	15374.2
4	11266.4	13303.3	15786.5	17753.8
5	12803.1	15244.1	18423.4	19791.7
		K-3 Schools		
1	893	901	907	939
2	892	901	907	939
3	893	900	907	938
4	892	901	907	938
5	892	900	907	938
	Percentage of students in free and reduced price lunch program			
1	0-19.3	0-19.3	0-19.2	0-17.2
2	19.3-38.9	19.3-40.6	19.2-40.8	17.2-39.7
3	38.9-57.9	40.6-60.3	40.8-61.0	39.7-60.4
4	57.9-78.4	60.4-80.2	61.0-80.3	60.5-79.8
5	78.4-100	80.2-100	80.4-100	79.8-100

8   It should be noted that the general trends discussed in this section are also covered in these studies; the reader is referred to them for more detailed analysis of the data.

9   Other ways to assess the socioeconomic status of students might be to use the percent of students that are nonwhite or of limited English proficiency. These variables are highly correlated with the percent of low-income, and all results are similar when using these other measures. For the rest of the chapter, SES and income are used interchangeably.

Media coverage of the inequities in teacher qualifications has often focused on the size of disparities after CSR, but it is important to point out that teachers were distributed far from equally even before CSR. Figure 8.3 shows the distribution of three K-3 teacher characteristics in 1995-96. Schools with the highest concentrations of poor students had 6 percentage points more inexperienced teachers than schools with the lowest concentrations of poor students (14.8% vs. 8.8%, respectively) and had double the proportions of teachers with only a bachelor's degree and of teachers lacking a full credential. As will be discussed in more detail later, schools with the most low-income students also had slightly higher pupil-teacher ratios[10] and paid slightly higher beginning salaries.

Figure 8.3. Teacher Characteristics, by Student Poverty 1995-96

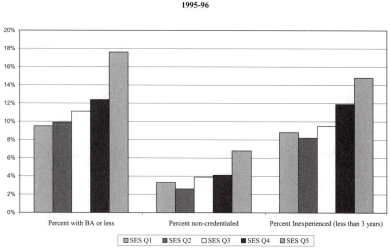

Figure 1.
Teacher Characteristics, by Student Poverty
1995-96

Figures 8.4 through 8.6 show how the distribution of teacher qualifications changed after CSR, both immediately (1996-97 and 1997-98) and in the longer-run (2000-01). There is no question that schools with the largest concentrations of low-income students suffered a large decrease in teacher qualifications. Schools in the lowest SES quintile saw a 12.9–percentage point increase in the proportion of inexperienced teachers and a .7–percentage point increase in the proportion of teachers with only a bachelor's degree. Most notably, by 1997-98, the percentage of teachers lacking a full credential almost tripled in the lowest-income schools to slightly more than 20%.

10 Pupil–teacher ratios are only an approximation of class size. Because teachers may spend part of their time engaged in nonclassroom activities, such as lesson planning, pupil–teacher ratios tend to be lower than actual number of students per class.

Figures 8.4. Percent of Teachers With Bachelor's Degree or Less

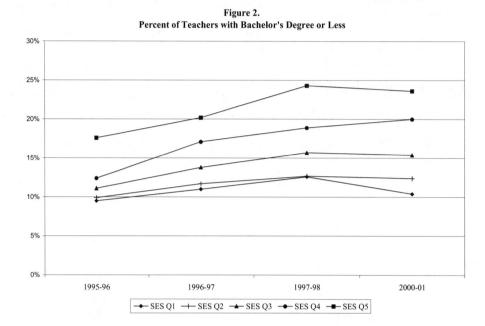

Figure 2.
Percent of Teachers with Bachelor's Degree or Less

Figure 8.5. Percent of Teachers With Less Than Three Years Experience

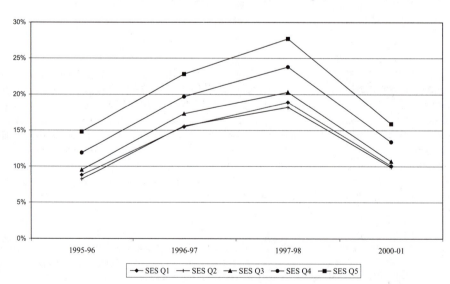

Figure 3.
Percent of Teachers with Less than Three Years Experience

Figure 8.6. Percent of Teachers Lacking Full Credential

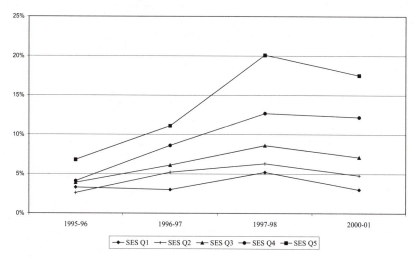

Figure 4.
Percent of Teachers Lacking Full Credential

From a certain perspective, one could argue that the effect of CSR on the distribution of teachers is perhaps not quite as bad as it has been made out to be. As mentioned, there were already large disparities in teacher qualifications between rich and poor schools previous to CSR. After CSR, schools in the highest SES quintile also saw large decreases in teacher qualifications such that the gaps in the proportion of teachers with a bachelor's degree or less and the percentage of inexperienced teachers stayed roughly the same. That is, although the levels for all schools deteriorated, a substantial portion of the differences already existed.

On the other hand, the gap in the proportion of teachers lacking a full credential doubled in size; by 1997-98, the lowest-income quintile had almost four times as many noncredentialed teachers as did schools in the highest quintile. Additionally, because the size of school and student income are correlated, schools in the lower SES quintiles tend to be larger; thus, even if the teacher quality measures change by similar percentages, that may represent a greater number of teachers (serving a greater number of students) in the lower-income schools.[11]

---

11 Because the unit of analysis here is the school, each quintile represents a different number of teachers and students. In particular, poverty, size, and urban environment all tend to be correlated such that the schools in the higher-poverty quintiles are also likely to be larger and part of the larger urban districts. To explore whether these large urban districts are driving the patterns here, the analysis was repeated excluding four of the largest districts: San Diego Unified, San Francisco Unified, Long Beach Unified, and Fresno Unified (Los

Finally, it is disturbing to note that the gaps are persisting, and even increasing, over time. Although it is encouraging that teacher qualifications are slowly improving overall, they are improving slightly faster for higher-SES schools. This could be explained in part by patterns of implementation. Schools with the most low-income students were the last to fully implement in all eligible grades (Bohrnstedt & Stecher, 2002a), thus they were still hiring for new positions in later years. As these teachers gain experience and earn their credentials, the gaps in these measures may shrink further. Phasing in implementation, beginning with low-income schools, could likely mitigate some of these problems.

CSR and Teacher Labor Markets

California's experience with CSR has clearly been difficult. Many schools are still struggling with staffing problems or recovering from the difficulties experienced during implementation. With a weaker economy straining state and local budgets, many districts are struggling to keep their small classes intact. At least a few districts have already abandoned the program in some grades (Hayasaki, 2002, Seaton, 2002), whereas others have only retained their programs through huge fundraising efforts by parents and teachers (Borgatta, 2002). For other states that are considering adopting large-scale CSR policies, an important question is whether California policymakers could have done things differently to avoid some of the problems. Other researchers have stressed that the speed and scale of implementation was a large factor (Bohrnstedt & Stecher, 2002b; Jepsen & Rivkin, 2002). In this section, I consider whether the way in which the program was financed may have contributed to the problems with the teacher labor market. I will discuss why certain districts are more likely to experience teacher shortages and lower teacher quality in general and why California's CSR policy likely exacerbated these inequities.

Even without the greater demand created by CSR, districts with many disadvantaged students usually have a harder time hiring high-quality teachers because they face the dual challenge of higher demand and lower supply.[12] On the demand side, these districts tend to be larger so there are simply more teaching positions to be filled. There also tend to be higher attrition rates out of such districts as teachers leave for positions in more attractive schools as well as other professions (see Imazeki, 2001; Theobald & Gritz, 1996).

On the supply side, it is often the case that fewer teachers want to work in these districts for a variety of reasons: the teaching jobs are more difficult because the students have higher needs and there is less support from parents and the community; the teaching jobs are usually in locations associated with higher crime and higher costs of living; and the schools themselves are often physically less appealing places to work (U.S. Department of Education, 1997b). As a result,

Angeles Unified has already been excluded). The patterns were roughly similar. Detailed data tables are available from the author.

12 See Imazeki, 2002, for a fuller discussion of the supply and demand problems of districts serving large populations of high-need students.

teachers of a given quality require higher wages to teach in these districts (Rosen, 1986). If wages are not high enough to fully compensate teachers for the harsher working conditions, teacher quality will be lower.

Because of these difficulties, schools and districts with the most disadvantaged students have the hardest time attracting and retaining high-quality teachers. A CSR policy can then exacerbate these problems. To see how, first consider a district's choice about the quantity and quality of teachers hired. Let us assume that the district chooses the number and quality of teachers to maximize school quality, subject to the district budget and the wages that must be paid to teachers. Both better teachers and smaller classes increase school quality. Note that choosing the quantity of teachers is equivalent to choosing class size, assuming that student enrollment is exogenous and relatively fixed. In California, the district budget is also exogenous, determined by the state, and is roughly equal per pupil across districts.

The wage that district i must pay teacher j can be broken down into two parts, a base wage and a premium for ability:

(1) $W_{ij} = w_i + p_i A_j$

+ The base wage, w_i, can be considered the price of additional teachers of some base quality level, whereas the premium for ability, p_i, can be considered the price of additional "units" of teacher quality, A_j. For example, if teacher quality is measured by experience, then A_j is the number of years of experience that teacher j possesses, w_i is the salary that district i must pay for a new, inexperienced teacher (with $A_j = 0$), and p_i is the premium that must be paid (per year of additional experience) for a more experienced teacher.[13]

For the sake of simplicity, assume that the only input is teachers' so that the entire budget is used for teacher salaries.

The wage bill for a district that hires N_i teachers will be equal to the district budget and can be represented as in equation 2:

(2) $W_i = w_i N_i + p_i A = B_i$

+ where is total teacher ability in the district (ie, the sum of A_j over all teachers), and B_i is the district budget. Thus, given a set budget, a district must trade off quantity and quality: buying additional teachers (higher N) to have smaller classes must mean a decrease in the total quality of the teachers purchased (lower). Specifically, hiring one more teacher of basic quality will cost the district w_i and they must therefore give up w_i/p_i units of total ability. In equilibrium, each district chooses the combination of class size and teacher quality that maximizes school quality without exceeding the district budget.

---

13 It should be noted that because of union contracts and the structure of teacher salary schedules, in reality, the only measures of teacher quality actually captured by Aj are usually experience and education.

If every district faces the same budget and the same prices (i.e., if B_i, w_i, and pi are the same for all districts), then every district will choose the same combination of class size and teacher quality.[14] However, as discussed above, some districts may need to pay higher wages to attract a teacher of even the most basic quality and may need to pay higher premiums to attract teachers of higher quality. Thus, in the model here, the base wage and the ability premium are both treated as district specific. Two districts may have similar budgets but face different prices, and they will end up with different combinations of teacher quality and quantity. It is straightforward to show that a district that must pay a higher base wage and/or a higher ability premium can end up with both fewer teachers (larger classes) and lower-quality teachers.

A policy requiring a particular class size (assuming it is lower than a district would choose on its own), without any increase in the district budget, must lead to a decrease in teacher quality. If a district needs to hire, say, five additional teachers, they must spend $5w_i$ simply to get teachers of basic quality and must therefore decrease teacher ability by $5w_i/p_i$. However, this trade-off only occurs because the district budget remains the same. If the budget were to increase by at least $5w_i$, the district could buy the additional teachers without necessarily decreasing total teacher ability. However, note that although total ability may remain the same, average teacher ability may still decrease because the number of teachers (N_i) has increased. For example, if all of the new teachers are inexperienced ($A_j = 0$ for each of the new teachers), then the sum of total experience of all teachers (A) may remain the same, but average experience (A/N) will decrease.

Consider two districts, A and B, that have the same student enrollment, but district A has characteristics that require paying teachers higher wages. That is, $w_A > w_B$.[15] Before the implementation of CSR, district A has fewer teachers than district B ($N_A < N_B$), and lower-ability teachers ($A < B$), although both districts have classes of more than 20 students. Under CSR, both districts hire enough teachers to decrease class sizes to 20 students. Because district A started out with larger classes (but the same number of students), it must hire more teachers while also paying a higher wage. Thus, simply to maintain the same ability level, district A will require a larger increase in its budget. However, both districts receive the same amount of money from the state (because enrollment is the same, and the policy gives each district a set amount per pupil). Even if this amount is sufficient to maintain teacher quality in district A, the same amount can buy both the

---

14 I am also assuming that all districts have the same production function for school quality. If there are differences in the marginal productivity of inputs (i.e., smaller classes and teacher quality have different effects on school quality in different districts), this will also lead to different choices of teacher quality and quantity. However, the basic implications of the model are the same.

15 We could also assume that $p_A > p_B$, but it is not necessary for the results that follow.

additional required teachers and higher quality in district B.[16] Thus, the gap in teacher quality is likely to increase under this policy.

Furthermore, this simple model assumes that wages are fixed. When CSR is implemented on a large scale, as it was in California, it is possible that the simultaneous increase in demand for teachers in all districts will lead to changes in wi and pi. In particular, the increased opportunities for teachers in more-desirable districts may cause a decrease in the supply of teachers of any given quality from less-desirable districts and a consequent increase in the salaries required to attract a teacher of any given quality into these districts. This further increases the cost of the CSR policy for these districts. Thus, even in districts in which salaries are increasing, teacher quality may still decrease, and the gap in teacher quality might increase even more.

Did Financing Matter?

The key issue is that the way in which California's CSR policy is financed does not take into account differing salary costs and hiring needs across schools and districts. By giving the same grant per pupil to all, and by beginning implementation for everyone at the same time, such a policy could exacerbate inequities in the distribution of teacher quality. There is an increasing awareness among researchers and policymakers that state policies to distribute general school aid should consider the differential costs of educating students with different needs (see Duncombe, Ruggiero & Yinger, 1996; Reschovksy & Imazeki, 2001). However, this may be equally important for financing specific school reforms as well.

To show how California's policy distributes CSR revenue, I simulate full implementation and compare the amount of CSR revenue for which a district was eligible in the first year of the program with the cost of hiring additional teachers.[17] In the first year of CSR, 1996-97, districts were eligible to receive $650 per K-3 student in a class of 20 students or fewer. Thus, the maximum amount of revenue a district was eligible to receive was equal to $650 multiplied by K-3 enrollment. The number of additional teachers needed depends on pre-CSR class sizes; the larger the average class, the more teachers needed to decrease class size to 20 students. To calculate how many additional teachers a district would need to hire, I assume that the number of teachers a district needs under CSR is equal

---

16 Conversely, if the amount is sufficient to maintain teacher ability in district B, it will be insufficient for maintaining teacher ability in district A.

17 Although the distributional analysis in the previous section was at the school level, the simulation here is at the district level. Although CSR revenue was technically distributed to schools, CSR revenue is only reported at the district level, and teacher salaries and other budgetary decisions are all set at the district level.

to total K-3 enrollment in 1996-97 divided by 20.[18,19] The difference between this number and the number of teachers employed in the previous year (1995-96) is used as a rough estimate of the additional teachers needed to implement CSR fully. It is then straightforward to calculate how much CSR revenue a district would receive per additional teacher needed.

Calculated in this way, 79 districts (9%) would not need to hire any new teachers. This does not necessarily mean that these districts already had K-3 classes of 20 or fewer students. However, most districts did have class sizes much closer to 20 students than the average California district and did not implement CSR in the first year. Theses districts are generally much smaller than others (the largest has 17 K-3 teachers) and are distributed across SES quintiles fairly evenly.

Figure 8.7 shows the results for the remaining districts. On average, salaries for new teachers vary only slightly across SES quintiles, although they are still highest in the lowest-income districts.[20] However, the amount of CSR revenue per new teacher needed is more than $10,000 less for the districts with the most low-income students than for the districts with the fewest. This may help explain the increasing gap in teacher experience and credentials discussed earlier: higher-SES schools received relatively more CSR revenue per new teacher needed and thus could afford to hire more experienced teachers.[21] This is consistent with the fact that in schools serving the highest-income students, 40% of new hires were experienced teachers, whereas in schools serving the lowest-income students, only 24% of new hires had previously taught elsewhere.

18 Note that this gives the number of teachers required to have a pupil–teacher ratio of 20 to 1. The number of teachers required for average class sizes of 20 students could be slightly higher (see footnote no. 10). Thus, this simulation gives only a lower bound on the number of teachers needed.

19 An alternative would be to calculate the additional teachers needed at each school and sum the total for the district (this is possible with the data). However, this may overstate the number of new teachers needed because in response to CSR, students and teachers were often reallocated across schools within districts to keep class size as close as possible to 20 students and to minimize the number of new teaching positions. The qualitative pattern of results is similar using either method.

20 It should be noted that when socioeconomic status is measured with the percent of minority students or those of limited English proficiency, there are larger differences in salaries across quintiles. Districts with larger populations of minority and low English proficiency students pay higher salaries.

21 It also possible that the additional revenue allowed higher-SES schools to offer bonuses or spend more on recruiting; however, data on specific expenditures for such items and activities are not available.

Figure 8.7. Simulation of Full CSR Implementation

SES Quintile	1995-1996 FTE	FTE for Full implementation of CSR	Additional FTE needed	CSR revenue per new FTE	Minimum Salary
1	49.81	73.53	23.73	$55,815.42	$26,989.56
2	63.75	95.78	32.04	$45,681.53	$26,760.56
3	72.26	109.71	37.45	$50,777.37	$26,614.96
4	96.34	145.13	48.79	$45,426.58	$26,773.74
5	63.67	97.56	33.90	$43,546.48	$27,032.68

This simulation is highly simplified and is intended only to give a general picture of the distribution of CSR revenues. There is no adjustment for changes in enrollment and, in that sense, the simulation may overestimate the number of new teachers needed specifically for CSR in districts with growing enrollments (i.e., some teachers would have been hired even in the absence of CSR). On the other hand, it almost certainly underestimates the number of new teachers actually hired because many schools decreased class size closer to 19, rather than 20, students to allow for fluctuations in enrollment (California Legislative Analyst's Office, 1997). The state's policy is that class size may be larger than 20 students on any given day but cannot exceed an average of 20.4 students; to ensure funding, many schools kept classes well under the maximum.

It should also be noted that although the numbers in Figure 8.7 imply that even the lowest-SES districts would have received adequate CSR revenue to cover the minimum salary of new teachers, this does not necessarily mean that it was adequate to cover the full costs of implementation. In addition to basic salaries, CSR revenue also needed to cover nonsalary costs such as benefits and training for new teachers, and, in later years, increased expenditures for recruiting and hiring bonuses. Together with the tendency of districts to hire more teachers than anticipated, this meant that, in many cases, the cost of CSR implementation was not fully covered by revenue from the state. In surveys conducted by the CSR Consortium, the majority of superintendents reported that CSR revenue did not cover the full costs of the program in the first year (Bohrnstedt & Stecher, 2002a). This was mitigated somewhat in later years when the per-pupil grant was increased; however, it still did not fully cover costs in many districts, particularly with salary costs increasing over time as new teachers gain experience and education, thus moving up the salary ladder.

Conclusion

California's experience with a statewide CSR program has not been trouble-free. Difficulties recruiting the large number of teachers needed to implement the program led to decreasing teacher quality across the state, particularly in schools with larger populations of high-need students. If this deterioration in teacher qualifications offsets the gains from smaller classes, policymakers must surely question whether a comprehensive CSR program is worth the expense.

Indeed, several California districts have begun to ask this very question. If California's experience with CSR is indicative of wide-scale CSR programs in general, this may not bode well for other states considering such policies. On the other hand, a better understanding of California's experience may provide valuable lessons about how to structure and implement CSR more successfully.

This chapter has provided an overview of the changes in the distribution of teachers under CSR. Teacher quality—as measured by experience, education, and certification—decreased across the state immediately after the implementation of the program, and the decrease was worse in disadvantaged districts. There is some indication that the situation is improving over time as hiring slows and as recently hired teachers gain experience and earn their credentials. However, the gaps between high-SES and low-SES schools still persist. Also, it should not be forgotten that there was a good deal of inequity even before the program began; thus, even returning to pre-CSR levels still means disturbing disparities in the education being provided to students of different income levels.

The way in which California's policy is financed may have contributed to the decrease in teacher qualifications. A policy that gives a per-pupil grant for each student in a small class, without accounting for salary levels or starting class sizes, may "buy more" for some districts than others. A simple simulation shows that, relative to the costs of the program, schools serving lower-income students receive less CSR revenue under this financing scheme because they start out with larger class sizes and must pay slightly higher salaries.

The popularity of CSR seems unlikely to wane anytime soon. Many states already target CSR programs at low-income students, and parents and teachers continue to advocate for wider adoption of these policies. As these programs are expanded to include more schools, the manner in which they are financed should take into account the differential costs of educating students with different needs. Hopefully, California's experience will help policymakers to maximize the effectiveness of CSR policies elsewhere.

References

Bohrnstedt, G.W., & Stecher, B.M. (2000). *Class size reduction in California: The 1998-99 evaluation findings.* Sacramento: California Department of Education.

Bohrnstedt, G.W., & Stecher, B.M. (2002a). *Class size reduction in California: Findings from 1999-00 and 2000-01.* Sacramento: California Department of Education.

Bohrnstedt, G.W. & Stecher, B.M. (2002b). *What we have learned about class size reduction in California.* Sacramento: California Department of Education.

Borgatta, T. (2002, May 8). Donations to maintain K-3 class-size limits in Irvine. Los Angeles Times, p. M1.

California Department of Education (2002). Class size reduction. Retrieved http://www.cde.ca.gov/classsize/.

California Legislative Analyst's Office (1997, February 12). Class size reduction. Retrieved http://www.lao.ca.gov/class_size_297.html.

Duncombe, W. D., Ruggiero, J., & Yinger, J. M. (1996). Alternative approaches to measuring the cost of education. In H.F. Ladd (Ed.), *Holding schools accountable: Performance-based reform in education* (pp. 327-356). Washington, D C: The Brookings Institute.

Ehrenberg, R.G., & Brewer, D. J. (1994). Do school and teacher characteristics matter? Evidence from high school and beyond. *Economics of Education Review* 13, 1-17.

Finn, J. D., & Achilles, C. M. (1999). Tennessee's class size study: Findings, implications, misconceptions. *Educational Evaluation and Policy Analysis*, 21, 97-109.

Grissmer, D. (2002). Cost-effectiveness and cost-benefit analysis: The effect of targeting interventions. In H. M. Levin & P. J. McEwan (Eds.), *Cost-effectiveness and educational policy* (pp. 97-110). New York: Eye on Education.

Hanushek, E.A. (1986) The economics of schooling: Production and efficiency in public schools. *Journal of Economic Literature*, 24, 1141-1177.

Hanushek, E. A., Rivkin, S. G., & Kain, J. F. (1998) Teachers, schools and academic achievement. NBER Working Paper No. W6691. Cambridge, MA.

Hayasaki, E. (2002, May 18). *Class-size reduction initiatives faltering*. Los Angeles Times, p. A1.

Imazeki, J. (2001, March). Moving on or moving out? Determinants of job and career changes for teachers. Paper presented at the meeting of the American Education Finance Association, Cincinnati, OH.

Jepsen, C., & Rivkin, S. (2002). *Class size reduction, teacher quality, and academic achievement in California public elementary schools*. San Francisco: Public Policy Institute of California.

Levin, H. M. (1988). Cost-effectiveness and educational policy. *Educational Evaluation and Policy Analysis* 10, 51-69.

Krueger, A. B. (1999). Experimental estimates of education production functions. *Quarterly Journal of Economics*, 114, 497-532.

Molnar, A., Smith, P., Zahorik, J., Palmer, A., Halbach, A., & Ehrle, K. (1999). Evaluating the SAGE program: A pilot program in targeted pupil-teacher reduction in Wisconsin. *Educational Evaluation and Policy Analysis* 21, 165-177.

Murnane, R.J. (1975). *The impact of school resources on the learning of inner city children*. Cambridge, MA: Ballinger.

Murnane, R. J., & Phillips, B. R. (1981). What do effective teachers of inner-city children have in common? *Social Science Research*, 10, 83-100.

Reschovsky, A., & Imazeki, J. (2001). Achieving educational adequacy through school finance reform. *Journal of Education Finance* 26, 373-396.

Rosen, S. (1986). The theory of equalizing differences. In O. Ashenfelter & R. Layard (Eds.), *Handbook of Labor Economics*, Volume 1 (pp. 641-692). Amsterdam: Elsevier.

Seaton, D. (2002, April 18). Class sizes to grow: the Riverside board decides to change the pupil-teacher ratio for third grades to save cash. *The Press-Enterprise*, p. B01.

Sonstelie, J. , Brunner, E.J., & Ardon, K. (2000). *For better or worse? School finance reform in California*. San Francisco: Public Policy Institute of California.

Summers, A. A., & Wolfe, B. L. (1977). Do schools make a difference? *American Economic Review, 67*, 639-652.

Theobald, N. D., & Gritz, R. M. (1996). The effects of school district spending priorities on the exit paths of beginning teachers leaving the district. *Economics of Education Review* 15, 11-22.

U.S. Department of Education, National Center for Education Statistics (1996). SASS by state, 1993-94 Schools and Staffing Survey: Selected results. Washington, D.C.: Author.

U.S. Department of Education, National Center for Education Statistics. (1997a). America's teachers: Profile of a profession, 1993-94. Washington, D.C.: Author.

U.S. Department of Education, National Center for Education Statistics (1997b). State indicators in education 1997. Washington, D.C.: Author.

U.S. Department of Education (2000). The class-size reduction program: Boosting student achievement in schools across the nation. Retrieved http://www.ed.gov/offices/OESE/ClassSize/class.pdf

9

Organizing Schools for Student and Teacher Learning: An Examination of Resource Allocation Choices in Reforming Schools

Linda Darling-Hammond
Stanford University

Jon Snyder
University of California, Santa Barbara

One of the major factors maximizing the gulf between educational goals and accomplishments has been the way resources have been defined.... There is a universe of alternatives one can consider and if we do not confront that universe, it is largely because we are committed to a way of defining who should be in the classroom...

Seymour Sarason (1982, p. 275, 284)

During the last two decades, public expectations of the United States education system have dramatically increased. Schools are now being asked not merely to... deliver instruction... or... cover the curriculum... but to ensure that all students learn to high levels. They are expected to offer challenging instruction while meeting the diverse needs of students who bring with them varying talents, learning styles, cultures, language backgrounds, family situations, and beliefs about what school means for them. However, although schools are expected to deliver much more powerful teaching and learning, they remain, for the most part, organized for assembly line results.

Recent analyses have suggested that how money is spent can make a large difference in school results. At the macroanalytic level, production function studies have suggested that teacher expertise (as measured variously by general academic ability, scores on teacher licensing examinations, certification status, degrees, background in content and teaching methods, and teaching experience) can make a substantial difference in student achievement (Darling-Hammond, 2000; Ferguson, 1991; Fetler, 1999; Goldhaber & Brewer, 2000; Greenwald, Hedges, & Laine, 1996; Monk, 1994; Monk & King, 1994; Strauss & Sawyer, 1986). Several studies have indicated that investments in higher-quality teachers make greater contributions to student achievement than other uses of educational dollars (Greenwald et al., 1996; Ferguson, 1991). Having found a strong relationship between district average teachers' scores on the National Teacher Examinations and student success on state examinations, Strauss and Sawyer (1986) note:

> Of the inputs which are potentially policy-controllable (teacher quality, teacher numbers via the pupil-teacher ratio and capital stock), our analysis indicates quite clearly that improving the quality of teachers in the classroom will do more for students who are most educationally at risk, those prone to fail, than reducing the class size or improving the capital stock by any reasonable margin which would be available to policy makers (p. 47).

In addition, some research has indicated that student achievement is higher, dropout rates are lower, and student affect and behavior are better in schools where students are well known by their teachers (for reviews see Darling-Hammond, 1997; Lee, Bryk, & Smith, 1993) and where there is greater opportunity for students to work intensely with a smaller number of teachers during longer periods of time (Gottfredson & Daiger, 1979; Lee & Smith, 1995). In addition to the positive effects of small school size, organizational forms that foster these strong, long-term relationships seem to produce unusually high levels of achievement for students who normally do not succeed in high school (Darling-Hammond, Ancess, & Ort, 2002). For example, in highly successful alternative schools, class sizes and pupil loads are decreased; teachers work intensively with smaller numbers of students for long periods of time; and teachers have large blocks of time each week to plan with their colleagues, build curriculum, make decisions, observe one another, and work with students and parents. Schools that have reallocated their resources to create these conditions have been found to be safer, more communal, and more successful in providing cognitive, social, and emotional support for students.

Researchers and reformers note that teachers need substantial time together to create new practices and engage in shared problem solving (e.g., Little, 1999). Studies of teacher development in other countries, notably China and Japan, point out how teachers appear to become more proficient when they work continually on curriculum, demonstration lessons, and assessments together (National Commission on Teaching and America's Future [NCTAF], 1996; Stigler & Stevenson, 1991). New curriculum reforms in the United States require substantial teacher learning that is content-based and tightly connected to teachers' ongoing classroom work (Ball & Cohen, 1999). Some extraordinarily successful schools have created time for these activities as a regular part of their operations (NCTAF, 1996; Miles & Darling-Hammond, 1998).

Together, these lines of research suggest that the ways schools organize their work may have important influences on what teachers and students learn and what they do. Yet, little research has been focused on how the reallocation of major school resources, such as time and staff, intersects with other school reform efforts to shape the possibilities for change and how the possibilities for such reallocations are influenced in turn by policies at the school, district, and state levels. This chapter examines how some districts and schools have begun to rethink the use of key resources—teachers and their expertise, staff and student time, and the direction of energy and focus within the organization—with the intent to better support high-quality teaching and learning. Our analysis focuses on how learning environments for students and teachers are shaped by the ways in which districts and schools structure staffing patterns, scheduling, and organization of students and teachers. We examine the outcomes of different approaches and the policy and organizational contexts in which these efforts have occurred, evaluating both the barriers that often impede such restructuring and the supports needed to enable the creation of more productive school organizations on a wider scale.

Trends in United States Education Resource Patterns

Many aspects of school design, including decisions about how key resources should be used, were developed in the last major era of school reform in the 1920s when scientific managers sought efficiencies in the use of staff and space to accommodate the large increases in enrollments brought about by compulsory education and mass immigration (Callahan, 1962; Tyack, 1974). To maximize the use of space and minimize building costs per pupil, they developed urban schools of 2,000 students or more. To use all of the classrooms at any one time and to minimize the required breadth of teacher knowledge, they adopted age grading and developed a "platoon system" for moving students from teacher to teacher, each of whom would teach a single subject for a single year. After specializing staff by grade level and subject area, they built systems of supervision and gradually added a variety of functions to serve other needs: counselors, special program managers, curriculum developers, and administrators of several kinds. As the system grew, staffing expanded along the model established during the early 20th century.

On the surface it would seem that schools should have the needed resources to create more individual time for students and to increase professional time for teachers. Real expenditures have doubled during the last 40 years, and pupil–teacher ratios have decreased substantially. From 1960 to 1999, the number of pupils per teacher in United States schools decreased from 26 to 17.6. Furthermore, in 1999, United States schools employed 1 adult for every 8 students; 1 professional staff person for every 12 students; and 1 classified teacher for every 16 students (National Center for Educational Statistics [NCES], 2001). Despite these generous ratios, class sizes exceeded 25 for most students most of time; student loads exceeded 100 for most teachers in secondary schools; and teacher planning time was both minimal and conducted in isolation from other teachers.[1]

---

1   Although public school teachers reported average class sizes in 1996 of 24 students for elementary teachers and 31 students for secondary teachers (NCES,

The Allocation of Resources Outside the Classroom

A key question is how resources are used. As the numbers of school staff have increased, the proportion of teachers has decreased. Since 1950, the proportion of school staff classified as "teachers" has decreased from 70% to 52% (NCES, 2001) (Figure 9.1). Approximately 80% of those classified as teachers work as full-time classroom teachers regularly responsible for one or more groups of students. The other 20% are engaged in administrative duties, such as department heads or supervisors for special programs; serve as demonstration teachers or mentors; or have other "pull-out" responsibilities.) Thus, just slightly more than 40% of school staff members are regularly engaged in classroom teaching (NCTAF, 1996).

Figure 9.1. Trends in School Staffing, 1950–2000

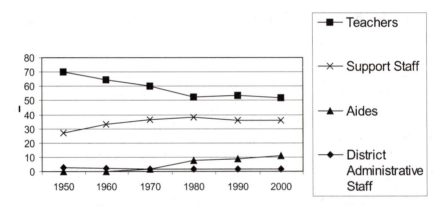

What do all of the nonclassroom teachers do? According to NCES (2001), in 1999, more than 34% of elementary and secondary school employees were engaged in administrative functions (this includes noninstructional support staff as well administrators), 3% were guidance counselors or librarians, and another 11% were aides.

An analysis of staffing and spending patterns from 1967 to 1991 in nine different districts across the country found that few of the newly added teaching staff were deployed to decrease class sizes for regular education students; most went to provide small classes to the growing number of students in special programs and to add a modest amount of time for teachers to be freed from instruction during the school day (Miles, 1997; Rothstein & Miles, 1995). In Boston, for example, 30% of students in the mid-1990s were identified for special education, bilingual education, or Chapter I programs, and 40% of teachers taught these stu-

2001), these averages are lowered by the small classes taught by special education and other specialist teachers, whereas most teachers teach notably larger classes (Rothstein & Miles, 1995).

dents in pull-out classes (Miles, 1995). Consequently, despite a teacher–pupil ratio of 1 to 13, most Boston classrooms averaged 23 students, and some have as many as 34 students. Miles notes:

> Using so many teachers outside regular classrooms means that all students, except those receiving completely separate education, spend the bulk of their time in larger instructional groups. In addition, Boston, like many school systems, has needed to develop administrative systems to monitor and coordinate the various teachers and service providers working with special students. This process diverts even more resources from the regular classroom, gradually making them larger. So, ironically, the very action designed to lessen the demands on teachers, referring a student outside the regular classroom, may increase them.... The pattern is self-perpetuating: the more schools designate specialists to respond to diverse learning needs, the less resources and pressure exist to help teachers in the regular classroom develop these skills.

Similarly, an analysis of school spending in New York State between 1979 and 1992 found that the most dramatic area of expenditure increase was for the... teaching of children with disabilities,... including special education teachers, school psychologists, and other nonteacher positions (Lankford & Wyckoff, 1995). Thus, the basic structure of schools has remained essentially the same across districts and across time, with new resources added largely around the regular classroom rather than into it. Despite recent calls for "restructuring," surveys suggest that public schools rarely engage in major reallocations of resources (Rettig & Canady, 1993).

In part, this may be caused by an increasing share of education funding between 1960 and 1990 coming to schools as categorical funds allocated for specific purposes by federal or state law. Audit trails encouraged the use of these funds for pull-out programs rather than investments in the core work of classroom teaching. Collective bargaining has locked some resource uses into formulas. Tradition has reinforced patterns that have gradually evolved.

In addition, the problems of teacher knowledge and personalized school organization are closely interrelated. Special programs have proliferated in part because many United States educators have received relatively little preparation for teaching learners with wide-ranging needs. Since the intervention of Taylor and the scientific managers of the early 1900s, teaching has been viewed as work requiring little training because it was fashioned as the implementation of routines outlined in curriculum packages and texts designed by those outside the classroom. Thus, most teachers have not been prepared to handle "special" students, i.e.,those who learn differently than lecture/recitation strategies allow; those who do not speak fluent English; those who develop at different rates or in different ways; and who have learning difficulties such as visual or auditory processing problems. In fact, many students fit one or more of these descriptions, and because "regular" classrooms—i.e., classrooms in which a single, limited pedagogy is used—are often too rigid to adapt to their learning needs, a large number of students fail. Paradoxically, the bureaucratic solution that places students in more costly special programs ultimately deflects funds away from both the teacher development and the teacher load reductions that might allow regular teachers to meet a greater range of student needs.

Miles (1995) identified several reasons for the suboptimal allocations of school resources in many schools. They include specialized programs conducted as add-ons; isolated instruction-free time for teachers; formula-driven student assignment; fragmented high school schedules and curriculum; and inflexible teacher work days and job definitions. Many of these practices are so pervasive that Tyack and Tobin (1994) call them the "grammar of schooling," and Sarason (1982) calls them the "regularities" of school. The tendency of bureaucracies to add specialists and adjuncts to schools rather than classroom teachers makes it difficult either to lower pupil loads or to increase time for teacher learning and planning. It is unlikely that schools can find ways to create more individual time for students or more shared planning time for teachers without prohibitively raising costs, unless they rethink the existing reorganization of resources.

International Differences

In contrast to United States staffing patterns, teachers comprise more than three fourths of all public education employees in Belgium, Japan, and Italy, and more than 60% in most other countries (Organization for Economic Cooperation and Development [OECD], 1995). These substantially larger ratios enable teachers in many other countries to have much more time for collaborative planning and professional development. United States teachers teach more hours per year than teachers in any other reporting country and are less well paid relative to other occupations than teachers in most European and Asian countries (Nelson & O'Brien, 1993). From a macroanalytic perspective, it might be said that these countries invest more of their resources in supporting the work of better-paid, better-prepared teachers who are given the time and responsibility for managing most of the work in schools rather than in external offices that inspect, monitor, and supplement that work. As Figure 9.2 illustrates, the United States surpasses all of the other OECD countries in the share of nonteaching staff it employs in its schools (OECD, 1995)

Figure 9.2. International Comparisons of Instructional and Other Staff

Country	Teachers (%)	Instructional Staff (Including Principals and Supervisors) (%)	Other Administrative and Support Staff (%)	Ratio of Teachers and Principals to Other Staff
Belgium	80.0	10	10.0	4.0:1
Japan	77.4	—	22.6	3.4:1
Italy	76.4	7.3	14.5	3.5:1
Australia	69.1	7.1	28.6	1.9:1
Finland	60.8	39.2	—	1.55:1
France	60.0	40.0	—	1.5:1
Denmark	57.9	28.1	15.8	1.3:1
United States	43.6	24.2	33.9	0.75:1

Source: *Education at a glance: OECD indicators. Paris: Organization for Economic Cooperation and Development, 1995. Cited in, Using what we have to get the schools we need: A productivity focus for American Education. (NY: Consortium on Productivity in the Schools, 1995), p. 44.*

Teachers in most of these countries also have broader professional roles that engage them in many aspects of schoolwork rather than in a single narrowly specialized function. They generally teach large groups of students only approximately 15 to 20 hours out of a 40- to 45-hour work week. In the remaining time, they engage in preparation, joint planning, curriculum and assessment development, school governance, their own professional development (including study groups, observation of other teachers, research, and demonstration lessons), and one-on-one work with students and parents (Nelson & O'Brien, 1993; NCTAF, 1996; Shimahara, 1985).

This time is made possible by the fact that there are more teachers and fewer nonteachers hired per capita and by the fact that staff roles are less bureaucratized. Specialists are not hired to supervise, write curriculum, and run special programs. Teachers develop curriculum with their colleagues, and they serve as guidance counselors for their students. Because they are trained to meet a broad range of learning needs, they rarely send "special" students off to pull-out classes. In many cases, they are trained to teach in more than one subject area and teach multiple subjects to the same students rather than one subject over and over again to different students.

There are, of course, good reasons for at least some amount of specialization. In some cases, individuals who have acquired deeper knowledge in a narrower field can better accomplish tasks that require specialized knowledge. The logic of specialization works best when individuals assigned to specialized roles have acquired high levels of expertise and when the organization of the work (1) allows them to have sufficient knowledge of the students for whom they are responsible and (2) allows them to be fully aware of the work of others in the organization that needs to be integrated with their own for the desired outcomes to be accomplished. Overspecialization occurs when tasks have been fragmented to a point where the client is no longer sufficiently well known to meet his or her needs, when the work is not adequately coordinated, or when tasks are highly specialized but the individuals assigned to do them lack the knowledge required. The organizational challenge is to find the right balance between specialization and a more integrated approach and to create structures that allow the knowledge of content and client needed for success.

Many other countries strike a different balance on this continuum than do schools in the United States. When there is adequate training for the range of tasks teachers are asked to undertake in different systems, the fact that teachers' roles are less narrowly specialized also allows them to be more effective in meeting students' needs. The more different ways in which teachers know their students—as counselors as well as teachers, for example, and over long periods of time—the more they can adapt instruction to meet their needs.

Teachers in other countries often share a workroom in which they spend breaks throughout the day and meet regularly to work on curriculum, assessment, and school management together. Japanese and Chinese teachers offer demonstration lessons to each other, intensively discussing the nuances of specific concepts, how they might be presented, what kinds of questions students might have, and what kinds of questions teachers should ask to elicit student interest (Stigler & Stevenson, 1991). German teachers hold "curriculum conferences" within the school to develop materials for their classes and to look at student work (Ratzki, 1988). These school structures assume that teachers must see students as whole beings and continually consult with one another to make wise instructional decisions.

By contrast, the twentieth-century teaching job in the United States was designed as piecework. Teachers are expected to perform the assembly line task of instructing large groups of students for most of the day according to texts and materials that are selected or developed by others in the system. "Regular" teachers are expected to teach only "regular" students because they have not been prepared to work with a wide range of learning styles and needs. "Special" children are sent off to "special" teachers for various services at various points in the day. Teachers stay with their students for at most 1 year and typically do not work with other teachers who serve the same students. When this approach to teaching is not effective, a demand for special programs creating new slots in the bureaucratic matrix is created.

In this conception of teaching, relationships among teachers or between teachers and students are believed to matter little. The design assumes little need for collegial consultation, for close work with individual students and parents, or for substantial professional development (Darling-Hammond, 1997; Little, 1999). Thus, most United States elementary teachers have 3 or fewer hours for preparation per week (only 8.3 minutes for every hour in the classroom), whereas secondary teachers generally have five preparation periods per week (13 minutes per hour of classroom instruction) (National Education Association [NEA], 1992). They typically have no time to meet with other teachers to develop curriculum or assessments, to observe each other's classes, or to meet with parents.

Another difference between United States schools and those in many other countries is the number of administrative layers that exist between schools and the governmental agencies that fund and administer them. In many other countries, a central ministry sends funds directly to schools and manages the leaner accountability system—largely comprised of curriculum frameworks, assessments, and periodic school reviews—that guides their work. In the United States, schools report to school district central offices (and, in most big cities, they also report to area offices that sit between the central office and the schools), to state education departments and intermediate units (the regional units that sit between the state department and districts in many states), and to the federal government. All of these levels increase the number of dollars spent on the management of schooling rather than its conduct. The many programs administered at each level also have separate reporting requirements and offices, so that the typical district organizational chart looks like a honeycomb of boxes, with assistant superintendents and directors for a large set of specialized core functions—elementary education, secondary education, adult education, pupil personnel services, staff personnel services, food services, research and development, finance and facilities, etc.—augmented by coordinators for a large set of special services—special education, bilingual education, compensatory education, health services, and so on.

This observation is not meant to suggest that all of the functions of agencies above the school level are unnecessary or that all of these units should be abolished. There are important functions for restructured districts and state agencies to carry out even if more decisions devolve to the school level. Nor are these observations meant to cast blame on the hard-working people who work in these agencies. They are doing the jobs set out by the current structures in the only ways those structures allow them to be done. Categorical approaches to program funding and regulatory mandates from legislatures have created needs for administrative management that these agencies are required to assume. If a substantially different allocation of funds is to occur, legislative strategies and administrative strategies must be changed in tandem while a new paradigm for organizing districts and state agencies is also developed.

Allocating Resources Within Schools

Some researchers have begun to look at how different within-school allocations of funds can create different possibilities for teaching and learning. A study of 820 high schools in the National Education Longitudinal Study (NELS), for example, found that schools that had restructured to personalize education and develop collaborative learning structures produced significantly higher achievement gains that were also more equitably distributed (Lee & Smith, 1995). The schools' practices included creating small units within schools, keeping students together throughout multiple consecutive years, forming teaching teams, assuring common planning time for teachers, involving staff in school-wide problem solving, involving parents, and fostering cooperative learning.

Redesigned Elementary Schools

Similar gains in shared time and personalization have been achieved in many elementary schools that have reduced class size by decreasing the number of specialists and nonteaching staff and increasing the number of classroom teachers. Such schools have restructured their staffing by "pushing in" special teaching expertise to teams and classrooms rather than "pulling out" children for fragmented special services. Many have also created shared planning time for teaching teams by creatively using clubs, "specials" (art, music, and physical education), local recreation services, and time banking. For example, at Hefferan Elementary School in Chicago, teachers teach four full days of academic classes each week and spend the fifth full day planning together with their multigrade teams while students rotate to "resource" classes in the arts, library, and other specials. At Ashley River Elementary in South Carolina, teachers have 80 minutes each day for planning, including shared time with their grade-level teams. Meanwhile, decreasing the number of specialists and counseling positions reduced class sizes; now 75% of staff members are classroom teachers. At Quebec Heights Elementary in Cincinnati, Ohio, teachers have found 5.5 hours a week to plan together and have lowered pupil–teacher ratios to 15:1 by creating multi-age clusters of students and teachers, by integrating special education teachers into cluster teams, and by eliminating separate Title I classes (Miles, 1995; Miles & Darling-Hammond, 1998).

These strategies are further supported by policies that enable teachers to spend 2 or more years with the same students and that allow teachers to work in teams with distributed expertise. These practices often decrease student failure rates and decrease referrals for special services because they result in greater knowledge of the child and family situation, more time to build useful teaching strategies for individual students, and more opportunities to gain advice from colleagues (Lieberman, 1995; Darling-Hammond et al., 2002). In all of these cases, evidence suggests that students are learning more than they did in traditional school structures as they benefit from more personalized settings and as teachers continually develop their expertise.

Redesigned High Schools

In studies of extraordinarily successful alternative high schools in New York City, researchers discovered strikingly different staffing patterns and organization of teacher time and student work than traditional schools provide (see Darling-Hammond, 1997; Darling-Hammond, Ancess, & Ort, 2002). Teachers in most of the successful new schools work in interdisciplinary teams with groups of 40 to 80 students to whom they teach a college-preparatory core curriculum framed by common "habits of mind." Teams of teachers often work with cohorts of students for 2-year periods. Class periods are 70 minutes or more in length, enabling intensive study and research. Portfolios that engage students in performance assessments are used for graduation. These are supported by advisors who work with students in small advisory groups as well as one-on-one. Teachers have many hours a week of joint time for curriculum planning.

A comparison of the use of school resources in these schools with traditional schools reveals how these intensive, personalized strategies are made possible.

Figure 9.3 compares the resource allocations in a typical New York City comprehensive high school with an enrollment of 3,380 students with those of two smaller alternative high schools in New York City. At least three organizational principles, similar to those in high-performance businesses, appear to guide the resource allocations of productively restructured schools.

Figure 9.3. Comparisons of Resource Use in Traditional and Restructured High Schools

Resource	Traditional Large School	Small School No. 1	Small School No. 2
Full-Time Teachers as % of Staff	58	67	73
Adults Teaching or Working With Advisories (%)	68	100	87
Ratio of Students to Adults	13.7:1	10.2:1	10.0:1
Average Class Size	33.4	25	18
Average Pupil Load[*]	167	75	36
Teacher Minutes Per Pupil Per Week[†]	6.2	13.6	33
Joint Planning/Staff Development Time[‡]	45 min	6 h/wk	7.5 h/wk
[*] Number of students the teacher is responsible for during the school year.			
[†] Load-to-time ratio: Number of students a teacher sees by the amount of teaching time each week.			
[‡] In addition to independent planning time of approximately 5 h/wk.			

First, the Taylorist divide between "planners" and "doers" is minimized or eliminated. (Frederick Taylor's organizational plans created supervisory structures so that those who plan and organize the work would not be the same people as those who did the work. The tasks were to be designed to be as narrow and repetitive as possible so as to allow the hiring of less skilled laborers who could be trained very specifically and who would not need to make nonroutine decisions.) Thus, in the large urban high school, more then 40% of staff are primarily nonteaching personnel: 1 principal, 9 assistant principals, 11 guidance counselors, 13 secretaries, 10 school-based services specialists (social workers, psychologists, etc.), and 17 security guards are employed along with 22 nonteaching school aides, 14 paraprofessionals, and 3 librarians.[2] "Big School" administrators and supervisors have little contact with students in a teaching or advising capacity. Their time is consumed by the tasks of planning and coordinating the fragmented work of the other personnel.

In the restructured schools, rather than assigning a cadre of people who work outside the classroom and a different cadre to work inside, nearly everyone both

---

2 Food service workers, janitors, and bus drivers are excluded from this analysis because their services are allocated through another process and formula.

teaches and plans. Most resources are devoted to core classroom teaching rather than to nonteaching functions or pull-out services. This reduces pupil–teacher ratios and permits more shared time for practicing teachers. At small school no. 1, for example, the principal, assistant principals, and all other staff work with students in advisories. Guidance counselors are attached to teaching teams and work with students in classes, seminars, and group sessions. The librarian is a classroom teacher who teaches classes and works with the school's media resources. Small school no. 2 offers a model with even less specialization: There are no guidance counselors, attendance officers, assistant principals, supervisors, or department heads. The codirectors teach classes themselves and have responsibility, as do all teachers and other professional staff, for counseling students in advisories.

Second, staff members are organized in teams responsible for an entire piece of work—in this case, a group of students. This creates a simpler work organization that demands less complex coordination while it allows the pooling of expertise and knowledge about students. Rather than a layer of planners who oversee the work of a layer of supervisors and coordinators who oversee the isolated work of individual "doers," work is structured to allow greater direct communication among workers who plan collaboratively. Rather than sitting on the side, specialists in such areas as counseling or special education are incorporated into teaching teams so that they can teach as well as help other teachers learn how to work more effectively with students.

Third, students and teachers engage in fewer separate classes per day for more extended periods of time. Rather than having eight classes per day of 42 minutes each, restructured schools create three to five class periods of 70 to 120 minutes each. As in a college setting, students take four or five courses at a time rather than seven or eight, studying each subject more intensely. This decreases teachers' overall pupil loads and the number of different "preparations" without decreasing instructional time for students. The smaller teaching loads make more teacher time available to students and more learning time available to teachers. The combined differences in staffing allocations and use of time result in very different possibilities for knowing students well and for working with them intensely. In the traditional school, pupil–adult ratios of 13.7 to 1 translate into average class sizes of 33 to 34. Teachers see 167 students per day, translating into only 6.2 minutes per week on average to spend with each student they teach. At small school no. 2, interdisciplinary clusters organize classes that are 70 minutes long and average 25 students each. Classes are offered three times per week, so that students get as much instructional time but teachers teach fewer courses. This gives them fewer total students, fewer "preparations," and more time to work together. These arrangements result in an average pupil load of 75, less than half that of teachers at "Big School." At small school no. 2, teachers of grades 7 through 10 teach two interdisciplinary classes that meet for nearly 4 hours daily for four times per week. With class sizes of 18, this results in a total pupil load of 36, less than one fourth the load of a teacher at "Big School." This organization gives teachers an average of 33 minutes per student per week.

In another resource allocation study, Cooper, Sarrel, and Tetenbaum (1990) found that only 32% of instructional staff time was spent teaching in regular high

schools compared with 60% to 85% of staff time in elementary schools, intermediate schools, and alternative high schools. Despite the fact that so little of the
total staff time is used for teaching, teachers have only one preparation period
daily, which is not organized for joint planning or staff development. Teachers, as
we found at our "Big School," meet collectively for at most one 45-minute staff
meeting per week. In contrast, shared time for curriculum planning, professional
development, and governance is much more extensive in the restructured
schools, ranging from 6 to 7.5 hours weekly, in addition to 5 hours of personal
planning time organized while students are in clubs, community service, and
other classes.

Through a combination of staffing choices (nearly everyone teaches), role
designations (teachers take on a broader array of responsibilities), scheduling
practices (block schedules with longer periods and fewer classes), and curriculum decisions (a core curriculum with no tracking), these schools are able to mar-
shal their resources to enable more intense and intimate work between and
among students and teachers.

Envisioning Alternatives to Traditional School Resource Allocations

The underlying logic of bureaucracy seeks (1) to make decisions hierarchi-
cally, thus requiring cadres of decision makers above the level of the school and
classroom; (2) to specialize functions, thus requiring a greater number of specialized personnel and large investments in the coordination of functions; and (3) to
manage work through the detailed specifications of procedures, which are then
monitored through elaborate reporting systems. These aspects of bureaucracy
increase complexity in school systems both vertically (through the extended hier-
archy) and horizontally (through extensive specialization), making it more difficult for parts of the system to connect to one another, for employees to know how
what they are doing relates to what others are doing, and for students to have
their needs addressed holistically.

Work Structures and Administrative Demands

Most United States schools are organized to allow specialization by grade
level and subject area as well as by special program areas added on to the core
program and administered separately. Students generally experience these programs as add-ons or pull-outs from their other classes rather than as enriched
resources within the main classroom setting. Teachers work in separate cells in
the matrix, which grow increasingly small after the primary grades in terms of
the amount of student life they cover. Teachers typically have time and opportunity to relate only to other teachers in their cell (e.g., the English department) and
to the supervisors who are also assigned to cover rows or columns in the matrix.
Students have to negotiate each cell separately, moving from one teacher to the
next, accommodating different settings, expectations, and groups of peers, and
making sense of the whole more or less on their own.

Adding new ideas for teaching and learning to these vestigial structures is
not likely to work well. Many districts are currently experiencing the frustrations

of trying to "do reform" without changing the underlying structures of schools and district organizations. The resulting clash of efforts decreases the capacity of the old system to do what it knows how to do well while impeding the efforts of reformers to undertake new strategies (Darling-Hammond, Ancess, & Ort, 2002). If new approaches to managing schools are to take hold, the old logic must be replaced with one that better accomplishes the goals and functions bureaucracy has tried to serve.

A new logic for building organizations will need to confront three fundamental assumptions of bureaucracies. One is the assumption that tasks will be performed most efficiently if jobs are highly specialized and broken down into small components that can become routinized, so that workers only have to have limited knowledge for the singular tasks they are assigned. The second is that organizations are most effective when they manage themselves from the top down, divorcing both the front-line workers and their clients or customers from major decisions. The third is that knowledge residing at the top of a bureaucracy can be codified in rules and procedures so that the workers need to have relatively little skill except in following orders.

New Alternatives and Professional Knowledge

Although the flaws in these bureaucratic assumptions are now more obvious, the solutions have been less so. Many states and districts have begun to decentralize decision making and expand teachers' roles. However, few have recognized the critical link between the knowledge base of educators and the success of new strategies. Consequently, the results of efforts to change curriculum, to create broader access to challenging content, to mainstream special education students, and to restructure school organizations have been extremely uneven. Success has occurred in places where educators have had the opportunity to develop the knowledge and skills they need to enact more complex practices; in many other settings, failure has resulted from these reform attempts.

Studying the Allocation of School Resources in Standards-Based Reform Settings

Standards-based reforms seek to make schools more aware of and more accountable for student learning results. Although some analyses have examined the influences of curriculum, assessments, or professional development on standards-based reform initiatives, few studies have looked at how allocations of resources influence or are influenced by reform efforts. As noted above, recent studies have begun to suggest that school organization and teaching possibilities are linked. To understand how, it is important to look in more detailed ways at how teacher capacity and school organization interact. What happens when schools are, or are not, organized for in-depth learning and collegial work? What happens to teaching and policy implementation when teachers have more, or less, time to collaborate with one another in studying children; to plan for lessons that use different learning approaches; to use assessment to provide more individually focused instruction; and to systematically focus on core ideas and "critical content"? What are the outcomes for children of school organizational decisions that differently support teacher learning and strong relationships between children and adults? What is the range of possibilities for reallocating human and time resources? And when does it make a difference?

A related set of questions concerns the interaction between the way in which schools allocate instructional resources and the features of the surrounding district and state policy environment. What kinds of district or state policies enable schools to (re)allocate their instructional resources to support teacher and student learning optimally? How do proactive attempts by the district and the state to improve the quality of teaching and learning "play out" in schools that organize their instructional resources differently—specifically, in schools providing relatively little time for teachers to collaborate or for teachers and students to develop personalized relationships compared with schools that have purposefully restructured their uses of time and other valued resources?

To pursue these questions, researchers must look closely at schools that configure their instructional resources differently in settings that are seeking to improve the quality of teaching and learning. During a 5-year period, the Center for the Study of Teaching and Policy (CTP) examined these questions through a multilayered set of state, district, school, and teacher case studies and surveys in four states undertaking standards-based reforms: California, New York, North Carolina, and Washington. The study followed up the development of these interacting policy environments over time and documented their consequences for learning, teaching, and teacher development.

The school level substudy sought to answer the following question: How do school-level choices regarding the allocation of resources influence the capacity of teachers to teach and students to learn? The study examined how schools' organization of people, time, and opportunities for student and faculty learning influences the implementation of curriculum and teaching policies. Three resource allocation choices are particularly central: (1) the allocation of professional expertise, i.e.,investments in the quantity and quality of teachers; the allocation of teacher time and expertise to different groups of students; and the organization of staff, including the extent to which there is shared responsibility for students and participation of teachers in planning, managing, and developing their work; (2) the allocation of time, i.e.,the amount of time teachers spend with the same students over a day, week, year, or years; the extent to which learning time is fragmented across subjects, teachers, and other staff; and the amount of time set aside for teachers to prepare and collaborate; and (3) access to content, i.e.,which students get access to what kinds of curriculum and teaching resources, and what kinds of specific professional development opportunities are available to which teachers.

The study used a comparative case study design contrasting 2 or 3 schools in each of four districts (10 total schools in four districts). In New York (New York City's Waverly District) and California (San Diego's Unified School District), the comparison schools are middle schools; in North Carolina (Pine River's County Public School District), the comparison schools are elementary schools; and in

Washington (Hobart's School District), the case study schools are high schools.[3] Case study schools within each district were matched as closely as possible on student demographics (socioeconomic status, racial and ethnic background, language background) and resources (core operating expenditures). We maximized variability on the resource allocation choices described above: professional expertise, time, and access to content).

Analysis of these data demonstrated the importance of examining teaching and learning investments at each level of the system—state, district, and school—rather than trying to understand reform from the school-level alone. Schools are constrained or enabled in their efforts by the ways in which states and districts manage the teaching labor force as well as they ways in which they shape within-school resource decisions. The study also pointed out the importance of considering development of teaching expertise as well as allocation of teacher and student time. Restructuring time to permit more teacher collaboration and personalization of student relationships may help spur some improvements but, by itself, does not compensate for a lack of faculty expertise. The combination of well-prepared teachers and resources organized to focus expert, personalized teaching on student needs appeared critical to those schools that showed the most substantial gains in student learning. We summarize findings on the elementary and middle school cases below because little restructuring of resources occurred in the high school sample.

Reallocating Resources to Support Student Learning and School Change

The states we studied had very different resource allocation strategies throughout the 1990s. In terms of overall spending, there were wide differences in 1999, with per-pupil expenditures, adjusted for cost-of-living differences, ranging from more than $8,500 in New York to only $4,700 in California, with North Carolina and Washington both just higher than $6,000 per student (Figure 9.4.) This was an increase for North Carolina and a decrease for California from a decade earlier. Although not the highest spender overall, North Carolina clearly did far more than any of the other states in terms of investing in teachers during the course of the decade: Beginning teacher salaries—adjusted for cost of living—were highest in North Carolina, and North Carolina's pupil–teacher ratio, like New York's, was below the national average. North Carolina had the steepest increase in teacher salaries of any state during the 1990s, nearly 12% for beginning teachers and 7% on average, whereas national salaries were nearly flat and some states actually lost ground. North Carolina also had the steepest increases in student achievement of any state in the nation during the 1990s and made the greatest progress in narrowing the achievement gap.

---

3 Pseudonyms are used for all of the districts (except San Diego, CA) and for all of the schools in the four districts.

Figure 9.4. State Investments in Instructional Staff and Teachers

		Ratio of Pupils to Staff	Ratio of Pupils to Teacher 1999[†]	Adjusted Per-Pupil Spending 1999 ($)[‡]	Adjusted Beginning Salary 2000[§]	Change in Beginning Salary 1990 to 2000 (%)[¶]	Change in Average Salary 1990 to 2000 (%)[¶]
		1993	1999				
United States Average	9.0	8.3	15.9	6,508	27,989	2.8	0.6
California	12.4	11.3	21.0	4,716	26,385	3.6	-3.6
New York	7.7	7.1	14.4	8,572	29,222	-4.3	-4.1
North Carolina	8.5	8.0	15.5	6,175	30,532	11.7	6.9
Washington	10.4	10.5	20.0	6,050	26,251	1.8	-1.5

[*] *National Center For Education Statistics, Digest of Education Statistics, 2001, table 86, fall 1999.*

[†] National Center For Education Statistics, Digest of Education Statistics, 2001, calculated from tables 85 (teachers as percent of staff) and 86 (ratios of pupils to staff).

[‡] *National Center For Education Statistics, Digest of Education Statistics, 2001, table 169, adjusted for cost-of-living differentials from American Federation of Teachers (2000).*

[§] *American Federation of Teachers (2000), pp. 8, 13. Beginning salaries adjusted for cost-of-living differentials.*

[¶] *National Center For Education Statistics, Digest of Education Statistics, 2001, table 79, change in constant dollars.*

North Carolina made major investments in teacher quality as well as salaries during the last 15 years, raising standards for teacher education, beefing up content and pedagogical requirements, raising admission and licensing standards, requiring NCATE accreditation for state teacher education programs, and funding professional development schools as well as extensive in-service professional development. North Carolina has more National Board Certified–teachers than any other state in the country, and Pine River County has more than any other district in the country. Pine River County may be the most professionalized district in this state that has invested so much in professionalizing teaching.

Within this supportive state and district policy environment, the two elementary magnet schools we studied allocate their resources in very different ways, which in turn has influenced the nature of the learning opportunities for both students and teachers and, in particular, has influenced the progress of the schools' lowest-achieving students. Both schools have approximately the same number of students and approximately the same number qualifying for free and reduced-price lunch. Both schools operate with approximately the same amount of funding, and both have fully qualified teaching staffs. During the study period, no unlicensed teachers were working at either school. Magnolia has a much more affluent subset of mostly white students attending from the well-to-do neighborhood surrounding the school combined with a group of low-income black students who are bused into the school. Nearly all of the Davis Valley low- to moderate-income students come to school on a bus. Its surrounding neighborhood comprises a long-standing, low-income African-American rural community.

Whereas Magnolia has traditionally shown high levels of average achievement, it has a large achievement gap between its white and black students that has not narrowed. Davis undertook a set of reforms that has substantially increased achievement for both black and white students each year since 1997 and has also begun to close the achievement gap between groups. Showing steep gains between third and fifth grade, fifth-graders at Davis performed nearly as well as those at Magnolia on state tests, even though as a group they scored much lower than their Magnolia counterparts when they were in third grade. In 2001, Davis's black students outperformed those at Magnolia on five of six end-of-grade tests given in reading and mathematics between third and fifth grades, and black students at Davis complete fifth grade ahead of those at Magnolia. The Davis Valley principal and teachers attribute this progress to a set of reforms that involved major reallocations of resources.

When a new principal arrived at Davis in 1992, she decided that the school needed to be radically restructured to create smaller classes and more personalization of instruction. In collaboration with faculty, class size was decreased dramatically to 15 students in grades K-2 and 18 students in grades 3 through 5. For comparison, average district classes sizes are 23 students in grades K-2 and 25.5 students in grades 3 through 5.) This was accomplished through the elimination of almost all classroom aides and three specialist positions. The schedule for specialist teachers was revised. Instead of seeing most classes in the school once a week, specialists did 15-day "extensions" with each grade in turn twice a year. For example, during the first 3 weeks of the term, the music teacher might see each third-grade class every day (during their regular teacher's preparation period), while the art teacher did the same with the fourth grade and so on. The school also delivers many specialized services directly in the classroom, such as some supplemental reading instruction, some special education services, and intellectually gifted instruction.

The much smaller classes allow substantial individualization of instruction and development of adaptive curriculum, which is supported by professional development for teachers and the weekly grade-level team meetings. Davis Valley has also used some of its magnet allotment to make its instructional resource teacher (IRT) position a full-time one. (This would otherwise be a half-time position.) The IRT, a writing specialist, spends her time consulting with teachers, team teaching, teaching demonstration lessons, and attending leadership and curriculum team meetings.

At more traditionally structured Magnolia, class size is at the average for the district with approximately 23 students in K-2 classes and approximately 25 students in grades 3 through 5. K-3 classes all have teachers' assistants, and upper-grade teachers share teachers' assistants. All children in the school have specialist classes in science, art, physical education, music, and computer laboratory; upper grades have specialist classes in Spanish and drama as well. An average fourth-grader spends only approximately half the day in the classroom with the regular classroom teacher. Additional pull-out programs are available for children who need extra help in reading and for academically gifted children.

Instruction at the school is largely traditional, with many teacher-dominated, whole-class lessons. Whereas students at Davis Valley, especially those in need of special help, are virtually always taught by a fully trained teacher, those at Magnolia Road who need special help are taught in small groups by teacher assistants, either in the classroom or in another room, or are tutored by parent volunteers.

To ensure more expert support for struggling learners, Davis Valley requested permission to reconfigure its district-funded Accelerated Learning Program (ALP), which targets struggling students. The school created a full-time position for an ALP teacher by eliminating transportation costs and custodial overtime for after-school and Saturday ALP sessions. The teacher allocation for ALP, which had been eight 1-month teacher positions, was thereby increased to one 10-month salary for a teacher who works with small groups of third- and fourth-graders both in their regular classroom and outside of the classroom. An additional grant from the district has enabled the school to pay third-, fourth- and fifth-grade teachers to tutor their own students after school. Because they know their students' needs and they are well trained to meet those needs, their students receive more knowledgeable and personalized instruction than they would in schools that use volunteer tutors. In general, Davis Valley gives priority to the classroom teacher working with children in the regular classroom, whereas Magnolia is more likely to rely on specialist teachers and pull-out programs (see Figure 9.5 for a comparison of resource allocations.)

Resource allocation decisions are also important in the different outcomes of two sets of three middle schools we studied in both New York City's Waverly District and San Diego, CA. In both cities, similar district-level reforms are aimed at investing in greater professional development organized around curriculum reforms in literacy and mathematics. The reforms are modeled after the work that Tony Alvarado undertook in District No. 2 in New York City before he became the Chancellor in San Diego. Alvarado decreased central office functions to the essentials, sent most staff back to schools, invested increasing amounts of resources in professional development, and focused the attention of managers on improving teaching. The investments, which have paid off in rapidly increasing student achievement in both District No. 2 and San Diego, include intensive summer institutes and ongoing study groups that focus on core teaching strategies and learning about new standards, curriculum frameworks, and assessments; school-based instructional coaching; and cross-school visits and peer networks designed to bring teachers and principals into contact with exemplary practices. Close, careful scrutiny of teaching exists at every level as does continual pressure and support to improve its quality (see Elmore & Burney, 1997; Darling-Hammond, Hightower, et al., 2002). The belief governing these efforts is that student learning will increase as educator knowledge grows.

Both Waverly District and San Diego have built on these approaches by introducing professional development institutes focused on literacy and mathematics as well as school-based coaching supports. Both have also worked to focus the attention of school leaders on instructional improvement. Key differences between the districts are the extent to which reforms have been voluntary or mandatory—San Diego's approach has been more insistent and pervasive across

Figure 9.5. Comparison of Resource Allocations in Two Elementary Schools

	Davis Valley		Magnolia	
Students	*572;* *One Third Free and* *Reduced-Price Lunch*		*468;* *One Third Free and* *Reduced-Price Lunch*	
Achievement Level 3 or 4 (%)	Third Grad-ers 1999 (%)	Fifth Graders 2001 (%)	Third Grad-ers 1999 (%)	Fifth Graders 2001 (%)
White Students Reading White Students Math	80 73	95 95	97 91	100 100
Black Students Reading Black Students Math	50 25	58 73	35 42	47 63
Average Class Size	15 (K-2) 18 (3-5)		23 (K-2) 26 (3-5)	
Staffing Ratios	34 teachers 3.5 aides		19 teachers 15 aides	
Use of Specialists	Eleven certificated special-ists work with students in classrooms (resource teach-ers work in classrooms; specialists join a teaching team to work 3 weeks with a grade level)		Nine certificated specialists work with students in pull-out settings	
Fragmentation	Students leave home class-room for 40 min/d to study in… community… centers in addition to spe-cialist periods (see above)		Students leave home class-room 3 periods/d (there are additional pull-outs for those in special-help pro-grams)	
Teacher Collaboration	Weekly grade-level team meetings; faculty use… optional… district profes-sional development days		Weekly grade-level team meetings in most grades; faculty chooses not to use most… optional… district professional develop	

its elementary and middle schools because of more centralized control of deci-sion making—and the extent to which within-school reforms have been based on a well-prepared teaching force.

In both of these cases, schools work within state contexts that have provided much less assured access to well-qualified teachers than in Pine River County, NC. Neither California nor New York had as focused a set of policies to improve teacher preparation and supply as North Carolina did throughout the 1990s, and both have large numbers of unprepared teachers teaching in urban areas. Whereas North Carolina's investments in teaching salaries grew dramatically during the decade (Figure 9.5), New York's teacher salaries decreased in real dol-lar terms, and California's salaries improved only slightly for beginning teachers and decreased on average overall. By 1999, in New York State, approximately 5% of its teachers were teaching without having appropriate certification (most of them in New York City). In California, approximately 15% of all teachers teaching were doing so without full credentials; these teachers were concentrated in high-minority, low-income schools in urban areas, some of which had a majority of teachers working without preparation.

However, San Diego worked hard to offset these trends with aggressive recruiting, salary investments, partnerships with local universities, and focused mentoring. By 2001 to 2002, the hiring of uncredentialed teachers had sharply decreased in San Diego; this was reflected in increases in the proportion of credentialed teachers in all the schools we studied to virtually 100% (Darling-Hammond, Hightower, et al., 2002). The New York schools we studied had widely varying proportions of certified teachers, ranging from approximately 80% to 100%.

These differences, along with differences in organizational structures and the allocation of key resources, appear to be associated with substantial differences in school outcomes. Among the three New York schools, "City Center, "the most traditionally structured school—a school within a school in a large building—invests least in well-qualified or -experienced teachers (approximately 20% are unlicensed, and approximately 30% have fewer than 2 years of experience), and these teachers have little opportunity to know their students well because they see approximately 140 students daily in classes of 30 students that take place in 42-minute periods. Teachers have little time to plan together with only one 42-minute period a week for grade-level meetings. These are not tied to a specific goal, such as curriculum planning, and as a consequence the time is often used for administrative matters such as exchanging trip forms or discussing class coverage. District staff developers come to the school but have only one day a week to spend there (large schools have no more coaching time assigned to them than do small ones), and they feel that they cannot readily meet the needs of the underprepared faculty. The school rarely taps other district professional development resources. Students merely enter and leave the school and perform poorly on state tests (Figure 9.6.)

Figure 9.6. Comparisons of Resource Allocations
in Three Middle Schools

	City Center	*Riverside*	*Cisneros*
Students	≈300 grades 6-8; 74% free and reduced-price lunch; ≈10% ELL; ≈33% identified as special education	≈200 grades 6-8; 75% free and reduced-price lunch; ≈5% ELL; ≈20% identified as special education	≈200 grades 6-8; 100% free and reduced-price lunch; ≈100% nonnative English speakers; ≈40% ELL
Achievement: Level 3 or 4 (%) in: Sixth-Grade CTB ReadingEighth-Grade ELA	28.7 4.9	40.6 41.0	20.0 46.6
Class Sizes Pupils/Day	30+ ≈140 students/d (with few "repeats")	15-17 ≈65 students/d (with many "repeats")	14-18 (for core classes and advisory) <100 students/d (with many "repeats")
Teacher Education/ Experience	≈20% unlicensed; ≈30% fewer than 2 years experience	≈7% unlicensed; ≈23% <2 years experience; ≈57% 3-5 years experience	All licensed ≈27% <2 years experience; ≈53% 3-6 years experience
Student Schedule	Five 42-minute periods; usually homogeneous ability groupings (by mini-school)	90-minute periods; mixture of heterogeneous and homogeneous ability groupings; students stay with same teachers for core subjects for entire year	45- to 60-minute periods; mixture of heterogeneous and homogenous ability groupings; students stay with same teachers for core subjects for entire year
Teacher Collaboration And Learning	42-minute weekly grade-level meetings (sparsely attended); little use of district support; few informal channels	140-180 minutes common preparation time weekly plus 1 afternoon/wk; use of district professional development support; multiple informal channels	2-3 preparation periods above contract; multiple informal channels; use of district professional development support; multiple informal channels
Personalization	Few if any visible opportunities or structures for knowing students well	Teacher teams work with groups of students for extended periods of time daily	Advisors serve 12-15 students in weekly advisories; Friday afternoon "clubs"; weekly school community meetings; after-school homework support

ELL; CTB; ELA; English Language Arts.

Cisneros, a dual-immersion language school, serves an economically needier and linguistically more diverse student body of approximately 200, all of whom quality for free or reduced-price lunch and virtually all of whom come from homes in which the first language is not English. Its students enter in sixth grade performing even more poorly on the state reading tests (only 20% reach level 3 or 4, i.e., "meeting" or "exceeding" the state standard); however, by the time these students reach eighth grade, they outscore those in most other district middle schools on the eighth-grade English Language Arts (ELA) examination. In eighth grade, 47% meet or exceed the standard, which is above the New York City average. Cisneros has invested its resources in a teaching force of fully qualified teachers, most of them trained in programs for bilingual teacher education at two well-known nearby universities with which the school maintains close relationships. Class sizes are smaller (between 14 and 18 students), and class periods are longer (between 45 and 60 minutes) than at City Center. Students stay with the same teachers for core subjects for the year, and many see particular teachers for more than one subject and for courses in more than 1 year. Teachers come to know students well both because of the way their teaching assignments are organized and because they teach weekly advisories to 12 or 15 students with whom they work closely as guides and advocates. School resources are used to provide teachers with additional preparatory periods and, although these are not used as systematically as at some schools to sponsor joint teacher planning, teachers talk frequently and make decisions together informally. The school also takes advantage of a wide array of district professional development supports in the form of workshops and institutes as well as coaching.

A third small middle school, Riverside, which serves approximately 300 students, has reorganized itself purposefully for greater personalization and teacher planning; however, its teaching force is more variable—approximately 7% are not licensed, and approximately one third are new to the school each year—and student achievement growth is not as great as at Cisneros. Although Riverside draws students who perform noticeably better on state examinations on entry (approximately 40% score at levels 3 or 4 on the CTB reading test in sixth grade), approximately the same proportion (41%) reach this level on the eighth-grade ELA examination, a lower proportion than at Cisneros, where the gains are much more dramatic. Riverside undertook a major restructuring when a new principal arrived in 1995 to revitalize what was viewed as a "chaotic" program that was then an extension of an elementary school in the same building. Teachers now work in grade-level teams of 3 to 4 teachers who are responsible for approximately 65 students. Most classes are at least 90 minutes long, and class sizes average approximately 16 students. Most staff feel that the school's efforts to use professional development resources and staff planning time toward the development of a project-based curriculum—accompanied by a system of performance assessments—has greatly improved students' learning opportunities in the humanities. Mathematics, an area in which many teachers lack specialized training, is an area of current concern that is now receiving attention. Despite greater affluence and fewer language needs, only 12% of Riverside students achieved a level of 3 or better on the state math examination in eighth grade compared with 35% of students at Cisneros.

These comparisons illustrate that, although refocusing school resources to enhance teacher planning and personalization for students may support school improvements, time reorganization strategies are not as powerful by themselves as when they are coupled with a well-prepared teaching staff who bring substantial knowledge into the resource mix.

In San Diego, all three middle schools have increased the qualifications of their teachers because of the district's efforts; in the two lower-achieving schools that had had more emergency-credentialed teachers, the proportions of emergency-credentialed teachers decreased from nearly 15% to 0% by 2001. All have reorganized scheduling to emphasize long blocks of literacy and math teaching time, with more expert teachers and coaches assigned to work with more educationally needy students; all have increased their participation in professional development by working with instructional coaches as well as attending institutes on literacy development and mathematics teaching; and all have increased student achievement while also increasing the proportion of students tested each year (Darling-Hammond, Hightower, et al., 2002).

The two middle schools that were previously lower achieving have shown the greatest gains as their staff composition has shifted more dramatically and educational opportunities have become more focused and equitable. A school with a larger middle-class population and a strong, collegial faculty (but with little formal shared time for most) has continued to use district reforms, as it always had, to build learning opportunities for teachers around the edges of a fairly traditional structure. This school has shown steady, modest improvements, but still shows a continuing large gap between higher- and lower-income students. The most traditionally structured junior high school—which had previously had the least collegial work organization, no shared responsibility for students, no shared time among teachers, large pupil loads, and short class periods—has modestly restructured, primarily in the sixth grade. However, it has struggled to create a collaborative, accountable teacher culture throughout the school. Although it has showed some gains in some years, this school has had the most uneven results thus far. The school that showed the steepest gains and the best performance for low-income students is also the school (1) that had previously organized all of its work around teaching teams working in small houses and (2) that maintained advisories for students and shared teacher professional development time for teachers as the district reforms took hold. This school had had a caring and personalized structure for students but large variability in teacher preparation and skills that has been substantially narrowed. Although aspects of its highly personalized structure were modified in the reforms, the continuation of aspects of this structure in a small school, coupled with staff that is more expert overall than it had been previously, has supported noticeable changes in achievement for students, especially those previously ill served.

Conclusion

No single "magic bullet" creates and sustains major school improvement, and there is no single school design that guarantees high achievement for students. However, school reforms that allocate greater resources to teaching, teacher learning, and time for students and teachers to build stronger relationships and participate more in-depth work appear to create new potential for student learning gains, especially for those students that have been least well served by systems in which they have previously had access to the least expert teaching in the most impersonal settings. Although much education reform energy and research has focused on the school level, it is also clear that state and district policy contexts are critically important in framing the possibilities and constraints under which schools struggle to develop stronger teaching. More conscious attention to how schools allocate resources for teaching may eventually lead to designs for schooling that can replace the century-old factory model with approaches that provide more opportunity for powerful teaching and learning.

Acknowledgment

This article draws on data collection and analysis for the Center for the Study of Teaching and Policy conducted in part by Carla Asher, Barnett Berry, John Denning, Michele Ferguson, Chrysan Galluci, Amy Hightower, Michael Knapp, Jeannette LaFors, Anneke Markholt, Milbrey McLaughlin, Susanna Ort, Joan Talbert, and Viki Young. The authors are grateful to these colleagues for their contributions.

References

Ball, D. & Cohen, D. K. (1999). Developing practice, developing practitioners: Towards a practice-based theory of professional education. In Darling Hammond, L., & Sykes, G. (Eds.) *Teaching as the learning profession: Handbook of policy and practice*. San Francisco: Jossey-Bass.

Callahan, R.E. (1962). *Education and the cult of efficiency*. Chicago: University of Chicago Press.

Cooper, B., Sarrel, R., & Tetenbaum, T. (1990, April). Choice, funding, and pupil achievement: How urban school finance affects students. Paper presented at the American Educational Research Association. Boston, MA.

Darling-Hammond, L. (1997). *The right to learn: A blueprint for creating schools that work*. San Francisco: Jossey Bass.

Darling-Hammond, L. (2000). *Teacher quality and student achievement: A review of state policy evidence*. Educational Policy Analysis Archives, 8(1). Retrieved

http://epaa.asu.edu/epaa/v8n1.

Darling-Hammond, L., Hightower, A.M., Husbands, J.L., LaFors, J.M., & Young, V.M. (2002, April). Building instructional quality: Inside-out, bottom-up, and top-down perspectives on San Diego's school reform. Paper prepared for the Annual Meeting of the American Educational Research Association. New Orleans, LA.

Darling-Hammond, L., Ancess, J., & Ort, S. (2002). Reinventing high school: Outcomes of the Coalition Campus Schools Project. *American Educational Research Journal*.

Elmore. R. & Burney, D. (1997). *Investing in teacher learning: Staff development and instructional improvement in community school district no. 2*. New York City. NY: National Commission on Teaching and America's Future.

Ferguson, R.F. (1991). Paying for public education: New evidence on how and why money matters. *Harvard Journal on Legislation*, 28(2), 465-498.

Fetler, M. (1999). *High school staff characteristics and mathematics test results.* Education Policy Analysis Archives, 7(9). Retrieved http://epaa.asu.edu/epaa/v7n9.html.

Goldhaber, D.D., & Brewer, D.J. (2000). Does teacher certification matter? High school certification status and student achievement. *Educational Evaluation and Policy Analysis,* 22, 129-145.

Gottfredson, G. D., & Daiger, D. C. (1979). *Disruption in 600 schools.* Baltimore: The Johns Hopkins University/Center for Social Organization of Schools.

Greenwald, R., Hedges, L.V., & Laine, R.D. (1996). The effect of school resources on student achievement. *Review of Educational Research,* 66, 361-396.

Lankford, H., & Wyckoff, J. (1995). Where has the money gone? An analysis of school district spending in New York. *Educational Evaluation & Policy Analysis,* 17(2), 195-218.

Lee, V., Bryk, A., & Smith. J.B. (1993). The organization of effective secondary schools. Review of Research in Education, 19, 171-267.

Lee, V., & Smith, J. B. (1995). *Effects of high school restructuring and size on gains in achievement and engagement for early secondary school students.* Madison, WI: University of Wisconsin, Wisconsin Center for Educational Research.

Lieberman, A. (1995). *The work of restructuring schools: Building from the ground up.* New York: Teachers College Press.

Little, J.W. (1999). Organizing schools for teacher and student learning. In L. Darling-Hammond and G. Sykes (Eds.), *Teaching as the learning profession: A handbook of policy and practice.* San Francisco: Jossey Bass.

Miles, K. H. (1995). Freeing resources for improving schools: A case study of teacher allocation in Boston public schools. *Educational Evaluation and Policy Analysis,* 17, 476-493.

Miles, K. H. (1997). *Spending more at the edges: Understanding the growth in public school spending from 1967 to 1991.* Ann Arbor, MI: University of Michigan Press.

Miles, K. H., and Darling-Hammond, L. (1998). Rethinking the allocation of teaching resources: Some lessons from high-performing schools. *Educational Evaluation and Policy Analysis,* 20(1), 9-29.

Monk, D. H. (1994). Subject matter preparation of secondary mathematics and science teachers and student achievement. *Economics of Education Review,* 13(2), 125-145.

Monk, D. H., & King, J.A. (1994). Multilevel teacher resource effects in pupil performance in secondary mathematics and science: The case of teacher subject matter preparation. In R.G. Ehrenberg (Ed.), *Choices and consequences: Contemporary policy issues in education* (pp. 29-58). Ithaca, NY: ILR Press.

National Commission on Teaching and America's Future (1996). *What matters most: teaching for America's future.* New York: Author.

National Center for Educational Statistics. (2001). *The digest of educational statistics, 2001*. Washington, DC: US Government Printing Office.

National Education Association (1992). *Status of the American public school teacher, 1990-91*. Washington, DC: Author.

Nelson, F. H., & O'Brien (1993). *How U.S. teachers measure up internationally: A comparative study of teacher pay, training, and conditions of service*. Washington, DC: American Federation of Teachers.

Organization for Economic Cooperation and Development (1995). Education indicators. Paris: Author.

Rettig, M. D., & Canady, R. L. (1993). Unlocking the lockstep high school schedule. *Phi Delta Kappan*, 7, 310-314.

Rothstein, R., & Miles, K.H. (1995). *Where's the money gone?* Washington, DC: Economic Policy Institute.

Sarason, S. B. (1982). *The culture of school and the problem of change*. Boston: Allyn & Bacon.

Shimahara, N. K. (1985). Japanese education and its implications for U. S. education. *Phi Delta Kappan*, 418-421.

Stigler, J. W., & Stevenson, H. W. (1991). How Asian teachers polish each lesson to perfection. *American Educator*, 15, 12-42.

Strauss, R. P., & Sawyer, E.A. (1986). Some new evidence on teacher and student competencies. *Economics of Education Review*, 5(1): 41-48.

Tyack, D. (1974). *The one best system: A history of American urban education*. Cambridge, MA: Harvard University Press.

Tyack, D., & Tobin, W. (1994). The grammar of schooling: Why has it been so hard to change? *American Educational Research Journal*, 31(3), 453-479.

Section IV

Teacher Compensation and Teacher Unions

10

An Early Assessment of Comprehensive Teacher Compensation Change Plans

Allan Odden

University of Wisconsin, Madison

New types of teacher compensation and related performance assessments of teachers are burgeoning all over the country. This chapter describes some of the most ambitious initiatives and proposals and from emerging research provides commentary on their design, operational features, and impact.

Before the 1990s, most efforts to change teacher compensation experimented with versions of merit pay (Hatry, Greiner, & Ashford, 1994; Murnane & Cohen, 1986) or career ladder programs (Freiberg & Knight, 1991; Schlechty, 1989), very few of which worked or lasted. Today's strategies are both different and more varied and include signing bonuses; housing supplements; higher pay levels for teachers in shortage areas like mathematics, science, and technology, or for teachers in hard-to-staff or low-performing schools; salary incentives for teachers who earn certification from the National Board for Professional Teaching Standards; more elaborate knowledge- and skills-based pay (KSBP) incentives (Milanowski, 2001); as well as school-based performance award programs that provide cash bonuses to everyone in a school for improved student performance (for an assessment of the latter, see Kelley, Heneman, & Milanowski [2002], and for examples of the others, see www.wcer.wisc.edu/cpre/tcomp/related).

This chapter describes and assesses key elements of these pay changes and related performance-based teacher evaluation programs in other districts. Section one provides a context for comparison by identifying various elements of employee compensation in any organization. Section two summarizes how and why various pay elements have been changing in the private sector and the parallel rationales for change in public schools. Section three describes the comprehensive new structures in Cincinnati, Philadelphia, and Iowa, focusing on the changes in their base pay structures and the underlying performance-based teacher evaluation systems. Section four analyzes strengths and weaknesses of these programs based on emerging research. Finally, section five identifies policy implications and needed research.

The Elements of Employee Rewards

Total employee cash compensation comprises two major elements: base pay and variable pay (Milkovich & Newman, 1999). Base pay includes salary that is paid consistently on a weekly, biweekly, or monthly basis. Base pay structures generally have a beginning wage, a top wage, and a system-based pay progression for navigating the base pay structure from beginning to top pay.

Most pay structures in the private and public sectors have years of experience as the primary factor in pay progression (Lawler, 1990), sometimes contingent on a satisfactory evaluation. In education, the single-salary schedule provides pay increases for both years of experience (steps) and education units and university degrees (columns). Teaches receive annual step increases up to some given year.

During the past two decades, many organizations in the private sector have created a different mechanism for base-pay progression called "knowledge- and skills-based pay." Under these systems, individuals' base pay is increased when they demonstrate that they have acquired and can effectively use a specified set of knowledge and skills in the workplace (Lawler, 2000). In most organizations, knowledge and skills assessments replace both seniority- and merit-based salary progression (Zingheim & Schuster, 2000).

Knowledge and skills-based pay in education would be very different from the current single-salary schedule (Odden, 2001). Years of experience and education units or degrees variables, indirect indicators of knowledge and skills not linked strongly to student learning (Hanushek, 1997; Murnane, 1983), would be replaced by or supplemented with more direct measures of teacher knowledge, skills, and professional expertise as the basis for pay progression.

The second pay element is variable pay, which is compensation provided in addition to base pay that is usually dependent on organization or group performance. Variable pay could be linked to a private organization's profits, revenues, stock price, or some other factor that is not necessarily economic. It is variable pay because it usually is contingent on meeting or beating a certain profit, revenue, stock price, or customer satisfaction target. In addition, variable pay is generally provided as a bonus payment, so it needs to be earned again each year. Moreover, because private sector firms organize work by teams and groups, variable payouts increasingly are provided to groups or teams of workers (Crandall & Wallace, 1998). School-based performance award programs would be the counterparts in education (Odden & Kelley, 2002). Total "cash compensation" is the sum of base pay and variable pay.

This chapter focuses largely on changes in base-pay progression for teachers represented by the shift from using years of experience and education units or degrees to using assessments of teachers' knowledge, skills, and instructional expertise. An assessment of the design and impact of variable pay elements in education is addressed elsewhere (Kelley et al., 2002).

New Approaches to Compensation and Their Rationales

For at least two decades, change in compensation structures has been rapidly expanding in the private sector (Crandall & Wallace, 1998; Lawler, 1990, 2000; Zingheim & Schuster, 2000). A primary factor for these changes has been change in work organization as a result of performance demands on private sector organizations (see, for example, Heneman, Ledford, & Gresham, 2000). As companies struggle to improve quality and decrease costs, they reorganize how the work is done, which requires individuals to develop and use new knowledge and skills. To reinforce skill acquisition, companies shift all or part of base pay to knowledge and skills, thereby decreasing the emphasis on seniority or years of experience. To help individuals and organizations "get it all right"—i.e., improve organizational results—some portion of pay is also conditioned on improved organizational performance; bonuses are provided to all members of an organization, plant, or team when that group meets or beats a performance-improvement target.

As a result, more companies are providing base pay and base-pay increases to individuals on the basis of knowledge and skills and variable pay to teams on the basis of improved organizational and team performance. In the process, they move away from providing pay increases on the basis of seniority (years of experience) as well as away from individual merit pay (Lawler, 2000; Rynes & Gerhart, 2000; Zingheim & Schuster, 2000).

Parallel Change in the Schools

Similar pressures and rationales for pay change are now affecting the education system (Kelley, 1997). Standards-based education reform seeks to dramatically improve student learning by quantum amounts. In response, nearly all states have developed rigorous content standards for what student should be taught as well as tests that measure student performance in those content areas. To accomplish these goals, initiatives to restructure the education system, including both the nature and quality of instruction and how it would be organized, are evolving (see for example, Bransford, Brown, & Cocking, 1999; Cohen, McLaughlin, & Talbert, 1993; Newmann and Associates, 1996; Wohlstetter, Van Kirk, Robertson, & Mohrman, 1997).

One restructuring emphasis is developing individual and school capacity to teach a standards-based curriculum so that more students learn to higher performance standards. Nearly everyone agrees that most teachers need enhanced knowledge, skills, and instructional expertise to be more effective in teaching students to higher performance standards (Corcoran & Goertz, 1995; Cohen & Ball, 2000).

One strategy, although not the only one, for creating this expertise is a KSBP teacher compensation system (for elaboration, see Conley & Odden, 1995; Mohrman, Mohrman, & Odden, 1996; Odden & Kelley, 2002). A knowledge and skills-based compensation system provides salary increases on the basis of demonstrated performance that new and higher levels of knowledge, skills, and professional expertise have been acquired and can be used effectively in the work environment. Such a system requires a set of teaching standards that describe the knowledge and expertise teachers are to acquire; a method of assessing individual teacher practice to different levels of performance; and linkage of the assessment results to a salary schedule. The teaching standards can also be used to organize professional development; the human resources system could be structured around the common vision of effective instruction reflected in the teaching standards. Such programs pay teachers for what they know and what they can do with what they know.

Such base-pay programs can be enhanced with school-based performance awards, which provide salary bonuses to all individuals in a school when the building as a whole meets preset targets for improved student performance. Such programs pay teachers for what they collectively produce in terms of student results.

Comprehensive Teacher Compensation Structures

Cincinnati, Philadelphia, and Iowa have each adopted or proposed new teacher compensation structures that include various combinations of all the above elements.

Cincinnati[1]

Cincinnati's new plan, jointly designed by teachers and administrators, includes both a KSBP salary structure and a school-based performance bonus (Kellor & Odden, 2000; Odden & Kellor, 2000).

The KSBP structure represents the most dramatic change. The district adopted teaching standards for all of its teachers by adapting the teaching standards in Danielson's (1996) Framework for Teaching. These standards complemented the state's use of the PRAXIS III standards for its new, performance-based teacher licensure system. The Cincinnati teaching standards are organized into four domains: (1) planning and preparing for student learning, (2) creating an environment for learning, (3) teaching for learning, and (4) professionalism. Each domain has additional components (17 total) and elements (66 total), which describe more behaviorally specific teaching practices.

Second, it restructured its teacher evaluation and began to revise its professional development systems around those standards. It replaced its previous traditional teacher evaluation system with a year-long performance assessment, linked to the new teaching standards, that must occur at least once every 5 years. For 2001-02, the new system included five formal observations of teachers, two by the principal and three by a central office teacher evaluator, both of whom were trained in the expertise to do such an evaluation.

The new teacher evaluation system collects multiple types of data—including that culled from the observations—for each of the 17 different teaching components and then, using a common scoring rubric, determines for each domain

---

1 This section draws from Odden and Kelley (2001).

four levels of teacher performance indicated by the data, with a rating of 1 (lowest) to 4 (highest).

Using these results, the district then created a new salary schedule that included five categories of teachers: apprentice, novice, career, advanced, and accomplished. To be placed in each higher category, teachers needed to demonstrate a higher level of professional practice through the new teacher evaluation system. Beginning teachers entered at the apprentice level. "Novice" reflected at least a "2" rating in all domains, and "career" reflected at least a "3" rating in all domains. The "advanced" category required a "4" rating in the instructional domain, a "4" rating in at least one other domain, and a rating of at least "3"in the other two domains. "Accomplished" reflected a "4" rating in all domains.

The goal for the salary schedule was to provide large salary increases for movement from lower to higher categories, i.e., from lower to higher levels of expertise and teacher instructional performance. Indeed, salaries were capped at a maximum within a category if a teacher did not improve his or her practice to the performance level of the next higher category. Teachers also had a fixed number of years to move out of the first two (the two lowest) categories or they lost their job. Thus, beginning teachers had to enhance their professional practice to at least the "career" category to remain teaching in the district.

Figure 10.1 provides details of that Cincinnati salary structure. Each category had a number of experience or "step" increases, but the salary for the top step in any category was below the beginning salary in the next higher category. The numbers shown were those that would have been used to pay teachers for the 2002-03 school year, but the union rejected the pay link in a May 2002 vote.

**Figure 10.1. Cincinnati's Proposed 2002-03
Knowledge and Skills Salary Structure**

Teacher Category	Performance Required	Salary Range Bachelor's Degree	Conditions
Apprentice	Entry level with teacher license	$30,000; no steps	Teachers who fail to advance to "novice" level within 2 years are terminated
Novice	Must be rated "2" or better on all knowledge and skill categories (on a scale of "1" to "4"); pass Praxis III review	$32,000 to $35,750; three steps	Teachers who fail to advance to "career" level within 5 years are terminated
Career	Must be rated "3" or better in all categories	$38,750 to $49,250; three steps	No maximum on number of years in category
Advanced	Must be rated "4" in two categories, including instruction	$52,500 to $55,000; three steps	No maximum on number of years in category
Accomplished	Must be rated "4" in all categories	$60,000 to $62,000; two steps	No maximum on number of years in category

The pay schedule also provided pay increases for other knowledge and skills, such as National Board Certification ($1,000) and a master's degree ($4,600) but only in the area of a teacher's license; for teachers who are licensed in two areas ($1,250); and for various teacher leadership roles ($5,000 to $5,500).

In addition, the new structure includes a school-based performance award program that, to schools that qualify, provides teachers and the principal with a $1,400 salary bonus; classified staff receives a $700 bonus. This pay element continues. Schools that consistently fail to improve performance are redesigned.

Implementation "glitches" for the new evaluation system (Milanowski et al., 2001) led in part to a change in teacher union leadership in May 2001. As a result, several changes were bargained and implemented during the 2001-02 school year. The evaluation system on which the proposed pay structure was based remains in place, unless the union and district negotiate a different system. It is also possible that a less-ambitious performance pay plan could be negotiated in the future. Most of the analytic comments below relate to the evaluation system that was in operation during the 2000-01 and 2001-02 school years. Only time will reveal the overall program's future.

Philadelphia[2]

The 2000 teacher contract required the Philadelphia school district to develop an "enhanced compensation system," largely based on teacher knowledge and skills, as a strategy to improve the quality of instruction and to substantially increase teacher salaries.

The design team, comprised of four administrators and four teachers, adapted the teaching standards in Danielson's (1996) Framework for Teaching. The Philadelphia Professional Teaching Standards include four domains: (1) planning and preparation for student learning, (2) creating an environment for student learning, (3) teaching and learning, and (4) demonstrating professionalism. Each domain has a number of additional components and elements that describe more behaviorally specific teaching practices.

At least once every 5 years, teachers must undergo a "comprehensive review" of their practice that provides a summative conclusion that their performance meets one of four different performance levels: teacher II, teacher III, teacher IV, or teacher V. In reaching this conclusion, the scores for each domain are weighted according to the following percentages: (1) 30%, (2) 20%, (3) 40%, and (4) 10%. Specific rubrics were developed to guide assessors in how to take all the evidence gathered from a multiple-month process and produce a teacher rating. The teacher I category is for the beginning teacher with no experience.

In addition to a portfolio and other material evidence—which likely includes lesson plans, examples of student work, teacher reflections on the effectiveness of their instruction, and logs of parent interactions—each teacher is observed four

---

2 Based on an April 2001 draft plan that serves as the basic outline for the 2002-03 pilot.

times during the comprehensive review year. The principal and peer assessors each conduct two observations. Both are trained and certified as being able to make reliable assessments of teacher practice to the performance levels.

In addition to performance, the team also added knowledge requirements for each teacher level. Passing the ETS Praxis II content and professional tests are required for the initial license. Then increasing numbers of either higher education or district provided content units are required for each level. Content knowledge may also be demonstrated via "authentic assessments," which are yet to be developed. Movement up through the levels requires both performance and content. Figure 10.2 shows how the system could be linked to a salary grid in the April 2001 plan.

The comprehensive review for the teacher II level excludes a few components in both domains 1 and 4. Teachers also must be reviewed and move to the teacher II level during either the second or third year of teaching or they lose their job in the district. For teachers at the teacher II, III, and IV levels, National Board Certification substitutes for a comprehensive review and demonstration of content knowledge and automatically moves the teacher to the next level. At the teacher V level, National Board Certification substitutes for three district knowledge credits. The district is still in the process of developing knowledge and performance requirements for movement into the teacher VI category. Finally, movement into both the teacher IV and teacher V levels can be done for either the content or performance dimension for half the salary increment, but both dimensions are required for movement to the next higher level.

Figure 10.2. Philadelphia's Proposed 2001-02 Enhanced Compensation Salary Structure

Teacher Category	Performance Required	Knowledge Requirements	Salary Range
Teacher I	Entry level with initial license (instructor I)	Praxis II content and professional tests	$34,000 to $38,000, including two $2,000 steps
Teacher II	Professional license (instructor II) Tenure Comprehensive review in all four domains	Twenty-four higher-education or 24 district-content credits	$40,000 to $42,000, including two $1,000 steps
Teacher III	Comprehensive review in all four domains	Master's degree in area related to K-12 or 15 additional district-content credits	$45,000 to $47,000, including two $1,000 steps
Teacher IV	Comprehensive review in all four domains	Master's degree plus 30 credits or 30 teacher IV district-content credits	$50,000 to $58,000, including four $2,000 steps
Teacher V	Comprehensive review in all four domains	Second certification in area of district need or teacher V district-content credits (number to be determined)	$60,000 to $68,000, including four $2,000 steps
Teacher VI	Under development	$78,000 maximum	

In addition, the enhanced compensation system provides salary incentives ($1,500) for teachers in shortage areas (bilingual education, special education, Spanish, chemistry, mathematics, and physics) and teachers in hard-to-staff schools ($2,000), most of which are high-poverty, low-performing schools.

The entire new plan will be piloted during the 2002-03 school year because of turmoil in the district during the 2001-02 year. The enhanced compensation system augments the district's school-based performance award program (Kellor, Odden, & Conti, 1999).

Iowa

In May 2001, Iowa's Governor Tom Vilsak signed a bill that established a new salary structure for all of Iowa's teachers to begin a process of substantially increasing teacher salaries, a reform led by the governor; the business community, whose point person was Marvin Pomerantz, a former President of the Iowa Board of Regents; and the legislature. The bill creates the structure within which the state is to design the specifics of both a KSBP structure, and a variable-pay bonus program.

The bill adopted a set of teaching standards based largely on the general standards of the Interstate New Teacher Assessment and Support Consortium (see Porter, Youngs, & Odden, 2001; Youngs, Odden, & Porter, in press). The bill requires the Department of Education to elaborate these standards to give them more specific meaning. The core state standards also may be enhanced at the local level.

The bill also developed a four-level career path for teachers based on performance to the teaching standards: beginning, career, career 2, and advanced. During the next 3 years, the department is required to develop an assessment system that will determine when a teacher's practice meets the performance standards for each level of the career path and to develop an aligned professional development system. The assessment for "career" and "career 2" is a comprehensive evaluation to be conducted by state trained local administrators at least once every 5 years. State-trained members of up to five new regional Review Panels will conduct the assessment for "advanced." Movement up the career path is contingent on passing both these state-designed evaluations and a local evaluation. Teachers will be able to move up the career path level by level, i.e., there will be no jumping over any level, but teachers can ask for a comprehensive review more often than once every 5 years to move up the career path more quickly.

Districts must create and administer a department-approved, 2-year teacher mentoring and induction program that is linked to the teaching standards and designed to help beginning teachers enhance their beginning instructional skills to the "career" level. New teachers may remain in the program for an optional third year, but if after that time period their practice does not meet the standards for the "career" level, they lose their jobs. Districts must also create ongoing professional development programs for "career II" and "advanced" teachers that also are aligned with the new teaching standards.

Figure 10.3 shows how the various performance requirements are linked to salary levels and the minimum salary levels to be in effect by July 2003. The goal of the fully phased-in program is to increase teacher salaries by $5000 to $6000 on average. Districts can create step increases within each category, but the top step must always be $2,000 below the beginning salary in the next highest category.

It is the goal of the legislature to implement a school-based, variable-pay bonus plan for all schools beginning September 2003. In the interim, the bill provides for local district-designed pilot programs for team-based variable pay for the next 2 years.

Figure 10.3. Proposed Teacher Salary Structure in Iowa

Career Path Level	Requirements	Minimum Salary
Beginning	Provisional license; passes Praxis II content test; participates in a state approved mentoring; and induction program	Increases by $1,500/y until reaches $28,000
Career	Passes comprehensive evaluation; successfully completes mentoring and induction program; participates in ongoing professional development	Must be $2,000 higher than beginning or at least $30,000; immediate increase for experienced teacher if current salary is less than $30,000
Career II	Passes comprehensive evaluation; participates in ongoing professional development	Must be $5,000 higher than beginning or at least $35,000
Advanced	Passes evaluation conducted by a regional review panel; possesses skills and qualifications to assume leadership roles	Must be $13,500 higher than beginning or at least $43,500

Assessment of the Programs

The theory of action for a KSBP evaluation and compensation system is much the same for both public and private sector organizations (Lawler, 1990; Odden & Kelley, 2002) and the following is the education version. First, classroom instruction is the key factor under the control of school districts that determines student achievement (Slavin & Fashola, 1998; Sanders, Saxton, & Horn, 1997; Wright, Horn, & Sanders, 1997). Improved student performance, therefore, is produced largely by improved instruction. Drawing from expectancy theory (Vroom, 1964), KSBP systems seek to provide incentives to teachers to improve their instructional capacity, hopefully enhancing teacher motivation to add to their instructional repertoire. By linking pay levels to knowledge and skills, the new salary structure will hopefully attract and retain teachers who develop the desired instructional practice and discourage those that do not. The result should be better classroom instruction and improved student performance. Finally, the entire human resources system can then be redesigned around a common vision of instruction, integrating the substantive focus of recruitment, induction, development, and evaluation of teachers around a set of teaching standards that reflect that vision (see Milanowski [2001] for an elaboration of this argument).

To work, then, KSBP and evaluation systems must identify the instructional strategies that produce improved student learning; the assessment system must be valid, reliable, and fully implemented; other human resources programs such professional development must be aligned to the standards so teachers have opportunities to improve their practice to the standards; the salary incentives must be large enough to motivate teachers to exert effort to improve their skills, provide the expected economic impacts, and be fully funded; and over time the link between higher teacher performance and improved student learning must be identified.

This chapter draws from some of the early findings of several research projects on these new pay programs (and similar performance-based teacher assessment systems in other districts) and addresses four key topics linked to their operation and potential impact: the nature of the standards, the assessment process itself, alignment to other human resources systems, and incentive levels and funding.

The Knowledge and Skills Identified, or, the Teaching Standards

The three jurisdictions adopted some variation of the teaching standards developed by Danielson (1996). These standards are quite far reaching and cover a teacher's activities from lesson planning, to classroom management, instruction, parental outreach, and involvement in professional activities. In this way, they capture most of the actions of good teachers.

However, three possible shortcomings must be addressed during implementation for such standards to incentivize improved instructional practices that will boost student achievement. The first is that the standards need specific content meaning. Understandably, Danielson (1986) provided a general framework for good teaching; the framework was designed for use by all teachers in all subjects at all levels. But good teaching is content specific and linked to the development level of the student (Bransford et al., 1999; Shulman, 1987). Thus, for teachers to show that they know content and how students learn that content, including the common errors students make for a specific aspect of the content, the teaching evidence gathered and assessed must be specific to the content and the grade level taught (Bruer, 1993). This knowledge is commonly called "content-specific pedagogy" and is key for teaching most students to high performance standards.

Unfortunately, getting systematic information about this kind of instructional practice may be difficult in the three jurisdictions. Neither principals, who are centrally involved in all three places, nor the small number of teacher assessors know all these content aspects for all teachers they evaluate. This means they may not gather data about content-specific pedagogy or have that focus pervade whatever instructional conversations occur. Indeed, early research on these kinds of teacher assessments suggests that this can be a shortcoming (Kimball, 2001; Milanowski et al., 2001).

A second possible shortcoming is that at some point evidence must show that standards describe teacher actions that lead to higher levels of student achievement. Although it is true that the standards already draw from research on effective teachers (see Danielson, 1996; Dwyer, 1994), there remains skepticism about whether what is actually collected on teacher performance represents teacher actions that produce higher levels of student achievement. This challenge is also true for the National Board's standards (see, for example, Podgursky [2001]). Over time, research needs to show that the actions in the standards are linked to improved student learning.

The third shortcoming is the comprehensiveness of the standard. The standards cover activities that go far beyond just instruction (eg, parent outreach, liaison with social service agencies, etc.). This makes the data-gathering process more complex and sends signals that instructional practices per se are not necessarily the top priority. Although good teachers engage in a variety of professional activities, jurisdictions might want to focus the summative performance assessment on just instructional practices, both to underscore its importance and to make the performance assessment system a bit simpler. Interim evaluation actions in between the comprehensive assessment periods could cover other important but noninstructional teacher activities. The results from both could be combined somehow to determine whether the teacher's overall performance warrants promotion to the next-higher performance and pay category.

The Performance-Based Assessment System

All three jurisdictions have, or in the future will implement, new teacher assessment systems, linked to the standards, which identify three to five different levels of teaching practice. As such, the systems represent dramatic improvements on traditional teacher evaluation system and improvements over these jurisdictions' previous evaluation systems. The new systems are more comprehensive, gather multiple forms of data over the course of a year, have guidelines for scoring all data items to different performance levels, and are specifically linked to explicit teaching standards, which in turn are linked to curriculum content standards.

Implementation and operation, however, must be carefully monitored. Research is showing that teachers are anxious about these new systems, at least during initial implementation (Milanowski & Heneman, 2001; Milanowski et al., 2001). Performance-based teacher assessment systems that are used to determine pay levels change the rules for teacher evaluation and pay and create something of a culture shock in the system. As a result, there is a high level of teacher anxiety. Teachers are used to getting a satisfactory evaluation to a low standard, which they interpret as indicative of doing well. The new evaluation systems provide a more varied profile of their practice, showing strengths and weaknesses relative to a high standard. Teachers are concerned about whether their performance will place them in a high-enough pay category. These systems make instruction much more public, opening the closed and private door of instructional practice to public scrutiny. These anxieties need to be recognized and addressed. Anxiety is a feeling, an emotional response. Districts must show understanding and empathy when these feelings emerge and work closely with and help teachers through at least the first cycle of evaluations. Getting the system up and running well will help ameliorate initial concerns; doing so should be the focus during initial implementation.

Several related issues might be raised about the operation of these performance assessment systems. The first is that they are complex and require considerable time and resources to implement (see Kimball, 2001; Milanowski et al., 2001). For example, 66 teaching elements exist in the Danielson framework; elements are the specific teaching behaviors that describe in detail a particular teaching component that is part of a teaching domain. Multiple types of evidence are gathered for most elements. These various data items are gathered using approximately 6 to 10 different data collection forms, including multiple observations of teachers, and teacher portfolios. Simply arraying all the data from all the sources across all the teaching elements, and then applying scoring rubrics to determine a level of practice indicated by the data, is a huge task. The question is whether it constitutes too large a task.

A related issue is the time-consuming nature of the observations. For example, the Philadelphia proposal would require four observations, two conducted by the principal and two by a peer evaluator. Initially, each observation also requires a preconference conversation, the observation, the write-up, and a postobservation conference. There also is a final summative conference with the teacher at the end of the year. This process could require, at a minimum, 8 hours of interaction with each teacher during the summative year by the principal and 6 hours by the other evaluator. That is a lot of time, and during the pilot, the initial conferences were eliminated. In Anoka-Hennepin (MN), which uses such a system but does not link it to pay, the principals conduct all the observations and raise issues of work overload (Kimball, 2001). In Cincinnati, teachers undergo five observations, but to save time, the preobservation and postobservation conferences were eliminated for the first year of full implementation. The question is whether live classroom observations require too much time and whether a less time-consuming strategy to gather evidence on active classroom practice, such as videotaping, is needed.

A third issue is that a complete picture of instruction, particularly content-specific pedagogy, is difficult to measure in a classroom observation. This is more appropriately revealed during the teaching of multiple lessons that comprise a curriculum unit designed to teach a specific concept in a content area (see, for example, Moss, Shultz, & Collins, 1998; Porter et al., 2001). Thus, not only are multiple classroom observations difficult to implement, but also they may not be the best strategy for identifying instruction comprehensively or that aspect of instruction, i.e., content specific teaching, that is most linked to having more students learn to high standards.

Fourth, and a dicey issue, none of these systems so far use evidence for an individual teacher about the learning gains of their own students as part of the evidence that is reviewed. Doing so would be controversial. Yet, there are techniques that could be used to gather such evidence at least for teachers of academic subjects (Stronge & Tucker, 2000). Some districts (Seattle [WA] and

Douglas County [CO]) are beginning to do so, as does the teacher evaluation model from the Milken Family Foundation (Schacter, 2000). Until such evidence on student learning growth is included at least to some degree in ambitious new teacher assessment systems, many will remain skeptical about the validity of the systems.

Finally, each system will need to prove the consequential validity of their systems, i.e., show over time that teachers who score higher actually do produce larger improvements in student academic achievement. Teaching matters in terms of student achievement, and some teachers are more effective than others (Sanders et al., 1997; Wright et al., 1997). Preliminary research in Cincinnati (Holtzapple, 2001) and the Vaughn Charter School in Los Angeles (Gallagher, 2002), which has a similar compensation system, has linked higher evaluation scores to greater value-added student achievement. However, more research is needed.

Alignment with Other Human Resources Elements

Both ongoing formative evaluations of the assessment systems (Milanowski & Kellor, 2000b; Milanowski et al., 2001)—and studies of the assessment systems in districts that have adopted teaching standards and performance assessments but not yet linked them to pay (Kimball, 2001)—suggest that operational complexities (discussed above) often diminish efforts to have rich interactions around effective instruction. If these new programs simply add to administrative complexity without furthering instructional improvement work, they will have difficulty sustaining themselves over the long-term because their prime rationale, to improve instruction, will not be attained.

With so much work exerted just to implement the standards-based teacher evaluation system, Cincinnati (Milanowski et al., 2001) and other districts (Kimball, 2001) also did not initially align other elements of their human resources system either with their teaching standards or with the new evaluation system. For example, completing all aspects of the performance reviews did not become part of principal evaluations, nor were professional development systems aligned with the new teaching standards. The latter was a major problem in Cincinnati, and the new teacher union leaders bargained with the district to postpone full implementation for 4 years during which professional development offerings are to be tailored to their new teaching standards.

A more subtle alignment problem in both Cincinnati and other districts was that the form of the evaluation system did not reflect what was done in typical professional development, so it appeared that the two systems were completely different. Connecting the two requires careful thought about how both systems can be designed. One way to make the two strategies look more similar would be to structure instructional improvement around standards-based curriculum units (Cohen & Hill, 2001) and to have the instructional portfolio in the comprehensive review also structured around a curriculum unit, as are the portfolios for Connecticut's performance-based teacher licensure system and the National Board Certification system. In this way, core pieces of both professional development and teacher evaluation would be the same, and teachers could more easily see a connection between their instructional improvement efforts and the nature and focus of the assessment and evaluation system.

Level of the Incentives, Costs, and Funding

All of the plans, on paper, provide substantial salary increases. Teachers in all three jurisdictions expressed general satisfaction with the proposed increases, concluding that the increases were "worth" the change in the salary system.

Whether those increases will be produced depends on whether the plans are fully funded. To date there are mixed data on whether the programs will be successful in garnering additional money. To be sure, new money for education—for whatever purpose—is hard to obtain and even harder in a weak national economy. But when teachers and their unions agree to a major overhaul in how they are paid—essentially shifting from the current, well-understood, and predictable single-salary structure to a different, knowledge and skills structure—they expect and deserve large salary increases. But dollars for higher salary are scarce in Cincinnati, provide only a small down payment in Iowa (they were borrowed from tobacco settlement funds rather than from the general fund), and are uncertain in Philadelphia (as was everything in 2002). Without concrete evidence that accepting dramatic new pay structures does produce substantial new dollars, other places may likely be more reluctant to embrace such comprehensive changes at least for the goal of boosting teacher salary levels.

Full funding is important for program sustainability because early research suggests that teachers like many aspects of these new approaches to compensation. In general, there is strong teacher support for explicit teaching standards (Milanowski & Kellor, 2000a, 2000b; Milanowski et al., 2001; Kimball, 2001) and, when the evaluation system is understandable and viewed as fair, for performance-based evaluation (Milanowski & Heneman, 2001) and compensation linkage as well (Milanowski & Kellor, 2000a). However, support is stronger among newer and mid-career teachers and weaker among senior teachers, which often leads program designers to provide "sweeteners" or opt-out provisions for senior teachers (Milanowski, 2001).

Research and Policy Implications

Several important research and policy implications have evolved from these programs already. Both are important not only for Cincinnati, Philadelphia, and Iowa but also for other states and districts that might adopt similar programs.

Implications for Future Research

Three important research implications are as follows. The first is determining whether and how the programs lead to change in instructional practice. This research should have a three-part focus: (1) Do the systems stimulate and/or reinforce district actions—such as different types of professional development; expanded numbers of professional development opportunities; and probably longer professional development programs that include some combination of summer institutes as well as ongoing coaching within an individual teacher's classroom—that help teachers' improve their instructional practice? (2) Do the programs stimulate district-wide discussions of quality instruction focused on improving instructional practice and if not, why not? (3) Do the programs increase the amount of content-specific pedagogical instruction? If none of these happens, the goals of the programs—to improve instruction in ways that increase student achievement—likely will be in jeopardy.

The second research issue is whether the changes in instructional practice that result can actually be linked to increased student achievement, i.e., to document the consequential validity of the systems. The hope is that the data collected in the new teacher assessment systems are the teacher activities that, if deployed in classrooms and schools, do produce higher levels of student learning. Research needs to identify those core teacher actions that do produce improvements in student achievement, and to make sure that those actions comprise the core of the teaching standards as well as the focus of the performance assessment systems.

The third is to identify what should be the appropriate minimum salary benchmarks for the various different categories of teacher performance (Goldhaber, 2001, provides some beginning evidence on this issue). One key goal of the new approaches to teacher compensation is to produce salary levels that enable schools to compete for teacher quality in the broader labor market. It would be a bitter disappointment to develop new approaches to compensation that were effective in helping teachers to develop an array of instructional expertise that improved student performance, only to have the private sector lure those accomplished individuals away with salary offers that were simply too high for an individual teacher to turn down.

Implications for District and State Policymakers

Several implications exist for district and state policymakers thinking about designing compensation changes as dramatic as those undertaken in Cincinnati, Philadelphia, and Iowa. The first is to spend sufficient time developing a specific set of teaching standards. Such efforts should show how a general framework would be implemented for different content areas, i.e., the framework should be clear about how it includes content specific pedagogy. In addition, the standards must be modified for teachers who do not teach traditional academic content, such as guidance counselors, librarians, social workers, and teachers of the disabled.

Second, jurisdictions should think about developing more focused and less complex teacher assessment systems and perhaps even to make distinctions between the teacher assessment systems and teacher evaluations. To do this, jurisdictions could decrease the number of "live" classroom observations by substituting videotapes of important aspects of classroom lessons for some if not all observations. Furthermore, if the videos were provided as part of a parsimonious teacher portfolio structured around the teaching of a specific concept in a particular content area, they could be one of many pieces of evidence showing how an individual taught a standards-based curriculum unit. Further still, expert teachers in the specific content areas could centrally assess these portfolios. This would insure assessment of content specific pedagogy by an expert as well as decrease the time required to administer the assessment system. Other aspects of teacher behavior, including some direct observations, could be covered in a broader evaluation structure.

The portfolio of the Connecticut performance-based teacher licensure system is already structured in the manner described above and, furthermore, has a four-level scoring rubric, only one of which is meant to be used for professional teacher licensure. This portfolio and its scoring rubric could serve as a model for streamlining and improving the current programs that rely so heavily on direct observations (Connecticut Department of Education, 2001; Pecheone & Stansbury, 1996).

Third, all individuals who are involved in the performance assessment of teachers, which for the next several years will include principals, need to know how to recognize good instruction and how to conduct reliable assessments of teachers. Thus, this expertise needs to be incorporated into requirements for earning a principal's license.

Fourth, both quality and efficiency arguments exist for doing all of the above on a statewide basis. Asking each school district to develop quality standards, a valid and reliable performance-based teacher assessment system, and related professional development on their own could exceed reasonable expectations. States could create the core elements of such systems, which could be elaborated at the local level if desired.

Summary

Cincinnati, Philadelphia, and Iowa and many other districts and states are creating and implementing fundamentally new approaches to teacher compensation and evaluation. Other districts are developing standards-based teacher evaluation systems without the link to pay. The scope of these efforts is both broad and deep. Their ambitious programs offer potential for dramatically improving teacher instructional performance, their pay levels, and their impacts on student learning. However, as is the case with any such pioneering new efforts, the leaders may not get all aspects of the programs right in the initial years of design implementation.

Early research on the design and operation of these and related programs show both promise and pitfalls. While these jurisdictions change and improve their programs as they move through the initial implementation period, it is hoped that others who follow will learn from their efforts and that over the next 10 years, the country will learn how best to design and implement new KSBP teacher compensation structures and their aligned performance assessment and professional development systems. We know that simply increasing salaries in the current structure produces neither enhances teacher quality nor better student performance (Ballou & Podgursky, 1997). KSBP salary structures—and perhaps others that have yet to be designed and implemented—do have this potential, particularly if the findings in the Vaughn Charter School and the Cincinnati Public Schools on the validity of their evaluation systems hold up under future research.

Acknowledgment

This chapter was prepared for the Consortium for Policy Research in Education, Wisconsin Center for Education Research, University of Wisconsin-Madison. The research reported in this chapter was supported by a grant from the United States Department of Education, Office of Educational Research and Improvement, National Institute on Educational Governance, Finance, Policymaking and Management, to the Consortium for Policy Research in Education (CPRE) (Grant No. OERI-R308A60003); the Carnegie Corporation; private donors; and the Wisconsin Center for Education Research, School of Education, University of Wisconsin-Madison. The opinions expressed are those of the authors and do not necessarily reflect the view of the National Institute on Educational Governance, Finance, Policymaking and Management, Office of Educational Research and Improvement, United States Department of Education; the Carnegie Corporation; the private donors; the institutional partners of CPRE; or the Wisconsin Center for Education Research.

References

Ballou, D. & Podgursky, M. (1997). *Teacher pay and teacher quality*. Kalamazoo, MI: W.E. Upjohn Institute for Employment Research.

Bransford, J., Brown, A., & Cocking, R. (1999). *How people learn*. Washington, DC: National Academy Press.

Bruer, J.T. (1993). *Schools for thought: A science of learning in the classroom*. Cambridge, MA: MIT Press.

Cohen, D., & Ball, D. (1999). *Instruction, Capacity and Improvement*. Philadelphia: University of Pennsylvania, Graduate School of Education, Consortium for Policy Research in Education.

Cohen, D.K., & Hill, H.C. (2001). *Learning policy: When state education reform works*. New Haven, CT: Yale University Press.

Cohen, D.K., McLaughlin, M., & Talbert, J. (1993). *Teaching for understanding: Challenges for policy and practice*. San Francisco: Jossey-Bass.

Conley, S.C., & Odden, A. (1995). Linking teacher compensation to teacher career development. *Educational Evaluation and Policy Analysis* 17(2), 219-237.

Connecticut State Department of Education (2001). *The Beginning Educator Support and Training (Best) program, handbook for the development of a teaching portfolio: Science, 2001-2002*. Hartford, CT: Connecticut State Department of Education, Bureau of Evaluation and Educator Standards.

Corcoran, T., & Goertz, M. (1995). Instructional capacity and high performance schools. *Educational Researcher* 24(9), 27-31.

Crandall, N.F., & Wallace Jr., M.J. (1998). *Work and rewards in the virtual workplace*. New York: American Management Association-Amacom.

Danielson, C. (1996). *Enhancing professional practice: A framework for teaching*. Alexandria, VA: Association for Supervision and Curriculum Development.

Dwyer, C.A. (1994). *Development of the knowledge base for the praxis III: Classroom performance assessment criteria*. Princeton, NJ: Educational Testing Service.

Freiberg, H.J. & Knight, S.L. (1991). Career Ladder Programs as Incentives for Teachers. In S.C. Conley, B.S. Cooper (Eds.), *The school as a work environment: Implications for reform* (pp. 204-235). Boston: Allyn & Bacon, 1991.

Gallagher, H.A. (2002). The relationships between measures of teacher quality and student achievement: The case of Vaughn Elementary (working paper TC-02-5). Madison, WI: University of Wisconsin, Wisconsin Center for Education Research, Consortium for Policy Research in Education.

Goldhaber, D. (2001). How Has Teacher Compensation Changed? In w. Fowler Jr. (Ed.), *Selected Papers in School Finance: 2000-2001. Washington, DC: National Center for Education Statistics.*

Hanushek, E.A. (1997). Assessing the effects of school resources on student performance: An update. Educational Evaluation and Policy Analysis, 19(2), 141-164.

Hatry, H.P., Greiner, J.M., & Ashford, B.G. (1994). Issues and case studies in teacher incentive plans (2nd ed.). Washington, DC: Urban Institute Press.

Heneman, R.L., Jr., Ledford, G.E., & Gresham. M.T. (2000). The changing nature of work and its effects on compensation design and delivery. In S.L. Tynes & B. Gerhart (Eds.), *Compensation in organizations: Current research and practice* (pp. 195-240). San Francisco: Jossey-Bass.

Holtzapple, E. (2001). *Report on the validation of teachers evaluation system instructional domain ratings*. Cincinnati: Cincinnati Public Schools.

Kelley, C. (1997). Teacher compensation and organization. *Educational Evaluation and Policy Analysis*, 19(1), 15-28.

Kelley, C., Heneman, H.G. III, & Milanowski, A. (2002). Teacher motivation, and school-based performance award programs. *Educational Administration Quarterly*, 38(3), 372-401.

Kellor, E., & Odden, A. (2000). *Cincinnati: A case study of the design of a school-based performance award program*. Madison, WI: University of Wisconsin-Madison, Wisconsin. Center for Education Research, Consortium for Policy Research in Education. [Available from: http://www.wcer.wisc.edu/cpre/pdfs.htm#rr].

Kellor, E., Odden, A., & Conti, E. (1999). *A case study of the school based performance award program in the district of Philadelphia public schools*. Madison, WI: University of Wisconsin-Madison, Wisconsin Center for Education Research, Consortium for Policy Research in Education. [Available from: http://www.wcer.wisc.edu/cpre/pdfs.htm#rr].

Kimball, S. (2001). Innovations in teacher evaluation: Case studies of two school districts with teacher evaluation systems based on the framework for teaching. Unpublished doctoral dissertation, University of Wisconsin-Madison.

Lawler, E.E. (1990). *Strategic pay: Aligning organizational strategies and pay systems*. San Francisco: Jossey-Bass.

Lawler, E.E. III. (2000). *Rewarding excellence: Pay strategies for the new economy*. San Francisco: Jossey-Bass.

Milanowski, A. (2001). The varieties of knowledge and skill-based pay design: A comparison of seven new pay systems for k-12 teachers (working paper TC-01-2). Madison, WI: University of Wisconsin-Madison, Wisconsin Center for Education Research, Consortium for Policy Research in Education.

Milanowski, A., & Heneman, H.G. III. (2001). Assessment of teacher reactions to a standards-based teacher evaluation system: A pilot study. *Journal for Personnel Evaluation in Education*, 15(3), 193-212.

Milanowski, A., & Kellor, E. (2000). *Preliminary report on the performance pay survey*. Madison, WI: University of Wisconsin-Madison, Wisconsin Center for Education Research, Consortium for Policy Research in Education.

Milanowski, A., & Kellor, E. (with assistance from Heneman, H. III & Odden, A.). (2000). *Teacher and evaluator reactions to standards-based teacher evaluation in the Cincinnati public schools: An evaluation of the 1999-2000 field test of the new evaluation system*. Madison, WI: University of Wisconsin-Madison, Wisconsin Center for Education Research, Consortium for Policy Research in Education.

Milanowski, A., Kellor, E., Odden, A., Heneman, H.G. III, White, B, Allen, J., & Mack K. (2001). Final report on the evaluation of the 2000-2001 implementation of the Cincinnati federation of teachers/Cincinnati public schools teacher evaluation system (working paper TC-01-3). Madison, WI: University of Wisconsin-Madison, Wisconsin Center for Education Research, Consortium for Policy Research in Education.

Milkovich, G,T., & Newman, J. (1999). *Compensation* (6th ed.). Burr Ridge, IL: Irwin/McGraw-Hill.

Mohrman, A., Mohrman, S.A., & Odden, A. (1996). Aligning teacher compensation with systemic school reform: Skill-based pay and group-based performance rewards." *Educational Evaluation and Policy Analysis*, 18(1), 51-71.

Moss, P.A., Schutz, A.M., & Collins, K. (1998). An integrative approach to portfolio evaluation for teacher licensure certification. *Journal of Personnel Evaluation in Education*, 12(2), 139-161.

Murnane, R. (1983). Quantitative studies of effective schools: What have we learned? In A. Odden & L. D. Webb (Eds.), *School Finance and School Improvement: Linkages for the 1980s* (pp. 193-209). Cambridge, MA: Ballinger.

Murnane, R., & Cohen, D. (1986). Merit pay and the evaluation problem: Why some merit pay plans fail and a few survive. *Harvard Educational Review*, 56(1), 1-17.

Newmann & Associates (1996). *Authentic achievement: Restructuring schools for intellectual quality*. San Francisco: Jossey-Bass.

Odden, A. (2001). Rewarding expertise. *Education Matters*, 1(1), 16-24.

Odden, A., & Kelley, C. (2002). *Paying teachers for what they know and do: New and smarter compensation strategies to improve schools* (2nd ed.). Thousand Oaks, CA: Corwin Press.

Odden, A., & Kellor, E. (2000). *How Cincinnati developed a knowledge- and skills-based salary schedule.* Accessed http://www.wcer.wisc.edu/cpre/pdfs.htm#rr.

Pecheone, R., & Stansbury, K. (1996). Connecting Teacher Assessment and School Reform. *Elementary School Journal*, 97(2), 163-177.

Podgursky, M. (2001). Defrocking the national board. *Education Matters*, 1(2), 79-82.

Porter, A., Youngs, P., & Odden, A. (2001). Advances in Teacher Assessment and Their Uses. In V. Richardson (Ed.), *Handbook of Research on Teaching* (pp. 259-297). New York: Macmillan.

Rynes, S.L., & Gerhart, B. (2000). *Compensation in organizations: Current research and practice.* San Francisco: Jossey-Bass.

Sanders, W.L., Saxton, A.M., & Horn, S.P. (1997). The Tennessee value-added accountability system: A quantitative, outcomes-based approach to educational assessment. In J. Millman (Ed.), *Grading teachers, grading schools: Is student achievement a valid evaluation measure?* (pp. 137-162). Thousand Oaks, CA: Corwin Press.

Schacter, J. (2000). *Teacher Advancement program performance-based accountability.* Santa Monica, CA: Milken Family Foundation.

Schlechty, P.C. (1989). Career ladders: A good idea going awry. In T.J. Sergiovanni, & J.H. Moore (Eds.), *Schooling for tomorrow: Directing reforms to issues that count* (pp. 356-376). Boston: Allyn & Bacon.

Shulman, L. (1987). Knowledge and teaching: Foundations of the new reform. *Harvard Educational Review*, 57, 1-22.

Slavin, R., & Fashola, O. (1998). *Show me the evidence! Proven and promising programs for America's schools.* Thousand Oaks, CA: Corwin Press.

Stronge, J.H., & Tucker, P. (2000). Teacher evaluation and student achievement. Washington, DC: National Education Association.

Vroom, V.H. (1964). *Work and motivation.* New York: John Wiley.

Wohlstetter, P., Van Kirk, A., Robertson, P., & Mohrman, S. (1997). *Organizing for successful school-based management.* Alexandria, VA: Association for Supervision and Curriculum Development.

Wright, P.S., Horn, S.P., & Sanders, W.L. (1997). Teacher and classroom context effects on student achievement: Implications for teacher evaluation. *Journal of Personnel Evaluation in Education*, 11, 57-67.

Youngs, P., Odden, A., & Porter, A.C. (in press). State policy related to teacher licensure. *Educational Policy.*

Zingheim, P., & Schuster, P. (2000). *Pay people right! Breakthrough reward strategies to create great companies.* San Francisco: Jossey-Bass.

11

Distributing The Pie: Allocating Resources Through Labor–Management Agreements

Julia E. Koppich
Koppich and Associates

When most people think about school improvement, education reform, efficient use of scarce fiscal resources, or responsible education decision making, "union" is not typically the first word that comes to mind. Conventional wisdom has it that, particularly where dollars are concerned, unions are singularly interested in enhancing the salaries of those whom they represent.

To be sure, unions (for purposes of this chapter, teacher unions) strive, through negotiated labor–management agreements, to ensure competitive salaries for their members. However, the notion that teacher unions are interested in using finite fiscal resources only to sustain and improve salary levels belies an emerging truth in a number of school district–union partnerships.

In the locales that are the subject of this chapter, union and management are reallocating existing funds, as well as generating new funds, for improved and expanded educational purposes. Minneapolis' Achievement of Tenure process, Denver's evolving Pay-for-Performance compensation system, Seattle's Weighted Student Formula, and Maryland's Montgomery County Professional Growth System all reflect the use of fiscal resources to structure different kinds of labor–management agreements than are the usual subject of discourse and critique.

In these places, labor–management agreements form the foundation of programs designed to improve teaching and learning. As a result, negotiating the allocation of dollars serves to broaden the purpose and scope of union–management accords well beyond standard salaries and benefits.

Minneapolis: Making Tenure Meaningful

The word "tenure" has taken on a life of its own where K-12 education is concerned. Often equated with a lifetime guarantee of employment, tenure is cited by its critics as the reason poorly performing teachers cannot be dismissed. Tenure is intended to be a guarantee of due process. It is meant to serve as protection from arbitrary firing by requiring that a teacher who passes a probationary period and achieves tenure earn the right to a hearing when the employer threatens dismissal for cause.

Over time, however, a combination of cumbersome bureaucratic requirements and poorly designed and administered teacher evaluation procedures has added to tenure's reputation as a lifetime employment sinecure. Teacher unions have helped to burnish this reputation by sometimes defending the honor of tenure without reaffirming its meaning as due process rather than protection of those who should not be teaching

Although tenure has acquired a particular, and often negative, connotation, probation—the period leading up to tenure—often has little meaning at all. In many school districts, passing probation and achieving tenure means little more than surviving the first 2 or 3 years of teaching. Although it is true that large numbers of teachers leave the profession within the first year or two, most who do so make this choice based on the difficulty of working conditions or because the job is not what they expected it to be. For those who choose to remain in teaching through the early years, evaluation of professional competence typically is less than rigorous (Darling-Hammond, Wise, & Pease, 1983; Haertle, 1986; Medley & Coker, 1987). The result is that nearly everyone who wants to achieve tenure does so.

A number of districts and their unions have taken steps to make probation more like what is meant to be. In these settings, a system of peer assistance and review (PAR) transforms probation into a period of professional induction in which novices continue to learn their craft and are rigorously evaluated to determine their readiness for independent practice. As a result of PAR, new teachers, who receive concentrated support, are more likely to remain in the profession long-term, and those beginners for whom teaching proves to be a mistaken career choice are not awarded continuing contracts (Bloom & Goldstein, 2000; Koppich, Kerchner, & Asher, 2001). However, PAR programs typically stop short of tenure decisions. For new teachers, these programs encompass only the first year of teaching. In the additional year or years before tenure, support and evaluation usually reverts to standard operating procedure.

Thinking Differently About Tenure

The Minneapolis Public Schools (MPS) and the Minneapolis Federation of Teachers (MFT) have taken a unique and comprehensive approach to tenure. Minneapolis' Achievement of Tenure process encompasses colleague support, professional development, and evaluative review in a systematic 3-year process designed to ensure that a teacher who receives tenure in that district is well prepared for the professional challenges ahead.

Minneapolis is an increasingly diverse school district of approximately 48,000 students. Seventy percent qualify for free and reduced-price lunch. Nearly three-quarters (71%) are students of color, and nearly 20% do not speak English as their native language. The district hires approximately 300 to 400 new teachers each year.

The idea for the Achievement of Tenure process derives from the experience of graduates of Minneapolis' residency program. This 1-year program provides a decreased teaching load and increased professional development for newly licensed teachers assigned to one of the district's professional practice schools. Matched with experienced teachers, residents participate in study groups, conduct action research, observe master teachers, and build their professional practice skills by working toward achievement of Minneapolis' contractually specified Standards of Effective Teaching.

The district and union came to recognize that teachers who complete the residency program are vastly better prepared than those who begin their careers fresh from student teaching. The MFT, in particular, began to consider the benefits of a residency-like induction program for all new Minneapolis teachers. Although the organization understood it was not possible to provide decreased teaching loads for all new teachers, the MFT believed it was worth pursuing a program that adapted many of the components of residency to a longer-term process leading to tenure. Such a program would have the double benefit of combining a comprehensive induction system with rigorous appraisal of new teachers' work.

As MFT President Louise Sundin explains, "We… were convinced that tenure in Minneapolis needed to mean something. It needed to be a process that those inside and outside the school system would view as worthy" (telephone interview, July 29, 2002).

The Achievement of Tenure process became part of the collective bargaining agreement between the MFT and the Minneapolis Public Schools in 1997. Developed collaboratively by the union and district, the 3-year process is designed to "ensure that all non-tenured teachers get a strong start in becoming highly skilled practitioners… " (Contract between MFT and MPS, 1999-2001).

Although taking on the issue of tenure was new to Minneapolis, negotiating reform was not. The tenure process became another piece of Minneapolis' comprehensive Professional Continuum of Teacher Development. Begun by the district and union in 1984, the continuum includes 1 year of mentoring for all new teachers; career-long professional development, much of it school based; support for teachers to seek National Board Certification; peer review; and multiple teacher leadership opportunities.

Achieving Tenure

Every teacher new to the Minneapolis schools is required to participate in the Achievement of Tenure process. Throughout this period, the novice teacher is supported by a school-based Achievement of Tenure team composed of the mentor, experienced teachers, and a school administrator. The team works with the beginning teacher throughout the probationary period to provide assistance, support, advice, coaching, encouragement, and—ultimately—determine @whether the teacher has demonstrated adequate professional knowledge and skill to be granted tenure in Minneapolis.

Each new teacher is required to develop an Achievement of Tenure plan, a kind of professional growth and development schema, which must be approved by the school team. The teacher must submit progress reports to the team in the winter and spring of each year. Artifacts illustrating the teacher's work during the term of the probationary period become the basis of a professional portfolio. The negotiated MPS-MFT contract spells out the requirements for achieving tenure, including the following:

1. Orientation: All new teachers are required to participate in a joint district–union orientation program.

2. Professional development: Forty hours of professional development, selected by the teacher and pegged to that individual's professional growth goals, must be completed within the 3-year probationary period.

3. Cognitive coaching: All new teachers complete a 20-hour cognitive coaching course offered by the district.

4. Videotape: New teachers videotape examples of their teaching and discuss these with members of their Achievement of Tenure team.

5. Surveys: Annual surveys of students and families, developed by the district's professional development department, provide beginning teachers with important feedback. Common student surveys are used for grades K–2, 3–5, 6–8, and 9–12. Family surveys are the same for all grade levels.

6. Action research: All new Minneapolis teachers are required to conduct an action research project. Each teacher selects a classroom-based problem and posits and tests possible solutions. Data gathered and results achieved are committed to writing and become part of the teacher's professional portfolio.

7. Evaluation: Annual evaluations, conducted separately by the principal and the mentor in the first year and by teacher colleagues thereafter, are based on Minneapolis' Standards of Effective Instruction.

Approximately 3 months before the conclusion of the probationary period, teachers seeking tenure present their portfolios to their Achievement of Tenure team. If approved, a final presentation is made to other school colleagues, administrators, and district headquarters representatives. Final approval to grant tenure comes at this point.

Teachers in Minneapolis who achieve tenure believe they have accomplished something important. They have passed a significant professional milestone and have earned tenure, not simply been granted it. Teachers who fail to successfully complete the tenure requirements lose their employment with the district.

Approximately 1,000 teachers have been through Minneapolis' Achievement of Tenure process. Although no formal evaluation of the process has been conducted, statistics would suggest that it has had an impact at least on the retention of new teachers. Whereas about half the teachers in urban districts leave the profession within the first 5years (Ingersoll, 2002), Minneapolis' new teacher attrition rate is less than 25%.

A Modest Investment

Minneapolis' Achievement of Tenure process reflects a relatively modest reallocation of dollars. The process costs less than $2,000 per teacher: hourly pay for the 20-hour peer coaching class; 1 day of a substitute's salary for a peer observation visit to an experienced teacher's classroom; and, on achievement of tenure, a $1,000 bonus that can be taken in the form of a laptop computer, $1,000 in cash, or a $1,000 contribution to a deferred compensation account.[1]

Assuming 300 new teachers are hired in Minneapolis in a given year, and all successfully complete the tenure process, the annual cost is approximately $600,000, or less than 1% of the district's $450 million budget. The import of Minneapolis' tenure review process is better calculated, not in terms of aggregate dollars expended for the program but as a significant policy departure from issues that are the traditional subject of labor–management agreements.

As a result of the negotiated contract, achieving tenure in Minneapolis has been transformed from a pro forma exercise to serious professional business. Tenure requirements frame Minneapolis' professional expectations for teachers and provide novices with an understanding of and appreciation for the complexity of good teaching. The process is a critical link in a joint labor–management chain of professional improvement. Says Emma Hixson, Administrator for Employee Effectiveness (a combination of the departments of Human Resources and Labor Relations), "What's been achieved [in Minneapolis] is the result of a highly evolved labor-management relationship. [This relationship] has made a huge difference and created huge opportunities" (telephone interview, August 20, 2002.)

Denver: Moving to Pay-for-Performance

Teacher salaries are much in the news. Discussion centers not just on rates of pay or whether higher salaries will attract and retain more and better teachers. The method of compensation itself has become a topic of discussion, political rhetoric, and research.

The standard single-salary schedule, which pays teachers according to years of experience and academic credits earned, has become something of an article of union faith. The system is defended on the basis of equity—teachers with similar qualifications earn like amounts of money.

Unions soundly reject compensation systems such as merit pay. They point to research that indicates merit pay reinforces a culture of isolation, that the

---

1   The new contract agreement between the school district and the MFT also grants teachers, at the completion of tenure, a district in-kind contribution of 20 hours to be credited to future movement on the salary schedule. The cost of this agreement has not yet been calculated.

determination of "merit" often is highly subjective, and that such systems have limited resources applied to them and thus tend to set quotas enabling only a few to actually receive the added compensation (Bacharach, Lipsky, & Shedd, 1984; Johnson, 1984; Murnane & Cohen, 1986).

Recent work on pay for knowledge and skills has reignited interest in alternative pay structures (Odden & Kelley, 1997). The national teacher unions also have taken a fresh look at their policies on new kinds of pay structures, although with quite different results. The National Education Association has come down firmly against differential pay except for teachers who earn National Board Certification. The American Federation of Teachers, in policy language replete with caveats, has endorsed (1) added pay for National Board Certification, for teachers who assume added responsibilities (e.g., mentoring), and for teachers in shortage fields; (2) knowledge- and skills-based pay; and (3) group performance awards for improved student achievement.

Pay-for-Performance Denver-Style

One of the most public pay-for-performance efforts underway is taking place in Denver. Through this work, the Denver Public Schools (DPS) and the Denver Classroom Teachers Association (DCTA) are defining pay-for-performance in Denver terms. Denver's pay-for-performance pilot project was launched in September 1999 as part of the contract settlement between the DPS and the DCTA. Negotiations leading to the contract, and the pay-for-performance pilot, were neither cordial nor collaborative.

The DPS and DCTA began negotiations for a successor to the then-current contract in March 1999. In April, the Denver school board proposed a pay-for-performance plan to replace Denver's salary schedule. Under the board's plan, the schedule, which consisted of 13 experience steps and 6 columns encompassing bachelor's degree to doctorate, would be replaced by earned academic steps based on teachers meeting instructional performance objectives.

The DCTA rejected this plan, arguing that a wholesale replacement of the existing salary structure—particularly without warning, preparation, or union involvement—was unacceptable. However, the DCTA also knew that pay-for-performance was an issue that was not going to go away. Neighboring Douglas County had had a form of pay-for-performance for a number of years. In addition, the state of Colorado was considering pay-for-performance policy and the DCTA itself, over the previous several years, had had five study committees on the topic of teacher compensation.

Moreover, the school board's plan, although not acceptable in its initial form to the DCTA, contained some good news for Denver teachers. The salaries of experienced teachers at the top of the schedule—40% of the DCTA membership—had essentially been "frozen" for some time. Under the school board's plan, these teachers, assuming they achieved the required instructional objectives, would receive a 4.5% raise for the first year of the contract and for each year thereafter. Stated another way, the school board's pay-for performance proposal would have increased pay for teachers in the "masters degree plus 30 units" column from an annual salary of $47,000 to $60,000 during the course of 5 years.

The reasons for the board's actions remain somewhat clouded. The district, according to school board documents, claims it wanted to change the way teachers were paid in Denver in order to "… link teacher compensation to student achievement." (Denver Public Information Office, 1999). Bruce Dickinson, Executive Director of the DCTA, remembers it differently. "The board said it wanted to save the district from bankruptcy" and saw the new pay plan as a way to accomplish this (telephone interview, July 30, 2002). What the district did not calculate, says Dickinson, is that the board's proposal would, 5 years out, have been unaffordable, costing the district $25 million more than the existing salary structure.

Whatever its genesis, the pay-for-performance proposal contributed to a breakdown in contract negotiations. With the help of a mediator, a contract settlement, including the pay-for-performance pilot, was reached. Teachers voted overwhelmingly to approve the new agreement.

The Plan

Denver's pay-for-performance plan requires that entire schools opt to participate. Although originally participation required an 85% affirmative vote of the faculty, that percentage was subsequently changed to 67%. Teachers in schools that are not part of the pilot continue to be paid according to the regular salary schedule. Teachers in pilot schools are paid according to that schedule as well, but with the bonus added.

The pilot began as a 2-year effort and was subsequently extended to 4 years. Twelve schools per year, or approximately 500 teachers, participate. Some schools remain in the pilot for just 1 year; others remain for multiple years. Each teacher in a pilot school is required to develop 2-year–long, classroom-specific instructional objectives. Tied to student achievement, objectives must be approved by the principal.

Three competing approaches are used to determine if teachers have met their objectives. One third of the pilot schools use scores on the norm-referenced Iowa Test of Basic Skills. Another third uses criterion-referenced assessments such as the Colorado Student Assessment Program or teacher-developed classroom tests. The final third of the pilot schools uses measures of teachers' increased knowledge and skills as they are related to student achievement.

Teachers who meet their objectives earn financial bonuses. For the first year of the pilot, each teacher received $500 for agreeing to participate and an additional $500 for each objective achieved. For each subsequent year, no participation bonus is offered. Achieving each objective is worth $750. Disputes about whether teachers have achieved one or more of their objectives is, by contractual agreement, subject to expedited binding arbitration. No cases have been submitted to arbitration.

Implementation of pay-for-performance is overseen by a design team composed of two members appointed by the district and two by the union. The process is being studied and evaluated by the Community Training and Assistance Center (CTAC; Pathway to results, 2001), a Boston-based technical assistance organization. According to Richard Allen, Assistant Superintendent for Budget and Finance for Denver Public Schools, "The CTAC study allows the union and the district to fix problems before they surprise us" (telephone interview, August 2, 2002).

Expanding Work Through the Joint Salary Task Force

A memorandum of understanding between the district and union established the Joint Salary Task Force to expand the pay-for-performance effort. Composed of DPS, DCTA, and community representatives, the task force began meeting in spring 2002.

Its multipronged agenda has three principal foci: (1) examining issues related to career-long compensation, such as attracting and retaining quality teachers; (2) reviewing options for motivational fiscal incentives, including pay-for-performance linked to improving teacher quality and student achievement; and (3) considering system compensation issues, such as whether various kinds of plans are affordable and under what conditions they could be successfully implemented by the district.

The task force is slated to present a draft compensation system, including but not limited to pilot-related pay-for-performance elements, in spring 2003. By November of that year, the final CTAC report will be published, and the design team will present the results of its own assessment of the pilot. In early 2004, the school district and the union are slated to release a joint recommendation for a new compensation structure. The teacher vote on a new pay plan is set for March 2004.

Paying for the Work

The district annually spends approximately $1.75 million out of its $528 million operating budget on the pay-for performance pilot. These dollars cover the cost of teacher bonuses and the salaries of design team members.

The most costly portion of the pilot—the research and evaluation components, including CTAC's work; the work of the Joint Salary Task Force; and communication to various school district and outside constituencies—is funded by the philanthropic community. The Denver-based Rose Foundation and the Los Angeles-based Broad Foundation, along with smaller local area foundations, is investing nearly $4 million during the course of 3 years to support pay-for-performance.

Both the union and district acknowledge that, whatever the result of the pay-for-performance pilot and the work of the Joint Salary Task Force, short of rejecting any new salary arrangement, the district's general fund revenues will not support a new pay system. A fall 2003 tax levy to generate added revenue is likely.

Preliminary Results

That Denver's pay-for-performance pilot has remained on track is something of an accomplishment in itself. Although union leadership has been consistent, the district has had five superintendents, as well as some turnover in school board membership, since the pilot began. It is too soon to know if Denver's version of pay-for-performance will contribute to improved student achievement. As CTAC's December 2001 formative report states:

> The task of producing individual student achievement data for teachers, and of linking student results to specific teachers, has proven more difficult than originally anticipated... The assessments upon which objectives are based and judgments of success are made must be fair, valid, and appropriate. Further, the set of assessments being used must be specific enough to reflect the instructional content of a particular classroom, and broad enough to provide a fair measurement across classes and schools. No single current assessment meets all these purposes. (Community Training and Assistance Center, 2001)

Both the union and district acknowledge that, as a result of the pilot, they now have a more complex and more sophisticated perspective than when the work began. Measuring and tracking student achievement is more complicated, they say, than either had anticipated. More importantly, perhaps, the union and district now view the pay-for-performance pilot not just as an effort to establish a different salary formula but also as part of the process to improve teaching and learning. Both recognize that a new compensation system cannot stand alone. It needs to be linked, they say, to improving teacher evaluation (a joint district–union evaluation committee has begun work on developing a new standards-based evaluation system) and enhancing professional development (particularly by helping teachers to better use data to improve instruction). In addition, says DCTA President Becky Wissink, "The pay-for-performance pilot has brought out into the open [the need to have] honest and intelligent conversations about students' different rates of learning" (telephone interview, July 30, 2002).

As a result of Denver's salary work, the union's role as a leader in education has expanded. Says DPS' Richard Allan, "The union leadership staked their reputations... on doing something better for their members." Whatever the outcome, district and union know they both will be held countable for the results.

Seattle: Allocating Resources According to Student Need

Most school districts allocate instructional dollars on the basis of a formula that assures equivalent dollars for all students. Educational need is not much part of the calculation except insofar as categorical funds are concerned. In Seattle, however, student need drives the distribution of resources. The weighted student formula (WSF) is an explicit recognition that equal dollars do not provide an equal education for all students.

The precursor to Seattle's WSF was an early 1980s strike settlement between the Seattle Public Schools and the Seattle Education Association (SEA). That agreement provided a modest sum of discretionary funds ($8 million spread, over time, across the district's 100 schools) to be used by building staff to make decisions related to student learning needs. Still, this distribution of funds fell short of enabling all schools to serve their students well.

Developing the WSF

When John Stanford became Seattle's superintendent and Joseph Olchefske its chief fiscal officer in 1995 (Olchefske is currently the district's superintendent), the district's fiscal condition was precarious. "We were about 18 months away from bankruptcy," says Olchefske (telephone interview, August 20, 2002). In addition, there seemed to be disconnection between resource allocation and educational goals.

The new administration and the SEA leadership, with whom it had formed a strong partnership, determined that the way to tackle both the resource and educational goal problems was to frame funding reform as academic reform. Doing this meant that if the district were intent on bringing every student to a common educational level, the funding system would need to acknowledge that different students require different levels of resources. Such a system meant there would also be fiscal winners and losers.

The district prepared a school-by-school analysis that compared school allocations using the standard distribution formulation and allocations using the WSF. This analysis showed that, under the proposed WSF, the predominately white, northend Seattle schools would lose money. Moreover, the WSF used in this initial calculation would render small schools not viable. Whatever the problems of the initial WSF formulation, however, the district's trial effort confirmed that a WSF was technically possible. After considerable debate, Seattle's school board voted unanimously to move forward with a WSF for the 1997 to 1998 school year.

The district appointed a committee composed of representatives of the SEA, principals, and central office instructional staff to refine the initial formula and, to the extent possible, mitigate some of the problems it raised. Chaired by Arlene Ackerman (then an official in the Seattle Public Schools, now superintendent in San Francisco), the committee was charged with reconciling three often-competing educational objectives:

1. Resources were to be directed to meet the educational needs of students.
2. Every school needed to be assured of having a viable educational program.
3. Any plan must comply with all district obligations, including the district-SEA contract.

How the WSF Works

Three decisions ultimately shape the resource allocation formula. First, relative student weights are calibrated according to student educational needs. A primary grade basic education forms the base-funding factor and determines the amount of revenue a 1.0-weighted student generates. Additional weights are calculated as the marginal cost of serving students with additional characteristics: poverty, using free and reduced-price lunch as the proxy; special education, by level of service; and bilingual education. Each characteristic drives additional funding to students beyond the base funding allocation. As a result, schools with larger numbers of students who are poor or who need special education or bilingual services generate more dollars.

Second, a foundation program guarantees the viability of small schools. The foundation allocation, which varies by school type, funds the basic administrative operation of the school and sets minimum school sizes. The basic foundation allocation for an elementary school (250 students minimum), includes one principal, one secretary, and one half-time librarian. A middle school (600 students minimum) receives enough resources to fund one principal, two secretaries, one librarian, and one counselor. A high school (1,000 students minimum) is guaranteed one principal, one assistant principal, two secretaries, one part-time data person, one librarian, one counselor, and one additional coordinator position.

Third, Seattle uses average, rather than actual, teacher salaries as part of the formula to deliver dollars to schools. The district and union maintain that using average salaries makes it more likely that staffing decisions will be based on quality and "fit" with a school rather than on salary costs. (Seniority is not a staffing issue in Seattle. As part of the district-SEA contract agreement, Seattle eliminated seniority 5 years ago as an assignment criterion.)

As the demographics of the Seattle teaching population shift, the average versus actual salaries issue becomes more academic than real. More than half the teachers in Seattle public schools now have 5 years or fewer of teaching experience, rendering pay differentials less pronounced.

Schools build their budgets and make resource allocation decisions based on their school plans. As a result of a 5-year multimillion dollar grant from the Gates Foundation, each school develops what is called a "transformation plan," a comprehensive program for school improvement. The school's budget must support its improvement goals.

The Seattle example is somewhat different from those of Minneapolis and Denver in that there is no written labor–management agreement around the WSF. The WSF composes part of district policy and, as such, is subject to the contract's grievance procedure. However, no contract or memorandum of understanding, per se, enshrines union participation. Nevertheless, the SEA is an active participant in and enthusiastic supporter of the WSF. The union has been involved every step of the way in the development and implementation of the resource allocation arrangement and currently is part of a joint union–management committee that oversees the WSF program.

Results

Seattle's WSF fundamentally redistributes dollars. It moves dollars from district headquarters to schools and it provides differential allocations to schools based on student educational need.

Has WSF made a difference in terms of student performance? Both the superintendent and union leadership demure on this question. Test scores are on a generally upward trajectory, albeit slowly and incrementally, and the drop-out rate has been cut nearly in half, from 17% to 9%, since the WSF was implemented. However, both district and union are quick to point out that no single reform is responsible for gains. The fiscal allocation formula is part of a package of education improvement efforts in Seattle. However, as a result of the way dollars are distributed, says SEA former Executive Director Roger Erskine, one of the original architects of the WSF, "decisions are more data driven" (telephone interview, August 2, 2002.) Schools are obliged to consider carefully how fiscal decisions will move them closer to meeting their educational goals.

Montgomery County: Focusing on Improving Teaching

With improving teacher quality high on policy agendas, many school districts have turned their attention to efforts to enhance the knowledge and skills of their teaching staffs. Some of these programs focus on developing induction programs for new teachers. Others concentrate on increasing opportunities for professional development among experienced teachers. Still others involve a new look at teacher evaluation.

Union involvement in shaping these programs has been variable. In some collective bargaining jurisdictions, these issues are statutorily required subjects of negotiations and therefore part of contract discussions. In others they are not. In some locales, the union has been willing, but the district has held the union at arms' length. In still others, the union has resisted change. In Montgomery County, MD, the teachers' union has been an outspoken proponent of reform and has forged a strong relationship with a school district committed to improvement.

Montgomery County Public Schools is an increasingly heterogeneous district of 136,000 students in suburban Maryland. The district is in the midst of a 5-year–long reform effort designed to transform the teaching and learning environment in its 189 schools. The long-run goal of this effort—the Professional Growth System (PGS)—is to create a professional learning community in each school focused on improving student achievement (Montgomery County Public Schools, 2001).

The principal components of the PGS include the following:

1. a job-embedded professional development process that includes individual teacher-initiated professional development plans and a staff development teacher in each school;
2. a multiyear professional growth and evaluation cycle; and,
3. a PAR program for those new to teaching and for underperforming experienced teachers.

A Brief Developmental History of the PGS

The early 1990s saw a serious economic slowdown in Maryland. Montgomery County, a fiscally dependent district whose budget must be approved annually by the local county council, experienced successive years of large cuts to its budget. In each of 3 years, for example, negotiated salary increases for teachers were eliminated because of lack of funds. Class sizes were increased. Negotiations between the union and district tended to be acrimonious owing not just to financial difficulties.

Then circumstances began to change. By the mid-1990s, the state's economy had turned around. New union and district leadership were in place. (The current superintendent, Jerry Weast, came to the district in 1999. The PGS was actually initiated under his predecessor.) A fortuitous confluence of events made the PGS possible.

A Teacher Evaluation Task Force, established by the Montgomery County Board of Education, recommended in 1997 that the district's then-20-year-old teacher evaluation system be replaced. That system was a "one size fits all" arrangement in which teachers, regardless of experience and skill, were evaluated on the same set of indicators. Moreover, that evaluation system, said the board's task force, relied on a deficit model that assumed the purpose of evaluation was to identify teachers' weaknesses but not necessarily build on their strengths. The new system, the task force recommended, should be calibrated to teaching experience and proficiency and reflect the principal goal of evaluation as improving the quality of teaching.

Fall 1997 also marked the beginning of negotiations for a new teachers' contract. The MCEA was emboldened by then-NEA President Robert Chase's declaration of a "new unionism" focused on labor–management collaboration for educational improvement. The union proposed, and the district agreed, to use interest-based bargaining for this round of negotiations.

Traditional contract negotiations are positional and thus adversarial. They stress the different interests and goals of the negotiating parties. Interest-based bargaining, on the other hand, tries to turn the process on its head by transforming collective bargaining into a union–management collaboration in which reaching mutually desired goals is the outcome.

Developed by the Harvard Negotiations Project, in interest-based bargaining, the parties endeavor to set aside personal animosities. They focus on interests—on what they hope to accomplish—rather than on hard-and-fast positions. They generate a range of acceptable resolutions before zeroing in on a single solution. Finally, the district and union reach agreements based on a mutually determined, reasonably objective standard of what is right and fair (Fisher & Ury, 1981).

Interest-based bargaining contributed to the achievement of a new, and a new kind of, contract for Montgomery County. The preamble to the 1998 to 2001 agreement emphasized improving student achievement, enhancing teacher quality, increasing staff development opportunities, and shared union–management accountability for results. The contract also framed a process for ongoing district–union collaboration through joint work groups and a commitment to develop new teacher staff development and evaluation processes, the latter based on the recommendations of the Teacher Evaluation Task Force, and a PAR program.

Between 1998 and 2000, what came to be known as the PGS began to take shape. The district and MCEA developed the PAR program, using as a model similar programs already in existence in places such as Toledo and Columbus, OH. PAR provides supported induction for beginning teachers, including modeling lessons, help with planning, coaching, and reviewing instruction under the guidance of consulting teachers, experienced practitioners selected by a joint union–management panel. PAR also operates for experienced teachers designated as "underperforming" based on the result of their previous year's evaluation.

Massachusetts-based Research for Better Teaching was contracted to develop the new evaluation system, including teacher performance standards and training for the administrators who would be responsible for implementing the system. Teacher evaluation now operates on 5-year cycles calibrated to years of experience. In the first 2 years of employment, teachers are formally evaluated each year. Thereafter, until their 10th year, teachers enter a 3-year cycle of evaluation. From 10 years of experience on, teachers are formally evaluated every fifth year. When not under formal review, they refine and implement their professional development plans.

Together, the district and union determined that enhanced professional development would operate on the principles of "school-based" and "job-embedded." Collaborative work was undertaken to design a professional development system that includes individual teacher professional development plans, aligned with school improvement plans, and the assignment to each school of a staff development teacher to coordinate and promote individual and group-based professional growth.

Formative Results

Montgomery County is now in the third year of a 3-year phase-in of the PGS. First-year evaluation results are encouraging. They show generally strong support from principals and teachers for the PGS. Teachers report that the new emphasis on professional growth has enhanced their repertoire of instructional skills and increased the variety of activities they use to reinforce student learning. As a result of the new evaluation system, teachers and principals now focus more intensely on multiple aspects of teaching and make clearer connections between teaching and student achievement.

Staff development teachers are viewed as boosting teachers' professional growth and facilitating the use of data to improve instruction. Finally, principals praise the PAR consulting teachers as effective mentors and teaching role models (Koppich, 2000). Subsequent years' evaluations will probe the PGS' impact on student learning.

Achieving Accord by Shaping the Budget

Montgomery County's PGS is not fundamentally shaped by specific language in the district–union contract. Each PGS element is acknowledged as part of the stated joint MCPS-MCEA commitment to continuous improvement. The PAR program is delineated in the labor–management agreement. The contract also outlines the use of staff development substitutes (eg., they are to be used only to provide time for job-embedded professional development) and states that the school district cannot unilaterally change the new evaluation system without consulting the union. However, much of the MCEA involvement that has influenced the form of the PGS stems not just from contract negotiations but from another source as well.

In Montgomery County, the teachers' union plays a key role, at the superintendent's request, in shaping the district's budget. In every school district, programs are driven by budget considerations. In districts with traditional labor–management relationships; however, the union rarely sees more than a finished budget. The organization often is not privy to fiscal data adequate to analyze budget allocation decisions or make informed choices about the availability or distribution of dollars.

In Montgomery County, the union is involved in the budget-building process. As a result, the MCEA participates in establishing programmatic budget priorities and designing programs. It also assumes a measure of responsibility, once the budget proposal is developed, for persuading the county's fiscal agency to fund it.

The PGS carried an initial price tag of $11 million, all of it new money. By 2002 to 2003, as the phase-in proceeded, the annual cost of the system was approximately $23 million. Although as a stand-alone number this figure is substantial, it actually represents just less than 2% of the district's $1.4 billion annual operating budget; in essence, it is a 2% investment in improving the quality of teaching.

Reshaping Labor–Management Relations

In the four districts that are the subject of this chapter—Minneapolis, Denver, Seattle, and Montgomery County—negotiating the distribution of dollars focuses to a considerable extent on education improvement efforts. Labor–management accords cited here, whether part of collectively bargained contracts or memoranda of understanding or other kinds of agreements, deal with difficult, often previously off-limits issues; among these are tenure, pay-for-performance, differential school allocations, and teacher evaluation. These examples represent the leading edge of a slowly emerging shift in the role and purpose of labor–management agreements, reshaping a system that was designed to deal solely with collective bargaining's statutorily authorized triumvirate of wages, hours, and working conditions.

The Historical Context

Collective bargaining in education took its cues from industrial-style unionism. Most state laws governing bargaining for public employees, including teachers, closely resemble the 1935 National Labor Relations Act, which legally sanctioned bargaining in private industry.[2]

Teachers embraced collective bargaining as a way of giving them a voice in the conditions under which they worked. Before collective bargaining, teachers did not speak for themselves; they were spoken for. Decisions of any consequence, from salaries to class sizes to transfer procedures, were made by school

---

2 Although private sector workers in industry are covered by federal law, collective bargaining for public sector employees' is authorized in state-level statutes. Approximately 37 states have such laws.

boards and administrators with little or no teacher involvement (Kerchner, Koppich, & Weeres, 1997).

Throughout the early decades of teacher collective bargaining—in the 1960s, 1970s, and into the 1980s—labor–management negotiations focused nearly exclusively on levels of compensation and the particulars of working conditions. Bargaining leading to contractual agreements typically was adversarial.

Adversarial labor–management behavior was part of the historical tradition inherited from private sector bargaining. The National Labor Relations Act discourages labor–management cooperation as a means of warding off the development of company unions. Public sector collective bargaining laws contain no such admonition, but wariness about union–management collaboration came as a borrowed consequence of industrial-style unionism.

The contract, in traditional collective bargaining terms, is designed to serve relatively limited purposes. It is meant to protect teachers from arbitrary and capricious actions of the employer through standardized work rules and to preserve fair and even-handed, across-the-district treatment of teachers. In addition, the traditional contract serves as a statement of the accrued rights of individual teachers. It establishes teachers' terms and conditions of employment by specifying the rights of those whose professional lives are governed by it (Kerchner et al., 1997).

A Turnabout

The labor–management agreements cited in this chapter, both those that are provisions of negotiated contracts and those that reflect implicit accord through union participation, represent a turnabout. In these agreements, individual teacher welfare—the rights and benefits of an employee—is subsumed by institutional welfare—the assessment of what is needed for the district or school to do well by its students. Management and union together assume joint custody of reform as they consider what makes sound educational sense for the school system and its students. (Kerchner and Koppich, 1993). The parties forge a professional partnership, negotiating agreements and the dollars attached to them, while focused squarely on education's bottom line: student learning.

The labor relations arena represented here both expands the scope of labor–management relations and replaces warfare with mutual cooperation. "Bread and butter" issues of wages, hours, and working conditions, the legal confines of collective bargaining, reflect only a portion of union and management's mutual interests. There is a broad and often consensual array of education policy challenges that both union and management have an interest in meeting. Management-union cooperation in this context is not simply cooperation for cooperation's sake. Union and management recognize that the product of true labor–management cooperation is not civility, it is education improvement.

Expanding scope requires change on the part of both union and management. Management, for its part, must be willing to discuss with the union those topics it traditionally has reserved for itself. The union must be prepared to work in areas from which it has conventionally been barred or has resisted.

Steering Toward the Future

Reforming unions face numerous challenges. They must persuade long-time members that a new way of doing business does not mean abandoning traditional union values or issues such as salaries and employment conditions. They are mindful of the fact that unions' ability today to focus energy and attention on an expanded range of educational issues owes in no small measure to the hard work and accomplishments of those who went before. At the same time, unions must also convince newer members and potential members that the union is an important vehicle for educational improvement. This is not an easy sell, even in the places where it is most consistent with reality.

As Harvard professor Susan Moore Johnson has written, teachers hired in the 1960s and 1970s, many of whom are on the verge of retiring, "… as a group… value job security, prefer autonomy to teamwork, tolerate isolation, eschew competition, respect administrative authority, [and] oppose differential treatment within their ranks. Newer teachers, on the other hand, prefer "jobs that feature variety, teamwork, risk-taking, [and] entrepreneurial opportunities" (Johnson, 2000). The first set of values is a good fit with the type of collective bargaining that built the power of teacher unions. The second is not.

Change in union–management relations is an evolutionary process. However, like the evolution of the species, evolution in education bargaining moves at a glacial pace. Current collective bargaining laws shelter and support industrial-style labor relations. They offer neither management nor union much incentive to change. Bringing about more counties like those of Minneapolis, Denver, Seattle, and Montgomery will require a new kind of bargaining statute that creates different expectations for labor–management relations and the agreements they produce.

References

Bacharach, S.B., Lipsky, D., & Shedd, J. (1984). *Merit pay and its alternatives*. Ithaca, NY: Organizational Analysis and Practice.

Bloom, G. & Goldstein, J. (Eds.) (2000) *The peer assistance and review reader*. Santa Cruz, CA: University of California at Santa Cruz.

Contract between the Minneapolis Public Schools and the Minneapolis Federation of Teachers, 1999-2001.

Czek, Laurie, Teacher Coordinator, Minneapolis Achievement of Tenure Program. Telephone interview with author, July 29, 2002.

Darling-Hammond, L., Wise, A.E., & Pease, S.R. (1983). Teacher evaluation in the organizational context: A review of the literature. *Review of Educational Research*, 52(3), 285-328.

Denver Public Schools Information Office (November 1, 1999). Unpublished background paper.

Fisher, R., & Ury, W. (1981). *Getting to yes: Negotiating without giving in*. New York: Penguin Books.

Haertle, E. (1986). The valid use of student performance measures for teacher evaluation. *Educational Evaluation and Policy Analysis*, 8(1), 45-61.

Ingersoll, R. (2002). *Out-of-field teaching, educational inequality, and the organization of schools: An exploratory analysis.* Research report for the Center for the Study of Teaching Policy. Seattle, WA: University of Washington.

Israel, Tom, Executive Director, Montgomery County Education Association. Telephone interview with author, August 19, 2002.

Johnson, S.M. (2000, June 7). Teaching's next generation: Who are they? What will keep them in the classroom? *Education Week.*

Jupp, Brad, Team Leader, DPS/DCTA Pay-for Performance Pilot. Telephone interview with author, July 10, 2002.

Kerchner, C.T., & Koppich, J. (1993). *A union of professionals: Labor relations and educational reform.* New York: Teachers College Press.

Kerchner, C.T., Koppich, J., & Weeres, J. (1997). *United mind workers: Unions and teaching in the knowledge society.* San Francisco: Jossey-Bass.

Koppich, J., Kerchner, C.T., & Asher, C. (2001). *Developing careers, building a profession: The Rochester career in teaching plan.* New York: The National Commission on Teaching and America's Future.

Koppich, J. (2001). The Professional Growth System in Montgomery County Public Schools: A report on first-year implementation results. Report prepared for the Montgomery County Public Schools

Medley, D.M. & Coker, H. (1987). The accuracy of principals' judgements of teacher performance. *Journal of Educational Research*, 80, 242-247.

Montgomery County Public Schools (2001). *The professional growth system in Montgomery County: Building professional community in schools.* Montgomery County, MD: Author.

Murnane, R.J., & Cohen, D.K. (1986). Merit pay and the evaluation problem: Why some merit pay plans fail and a few survive. *Harvard Educational Review*, 56(1), 1-17.

Murphy, Nancy Executive Director, Seattle Education Association. Telephone interview with author, July 23, 2002.

Nordgren, Lynn, Professional Development Coordinator, Minneapolis Public Schools. Telephone interview with author, August 16, 2002.

Odden, A., & Kelley, C. (1997). *Paying teachers for what they know and can do: New and smarter compensation strategies to improve schools.* Thousand Oaks, CA: Corwin Press.

Pathway to results: Pay for performance in Denver. (December 2001). Denver, CO: Community Training and Assistance Center.

Index